THE SUCCESSION
TO THE
THRONE OF DAVID

by

LEONHARD ROST

HISTORIC TEXTS AND INTERPRETERS IN BIBLICAL SCHOLARSHIP

General Editor:
Professor J. W. Rogerson (Sheffield)

Consultant Editors:
Professor C. K. Barrett (Durham)
Professor R. Smend (Göttingen)

THE SUCCESSION TO·THE THRONE·OF DAVID

LEONHARD ROST

The Almond Press · 1982

HISTORIC TEXTS AND INTERPRETERS
IN BIBLICAL SCHOLARSHIP, 1

THE SUCCESSION TO THE THRONE OF DAVID
by LEONHARD ROST

Translated
by MICHAEL D. RUTTER and DAVID M. GUNN

With an Introduction
by EDWARD BALL

This book contains a translation of Die Überlieferung von
der Thronnachfolge Davids, by Leonhard Rost, first published by Verlag von W. Kohlhammer, Stuttgart, 1926, in the
series, Beiträge zur Wissenschaft vom Alten und Neuen
Testament, edited by Rudolf Kittel (Third Series, Vol. 6 [=
Vol. 42 inclusive]). Reprinted (with typographical errors
corrected and notes collected at the end) in Rost's Das
kleine Credo und andere Studien zum Alten Testament, pp.
119-253, by Quelle & Meyer Verlag, Heidelberg, 1965, and
translated here by permission.

British Library Cataloguing in Publication Data:

Rost, Leonhard
    The succession to the throne of David. - (Historic
    texts and interpreters in Biblical scholarship, ISSN
    0263-1199; 1)
    1. Bible. O.T. Samuel - Criticism, interpretation,
    etc.
    I. Title   II. Die Überlieferung von der
    Thronnachfolge Davids. English   III. Series
    222'.406   BS1325.2

    ISBN 0-907459-12-9
    ISBN 0-907459-13-7 Pbk

Published by
The Almond Press
P.O. Box 208
Sheffield S10 5DW
England

Printed in Great Britain
by Redwood Burn Limited
Trowbridge, Wiltshire
1982

CONTENTS

PREFACES · AND
INTRODUCTION

GENERAL PREFACE TO THE SERIES

Historic Texts and Interpreters
in Biblical Scholarship

It is becoming increasingly recognised in English-speaking scholarship that the study of the history of biblical scholarship is an integral part of Biblical Studies. This fact has, of course, long been acknowledged in Germany. Not only are the standard and the most detailed books about the history of biblical scholarship German works, there exist many monographs and unpublished dissertations in German dealing with important biblical scholars and their most significant writings. The growing interest in this whole area on the part of English-speaking scholarship can be indicated in several ways. A recent major contribution has been The Cambridge History of the Bible (3 vols. 1963-1970), although its coverage is necessarily somewhat restricted. The American Society of Biblical Literature has initiated a series entitled "Studies in American Biblical Scholarship, Schools and Scholars" of which the first numbers have begun to appear. At a more popular level, R. E. Clements's A Century of Old Testament Scholarship (1976) has provided valuable orientation for present-day students, while another welcome development has been the translation (in 1973) of W. G. Kümmel's The New Testament: The History of the Investigation of its Problems.

The study of the history of biblical scholarship contributes to current Biblical Studies in several ways. First, it disposes of the simplistic generalisations in terms of which past biblical scholarship is often viewed, generalisations which sometimes only serve to reinforce our own prejudices. Second, it introduces a necessary element of self-criticism into Biblical Studies. Standpoints which may have been widely and uncritically accepted into modern Biblical Studies can be shown to rest upon flimsy evidence or reasoning, and the necessity for a new approach can be underlined. Third, the study of past scholars often indicates what giants they were, how incredible were their achievements, and how great their stature as scholars. It is difficult not to become diffident and modest about the achievements of present-day scholarship when they are viewed in the light of what was achieved in the past, without many of the technical resources of scholarship which are taken for granted today. Fourth, a study of scholars in the context of the theology and philosophy of their time reminds us that Biblical Studies is something carried out in the real world, and that it is profoundly affected by external events and movements of thought. Nothing is more misleading than to suppose that Biblical Studies consists merely of "results". Behind each "result" is a human being wrestling with the biblical text in a particular situation. Fifth, it can be argued that the same basic problems in Biblical Studies present themselves afresh to every second or third generation of new scholars. Better knowledge of the past of the discipline may afford important insights into problems that may seem today to be new and insoluble.

Historic Texts and Interpreters in Biblical Scholarship is designed to fill a gap in the English-speaking contribution to the history of biblical scholarship. The series will make available in English translation texts that have been influential, but which have remained in their original German or Latin or French. These texts will date predominantly from the 18th, 19th and early 20th centuries. The series will also translate some previously unpublished dissertations, as well as important monographs and articles which have already appeared in other languages. Finally, the series will encourage English-speaking scholars to contribute to this area of research, by publishing dissertations in English, and by inviting original monographs on biblical scholars and their work. The history of biblical scholarship, for all that has been achieved so far, is a field in which very much remains yet to be done. It is to be hoped that Historic Texts and Interpreters will further stimulate interest in the field, to the increase of our knowledge of the past, and to the more effective practice of biblical scholarship in the present and future.

John W. Rogerson
The University of Sheffield

TRANSLATOR'S PREFACE

The principal foundation of this translation is the work of Michael D. Rutter. I have revised it and edited the book as a whole. Others have contributed along the way and I express here my considerable gratitude to them: to my colleagues in the Department of Biblical Studies, John Rogerson and David Clines; to Bernhard Lang of the University of Mainz; and to Ed. Ball of St. John's College, Nottingham, who also very kindly contributed his expertise by way of the Introduction. It need hardly be said, of course, that any failings in the translation remain my own and Mr. Rutter's responsibility. A last word of thanks goes to Dr. Diether Kellermann of Tübingen, whose friendly cooperation helped make this book possible.

I have made various changes to the presentation of the material. First, English translations often replace, or supplement, Rost's Hebrew quotations. Second, I have moved the long list of "ark narrative" vocabulary from its original position in the body of the text (see pp. 14-15 below) to an appendix at the end. Third, the notes have been revised: the system of reference has been clarified, some notes have been combined, and the resulting sequence has been numbered by chapters (as was the case in the 1926 edition). A bibliography at the end of the book provides details of works cited (a partial list appeared in the 1926 edition, omitted in 1965), and an index of authors has also been supplied.

Finally, to the substance of the book itself. As some readers may be aware, my own studies in the Books of Samuel have been no little concerned with Rost's work, and as well as drawing freely upon it I have also voiced some criticism. Familiarity, they say, breeds contempt. A renewed, and close, acquaintance with his thesis over the past year or so has indeed produced its occasional dismissive moments. I come away, however, with one feeling overwhelmingly predominant. And that is, unquestionably, sheer admiration.

David Gunn
The University of Sheffield
7th September, 1982

AUTHOR'S PREFACE TO THE 1926 EDITION

I owe the stimulus for this work to Professor Alt of Leipzig. He has maintained his kind interest even after the original subject had changed somewhat. I offer him my sincere thanks for all his kindness. Professor Procksch, since his appointment to Erlangen, has most kindly taken an interest in the present study, and for this I owe him my humble thanks.

The publication was made possible with help from the Notgemeinschaft für die deutsche Wissenschaft, secured through the good offices of Councillor Dr. Kittel of Leipzig. I am deeply grateful to him, as well as to the Notgemeinschaft, and I thank him especially, also, for accepting my work in his series, "Beiträge zur Wissenschaft vom Alten und Neuen Testament."

L. Rost

LEONHARD ROST - BIOGRAPHICAL NOTE

Born Ansbach, Germany, 30th November, 1896. Served in First World War. Studied theology and and oriental languages at Erlangen University: Doctorate, 1921, in Arabic studies; Licentiate in Theology, 1925; Habilitation in Old Testament Theology, 1926 (Die Überlieferung von der Thronnachfolge Davids). Berlin University, 1929; personal chair, 1936. University of Greifswald, 1937; established chair, from 1938. 1940-45, stood in, additionally, as Old Testament Professor, Berlin. Honorary doctorate, Erlangen University, 1943. 1946, Humboldt University; Vice-President of the Diet of the Theological Faculties in the DDR; Guest Lecturer at the Kirchliche Hochschule in Berlin-Zehlendorf; church work in Berlin. From 1956, Professor of Old Testament Theology, Erlangen University. Retired 1966. Honoured by BRD President, 1970, for services to learning and culture. Died 5th December, 1979.

Edited and co-edited various series, collections of essays, lexica and text editions. Among his published work: an edition of the Damascus Document (1933); Israel bei den Propheten (1937); Vorstufen von Kirche und Synagoge im Alten Testament (1938, 2nd edn. 1967); Das kleine Credo und andere Studien zum Alten Testament (1964); Einleitung in die alttestamentlichen Apokryphen und Pseudepigraphen (1971 [ET 1976], 2nd edn. 1979).

INTRODUCTION*

f the many contributions to Old Testament scholarship by Leonhard Rost (1896-1979),[1] none has been more widely and enduringly influential than his study of the narrative concerning the succession to the throne of David (II Sam 9-20, I Kgs 1-2), and of the traditions in II Samuel which he believed to stand in a close literary relationship with it, which is here presented for the first time in an English translation. The work was first published in 1926, when its author was barely thirty (and in which year he became Privatdozent in the University of Erlangen), in the established series "Beiträge zur Wissenschaft vom Alten und Neuen Testament"; and through the following decades, Rost continued to adhere to the views which he had set out there with such obvious skill and clarity - to say nothing of freshness and originality.[2] It would be conceded on all sides, even - or perhaps especially - by those who would dispute many of its basic conclusions, that Rost's study plays a quite central role in the developing study of the historical books of the Old Testament. Brevard Childs, for example, speaks of "Rost's brilliant thesis,"[3] while H. J. Stoebe rightly says that his work "has provided a contribution of decisive importance for our knowledge of the traditions in the Books of Samuel, as regards their origin, their form, and their objectives - hence for the understanding of these books in general."[4] Such testimonies could easily be multiplied.

The first major reviewers of Rost's book would perhaps not have guessed the success it would come to have over the following four decades. There was, indeed, general agreement that Rost had made many new and significant observations. His results, said Kuhl, were gained "through a very cautious and delicately conducted investigation of the style, structure, and world of ideas of the separate narratives,"[5] while Gressmann observed that "we may be glad not only of many new and noteworthy findings, but also of the complete skill

---

* Dedicated to the memory of Norman Henry Snaith.

with which these narratives are examined in depth from the aesthetic, critical, and theological viewpoints."[6] At the same time, both scholars disputed Rost's judgement that II Sam 6.16, 20-23 should be considered part of the succession narrative, and neither could accept that parts of II Sam 7 belonged to it (I Kgs 2.24 is regarded, against Rost, as a redactional addition), or that II Sam 10-12 could properly be called "the early history [or "background story"] of the successor to the throne," since these chapters speak only of the birth of Solomon. Kuhl regards II Sam 11.2-12.23 as an independent story, complete in itself, and disputes also whether the "Tamar-Novelle" in II Sam 13-14 belonged originally to the succession story, noting the fresh beginning at 15.1 as compared with 13.1.[7] Gressmann claims that he is already sure that II Sam 13-20, I Kgs 1-2 form a unified source which may be designated as the "history of the succession to David" (though this is not, in fact, clear in his commentary on this material, published a few years previously).[8]

In these criticisms, we may detect a number of possible weak spots in Rost's case, which would emerge again in later studies. Others drew attention to what were claimed to be weaknesses of method in Rost's delimitation of the boundaries of his source materials. Thus H. M. Wiener[9] notes links between the succession narrative and earlier material which Rost had underplayed: he himself would postulate a document "N" (the work of Nathan or an associate), written indeed in Solomon's reign, but reaching back as far as the stories of Gideon and Abimelech in Judges. Rost's stylistic considerations are insufficient to sever the succession story from what precedes, and there is no independent "ark narrative."

But the most important review of Rost's work was that by Otto Eissfeldt in the "Orientalistische Literaturzeitung."[10] Eissfeldt, like other reviewers, expresses appreciation of "many fine features" including the stylistic investigations, the quest for "settings-in-life" for the separate narratives, and the commitment to the analysis of wider literary units; yet he also expresses a number of basic disagreements which made him throughout the following decades[11] a most penetrating critic of Rost's views regarding the scope and original independence of the larger narrative units postulated in the present work. Rost, says Eissfeldt, confuses literary unity with unity of content, so that he detects once independent, separate narratives such as the "ark narrative" or even the "succession narrative," when they never existed as such; he misses significant links connecting the succession story with what precedes; both the beginning of the narrative in II Sam 6.16b, 20-23, and its ending at I Kgs 2.46b are arbitrarily determined and unconvincing. In all this, Eissfeldt argues, there are two basic errors: first, instead of trying to explain the present form of the Books of Samuel, Rost confines his attention from the outset to a part which he regards as a unity primarily on grounds of its content, and not really for literary and stylistic reasons - since, says Eissfeldt, "to ask about the theme of a writing is to regard it from the point of view of its content" (col.805). For Rost to have confined his study in this way was dangerous. Secondly, Rost "postulates for a narrative work a unity of style and makes the boundaries of the literary unit coincide with the boundaries of the identity of style" (col.806). Noting the important part played by stylistic arguments in Rost's study, Eissfeldt claims that in antiquity style was much less the possession of a particular author than Rost believes (see pp. 3f.). If this is so, he argues, then such arguments need to be used with great caution: a good deal of what Rost says of the style of the "ark narrative" is true of Hebrew narrative style in general, and so can hardly be used to support an understanding of this story as an independent source.

Eissfeldt was in fact making a number of significant points regarding Rost's methods and results. Much later he was to summarise his disagreement in these terms: "in spite of its detailed examination of stylistic criteria, this defining of the limits of an apparently fixed and complete historical work rests ultimately not upon literary criteria but upon considerations of content, as to whether the narratives reveal relationships to the theme of the succession to David or not; and the conclusions are anything but certain."[12]

Eissfeldt's own study of the sources of Samuel, which appeared a few years after Rost's work,[13] divided the material of these books into three continuous strands designated I, II, III, which he came to identify, with varying degrees of hestitation, as continuations of the L, J, and E sources which were to be found in the preceding narrative books. Certainly, modifications in Eissfeldt's views may be detected. He later came to stress rather more the relative independence of II Sam 9-20, I Kgs 1-2 as a "new entity" (Introduction, p. 276), but still declined to see it, with Rost and others, as a quite separate source, arguing rather that it should be regarded as the continuation of the J strand. Clearly, he noted, a good deal here depends on how we understand the intermediate stages between those smaller narratives which may be detected behind even the relative compactness of the succession narrative, and the larger narrative complex labelled J.

Rost's position was to assert that, with the odd exception (the narrative of the Ammonite war), no even relatively independent shorter units may be detected within the succession story; and, conversely, his work shows little interest in the overall disposition of the material in Samuel.[14] His claim is that no continuous strands existing as collections of older material have been combined to make up the present work: on the contrary, we are dealing with a grouping and linking of originally separate source "blocks" - the ark narrative, the succession narrative, the story of the rise of David to kingship - though Rost does claim that the ark and succession stories were linked by the author of the latter as he incorporated the first element of the succession story into the end of the ark narrative, and that the ancient fragments concerning the divine revelation to David in II Sam 7.11b, 16, were also taken up by him (see pp. 85-8).

Rost was here laying the foundation for a new view of the composition of Samuel, in seeing the major components of the present work not as intertwined or juxtaposed source strands running "horizontally" through the books, but as "vertically" divided blocks laid, roughly speaking, end-to-end, and defined on the basis of their theme and style. Later scholars have in broad terms, and whatever their quite substantial disagreements in detail, largely followed Rost's model for the composition of Samuel - and indeed of the historical books from Joshua to II Kings as a whole - rather than that of Eissfeldt.

Here, then, is one significant indication of the importance of Rost's work: he provided a fresh way of looking at things. We should certainly not underestimate the weight of Eissfeldt's criticisms, and it may be that the two approaches do not stand quite so far apart as has sometimes been thought - there are in Eissfeldt's later work, as we have noted above, at least some indications that the lines of division in this discussion may frequently have been drawn too sharply. Yet there is no doubt that with Rost, the balance of understanding shifted in a quite striking way within Old Testament scholarship.

It may be of some interest and importance to consider the possible reasons for the success of Rost's study not only in its general approach, but also down to its details, and for the comparative decline of the approach best exemplified by Eissfeldt.[15] First, however, it will be useful to attempt a brief characterisation of the scope and methods of Rost's work.

II

He begins (pp. 3-5) with some general observations, which will play an important part in the subsequent investigations, on the need to take proper account of the style of a text. Unlike vocabulary and content, which are naturally deter- mined by the subject under consideration, "the style is the man," it belongs to him as an individual, and a consideration of style will not only provide great help in marking out the separate sources, but will also bring the authors before us, no more as "lifeless stereotypes," but as "flesh-and-blood people, with living personalities" (p. 4). In this, Rost shows at least some degree of agreement with Gunkel, for whose "literaturgeschichtlich" approach, a consideration of the author's views and personality reflected in a text is of prime importance in reflecting the life of the people. It is possible to detect something both of the individual and of the typical: "we can look into their hearts and perceive their piety, nurtured in the same soil, but in each person shaped somewhat differently. The portrait of a period then becomes richer, livelier and more realistic" (p. 4). (We may here pause briefly to set this approach in the context of more recent discussion regarding the extent to which it is possible, or profitable, to use literary texts in this way - and one does not need to have a wholehearted conviction of the fallaciousness of "intentionalism" [itself a rather complex notion] to sym- pathise with the problems involved in such uses.[16]) Through- out Rost's work, this will be the kind of position for which he is aiming: how far do the sources considered contribute to a deeper and richer understanding of the intellectual and religious outlook of their authors and of the period to which they belong?

In the discussion of each block of material considered, such delineation of the theological and religious outlook of the writers plays an important part (see especially pp. 5, 30-3, 41, 50-2, 56, 61f., 63f., 106-8). To some extent such de- lineation of differing views is used to support the literary demarcation of the sources, but its main purpose is to contribute "to our knowledge of the theological outlook and religious devotion of the early monarchic period," by which "we are afforded remarkable insight into the richly varied climate of contemporary religious thought" (p. 115). It may be that Rost does not always sufficiently distinguish between the ideas expressed within a particular author's work and the general intellectual and religious climate of a particular period, though he is to some degree aware of this difficulty. This problem, however, is clearly related to that of the connection between the individual and the typical, noted above, and so to wider questions about the historicity of the sources and the extent to which we may use them (however historically trustworthy they may be in general terms) in trying to reconstruct the ideas of the participants, whether individuals or groups.

While Rost's main concern is with the succession story, he pays considerable attention to the "subsidiary sources" (Unterquellen) which have been linked with that source. We may illustrate his procedure from his consideration of the ark narrative. First, against previous opinions which had seen the stories about the fortunes of the ark in I Sam 4-6, II Sam 6 as parts of more extensive narrative sources and also as composite in themselves, Rost argues that the various analytical criteria used by Budde and others fail to prove a division of the material into distinct but interwoven sources. It is far better, he suggests, to suppose that this material goes back to one independent source in which the ark stood at the centre of interest. This suggestion, then, is based in a preliminary way on criticism of earlier studies, and on a prior decision to make fuller use of the criterion of content or theme:[17] "the question of sources can only be solved by combining all narratives in which the ark has a central importance" (p. 10). Thus, after a critical examination of the text[18] in which Rost engages especially with Gressmann's attempt to excise a good deal of material from the original narrative, he is able to suggest a more accurate delineation of the original extent of the story (p. 13), and it is this delineation which provides "the basis for further examination" of vocabulary, style and so forth. There is no need here to examine in detail the use Rost makes of his perhaps rather crude analysis of vocabulary,[19] though we may properly pay tribute to his sensitivity in handling the phenomenon of style in its different aspects. Miller and Roberts have, indeed, spoken of the weakness of Rost's stylistic arguments,[20] but when we bear in mind the comparative lack of stress on such features in much Old Testament study prior to his time, the lively character of this work demands sympathetic treatment.

From the examination of style, Rost passes on to a consideration of structure and purpose (pp. 22ff.), to which the
preceding discussion is believed naturally to lead. Thus we
may conclude, he says, "that the narrative consists of an
account of the fate of the ark from the time of its removal
from Shiloh to the day on which it was installed in Jerusalem"
(p. 23). Next, there is a fuller consideration of the question
as to whether we really are dealing with "a complete and
independent narrative devoted to the ark," and this is
answered in the affirmative. At each stage of his argument
(as here, p. 26), Rost offers summaries of the conclusions to
which the preceding investigation has led him, and the work
thus has, without doubt, an attractively articulated and most
imposing cumulative effect. From this we are rushed on to a
consideration of the purpose of the narrative. It is here
interesting that Rost thinks it possible that the narrative
"could have been the result of sheer pleasure in story-telling"
(p. 26), but this is very quickly brushed aside in favour of the
"possibility," which immediately becomes a certainty ("without a doubt" - doch wohl), that we are dealing here with the
cult legend of the shrine of the ark in Jerusalem. The study
continues with a consideration of the authorship and dating,
and a sensitive assessment of the historicity of the story. But
"much more important" (p. 30) than the degree of historicity
(as a modern reader might understand it) is the issue of the
narrative's theological content (pp. 30-3). In particular we are
interested in "its underlying conception of God" from which
we may "get an insight into the spiritual life and religious
devotion [das Geistesleben und die Frömmigkeit] of the early
monarchic period" (p. 30). Here, as already indicated, we may
see what Rost conceives of as the end purpose of his study: an
understanding of the theological and religious outlook of a
particular author and of (in this case) the priestly group in
Jerusalem to which he belonged.

We need not here pause to consider Rost's treatment of II
Sam 7,[21] and of the account of the Ammonite war,[22]
except to underline the way in which, "mutatis mutandis,"
similar procedures are followed, leading in each case to a
sketch of the proposed religio-historical content of the
different materials. Rost finally turns, however, after these
rather detailed preliminaries (!) to a study of the "succession
narrative," that "Lieblingsstück der Literarkritik" as Budde
has it.[23]

Once more, the discussion begins with a brief, critical
consideration of previous work on this material, and es-

pecially of the then dominant tendency to see II Sam 9-20, I Kgs 1-2 as part of some larger whole. (It is interesting to note that, as with the ark story, Rost finds some pre-figuration of his own views of the literary delimitation of the material in the work of Carl Steuernagel, whose great "Introduction," published in 1912,[24] is sometimes regarded as a final monument to a century and more of concentration on source-criticism, though in fact he already shows the influence of Gunkel's form-criticism (see pp. 205ff.).) But Rost disagrees equally with those like Caspari and Gressmann who would divide the section into a number of more-or-less independent "Novellen," since it is impossible to detect real distinctions of language and style, and since the different supposed units are unified as regards their content (pp. 67, 83f.).

Rather, in trying to ascertain the scope of the succession story, we must once more begin from its <u>theme</u> - which Rost finds most clearly expressed in the insistent question of I Kgs 1, "Who shall sit upon the throne of my lord the king, and who shall reign after him?" - and use this as a basic guide to the delimitation of the story. Here we have "the key to understanding the whole work" (p. 68, cf. p. 89). This "key" then serves to show the necessary continuation of the story in I Kgs 2 (pp. 68ff.), while its antecedents are to be found in II Sam 9-20, where the question of the "hero's" background (chs.11-12 framed by the account of the Ammonite war), and the story answering the question why it was he and not some other son of David who succeeded to the throne (chs.13-20), are handled. The whole content of the succession story, including ch.9, is interwoven; every part is necessary to the overall thrust of the narrative (p. 85).

But the beginning must be found even before II Sam 9, since, among other points, I Kgs 2.24 (see pp. 41, 86) pre-supposes some form of divine promise to David such as we find in the oldest level of II Sam 7 (verses 11b, 16), while II Sam 6.16, 20-23, though now standing within the context of the ark story, nevertheless concerns the question of suc-cession: no descendant of Saul, through his daughter Michal, shall follow David. Rost argues that the linking of the ark and succession narratives was the work of the author of the latter (p. 88).

Having thus delimited the scope of the narrative, Rost con-tinues with a discussion of its style (pp. 90ff.),[25] including considerations of its structure and development. In contrast to the style of the ark story, we find here, he says, a rich depiction of character (pp. 102ff.). Next, we have some consideration, as with the analysis of the ark narrative, of the historicity, the date and authorship,[26] and the theological and religious outlook expressed in the succession story (pp. 103ff.); and, finally, Rost returns to the question of the narrative's original independence from other collections of material, both those preceding it in Samuel, and the material which follows it in I Kings, but once more concluding that in the succession narrative as defined (p. 87) we have "an integrated, self-contained story" (p. 114). We may observe how he concludes this chapter, not with the summary of the religious content of the story, as in the case of the ark narrative, but with a restatement and defence of his view that J and E as we know them from the "Hexateuch" cannot in any meaningful sense be found in Samuel and Kings - for this has been throughout an important result (or presupposition?) of the investigation, even if its main aim, ostensibly at least, is a religio-historical one.

At this point we may offer a few preliminary observations on Rost's thesis, which in part serve to underline points already made by the early reviews considered above. To begin with, we may note once more the similarity of Rost's method in his handling of the ark narrative and of the succession narrative. The main point of departure lies in the preliminary definition of the "theme" of the narrative, and this then serves as a major factor in the delineation of the boundaries of the story. There are differences, however. In the case of the ark narrative, Rost proceeds from a rather general consideration of <u>content</u> - materials concerning the ark are grouped together, though he sees grounds for excluding II Sam 7.1-7 (see pp. 13, 16, 25, 52f.). But this is a rather loose statement of <u>theme</u>; so we quickly pass to the analysis of vocabulary (see the Appendix and cf. p. 14), one of whose functions is to suggest the relative isolation of the ark narrative within the Books of Samuel (p. 14). We have already seen some reason for caution in the interpretation of this listing of vocabulary usage. In the case of the succession story, on the other hand, we appear to have a clear statement of theme in the repeated question of I Kings 1. Yet we must note how Rost simply <u>assumes</u> that we have here the "key" to understanding and isolating the whole work (p. 68). In a similar way, Rost simply assumes "a priori" that the nature of the question is such that the narrative will include II Sam 11-12 and 13-20 (p. 73), and that "as the writer concentrated on the succession to David as his theme, he could hardly avoid dealing with the figure of Michal" (p. 88). Again, we need not here attempt to judge whether Rost is justified in making such assumptions, but it is important to note that he does make them and to be clear as to the role they play in his argument.

In addition, we have noted above (n.17) how a recognition of the importance of the succession issue in I Kgs 1 need not in itself mean that we have here an implicit statement of the theme of the whole narrative work.[27] We come back once more to the central question of theme. D. M. Gunn has nicely stated the problem:

> ... there is a methodological difficulty in too great a reliance on the thematic method of defining the boundaries of a narrative such as this, since it entails a large risk that the crucial definition of the theme will be arrived at before the boundaries of the material are known. This is in fact what happens in Rost's analysis. Yet strictly speaking (though one cannot be rigid in this matter) the reverse procedure ought to be followed. How can a critic be to any degree certain that he has accurately characterized the theme of a piece of literature, at any time a delicate and intricate business, unless he knows what that piece of literature consists of?[28]

As regards the other major narrative blocks considered by Rost, he appears to have been the first scholar to think expressly of a connected narrative work concerning the rise of David to kingship (see pp. 8f. with p. 121 n.12, 105, 109-12), though this is not considered in any detail; but here too, Rost's view has proved to be durable and fruitful.[29]

In the case of the ark narrative, A. F. Campbell argues that Rost "went far beyond his predecessors, and his successors have not gone very far beyond him";[30] he himself assumes the essential correctness of Rost's delimitation of the narrative, though he includes within it some passages deleted by Rost (not least II Sam 6.16, 20b-23; pp. 142, 163) and suggests a broader purpose than that of the cult legend (p. 165).[31] Campbell also makes the important point that the text should be examined as a narrative in its own right, rather than on the basis of the presumed history (or non-history) which may be thought to be behind it (cf., e.g., pp. 60 n.1, 100 n.2, 247f.). It is as well to underline this point here, since such confusion may well also lie behind a good deal of study of the succession story. But more radically,

Miller and Roberts[32] deny that II Sam 6 should be regarded as part of an "ark story," while admitting that "the author of II Sam 6 had the earlier narrative I Sam 4-7 before him, and his shaping of the later material, particularly the incident of the death of Uzzah, has been influenced by the theology of the earlier ark narrative" (p. 24). On the other hand, they link I Sam 2.12-17, 22-5, 27-36 with 4.1b-7.1, and see the subject of the narrative not as the ark, but as Yahweh himself, his power and his purpose (p. 60). We may remind ourselves of Wellhausen's judgement that "the relationship of II Sam 6 to I Sam 4.1-7.1 is only a unity of content, and not a literary unity,"[33] and note how here, as in discussion of the succession story, Rost has been accused of confusing these properly separate issues.

III

We are now in a position to return to the questions - and from now on we shall confine ourselves mainly to the succession story - why and how did Rost's work come to enjoy the success it did, in the decades following its publication?

We have noted already the considerable degree of freshness in his study. His linking of parts of II Sam 6 and 7 to the succession story (understood as an originally independent work) was new, though the connection of I Kings 1-2 with II Sam 9/10/13-20, an essential presupposition of Rost's analysis, was a long accepted result of scholarship.[34] Fresh, too, was his emphatic and detailed rejection of the original setting of this narrative within a larger complex such as a continuation of a pentateuchal source, though (we can say with hindsight) some steps in this direction had already been taken.[35]

On the other hand, the early dating of the material, and the connecting of it with eyewitness knowledge of the underlying events, was not new, as we shall see below, though the comparatively cautious terms in which Rost expressed this point, and its relationship to the historical character of the narrative (p. 104), should certainly be noted. Rost's minimalist view of the redactional reshaping of the story had long been current; and while he was certainly the first scholar to work out an overall thematic articulation of the narrative in terms of the succession issue, others before him, as he occasionally implies in passing, had seen this as a concern of this material.[36]

What, then, are the reasons for the impact made by Rost's "classic study?"[37]

To begin with, we must once more underline the intrinsic merits of the work. There is, first, the well-structured nature of the discussion (whether or not one always agrees with the starting-points). We have observed how in each chapter Rost carefully proceeds step by step, from a consideration of the difficulties he sees in prevailing views and a statement of his own initial premises, through each stage of his argument. We have seen how at the end of each element of the discussion a succinct summary of the results thus far is offered. However familiar one may be with the arguments which have been levelled against the study, it is difficult to deny that it has about it a sheer compelling clarity; and this impression is itself sufficient to suggest that we are handling something of a "classic."

We need also to try to put ourselves back into the context in which Rost was writing. When we attempt this, we may discern rather clearly that the work is essentially an exercise in simplification. In outlining the scope of the monograph, we noted how alongside the major aim of sketching some of the religious and theological attitudes of the early monarchy period, a great deal of stress is placed on the results of the source-critical investigation. The clarity and economy of Rost's procedure stands in marked contrast to the dominant source-critical views of Samuel.

Rost himself refers to, and criticises, the (then) still influential theory that the pentateuchal sources, or something closely related to them, could be traced through some, if not all, of the historical books down to Kings. The view that at least two lengthy connected sources can be traced, interwoven or juxtaposed, through the Books of Samuel goes back at least as far as the work of Gramberg, and the idea of their link with the source-strands of the Pentateuch was discussed favourably by Stähelin and Schrader.[38] It was Karl Budde, however, who expounded this view in a thoroughgoing way for Judges and Samuel, within the framework of the Graf-Wellhausen hypothesis, and in this he found a great deal of support - though exponents of the JE view of Samuel did not always make clear precisely in what sense they were attaching these labels to the sources.[39] In fact, we find around the beginning of this century a whole spectrum of views, ranging from those who would see the sources of Samuel as simple continuations of the J and E sources at least some way into the historical books, to those who, even if they saw continuous interwoven sources, nevertheless denied any connection with the pentateuchal strands - except perhaps some vague community of ethos. Those who argued for continuations of J and E into the historical books usually stressed, however, the different levels within these documents. Budde, to take the classic case, saw J as the product of a complex development, beginning with near-contemporary material in the "succession story," and working backwards in stages through the earlier periods of Israel's story.[40] On the other hand, Rudolf Kittel[41] argued strenuously against Budde's understanding of the composition of Samuel and the preceding books, seeking to demonstrate that the linguistic and other contacts between the sources of Samuel (and Judges) and those of the Pentateuch are due simply to a common background of thought, not to the identity, of their respective authors. There is, for him, little point in trying to connect a block like II Sam 9-20 with J; it is better seen as independent, and investigated in its own right, along with other clusters of stories in Samuel, particularly as these are grouped around individual figures.

In Kittel's work we may see hints paving the way for Rost's understanding of the composition of Samuel, though Kittel continued to hold to the idea of "horizontal" sources running through the clusters of material. But the general impression of the period may be described as one of stalemate between the proponents of the "horizontal" source-strata view. It is true that it could be claimed with some justification that to Budde "we owe what is now a generally accepted opinion in the critical school, that the J and E elements of the Hexateuch are continued into the books of Judges and Samuel",[42] but it was equally true that such analysis seemed able to pay fewer and fewer dividends. This applied to both the Pentateuch and the historical books. We may recall von Rad's starting-point for his study of "the form-critical problem of the Hexateuch":

> No one will ever be able to say that in our time there has been any crisis in the theological study of the Hexateuch. On the contrary, it might be held that we have reached a position of stalemate which many view with considerable anxiety. What is to be done about it? So far as the analysis of source documents is concerned, there are signs that the road has come to a dead end.[43]

Much earlier - perhaps around the beginning of this century - and more vehemently, Hugo Gressmann had written:

> Literary criticism has, under Wellhausen's leadership,
> lived to see a striking march of triumph ... But it is
> impossible to close one's eyes any longer to the fact that
> a one-sided literary criticism, and with it the school of
> Wellhausen, has played out its role ... The younger
> scholars and perhaps even more, the impartial observers,
> will feel as I do: we are sick to death of a diet of literary
> criticism.[44]

In 1924, Gressmann succeeded Karl Marti as editor of the
"Zeitschrift für die alttestamentliche Wissenschaft" - itself
an eloquent testimony to the way an old order was beginning
to give way to a new. Gressmann made clear that he still
accepted the importance of source-criticism, but stressed the
need to push beyond it into the earlier history of the
material.[45]

If we may see in all this some accurate reflection of the
mood of the times, it is not altogether surprising that Rost's
work attracted attention, in so far as it seemed to offer a
clear, compact alternative to the old source-critical views,
at least as far as the Books of Samuel were concerned. That
is to say, in general terms, that it fell on fruitful ground.

A little more may be said, however, about the relationship
of Rost's work to that of the pioneers of form-critical and
traditio-historical work, Gunkel and Gressmann.

Those scholars fiercely criticised what they took to be
Wellhausen's excessive concentration on the literary sources,
and his comparative lack of interest in trying to press back to
the earlier stages in the formation and transmission of their
contents.[46] Gunkel commented:

> The school of Wellhausen was and is still inclined, in its
> constructive historical work, to be too subservient to the
> literary documents, overlooking the fact that special
> precautions must be taken if the actual history is to be
> successfully reconstructed from the sources, however
> carefully these may have been sifted.[47]

For all their indebtedness to their predecessors, there is
nevertheless a parting of the ways. There is a growing stress
on the history of the smaller units of material lying behind
the sources.

How then does Rost's work stand in relation to this development of method? R. E. Clements has said of his study of
the succession story that

> What was significant in Rost's treatment was the argu-

ment that the study of the separate narrative incidents needed to be supplemented by a recognition of the overall redactional purpose which they had been made to serve. What Rost was in fact doing was to develop Gressmann's approach, recognizing that the separate narratives have been strung together into chains, or complexes.[48]

This statement of the relationship could, however, be a little misleading. Obvious points of contact there certainly are. We have already noted Gressmann's appreciation of Rost's work, not least its aesthetic criticism which was so important to the pioneers of form-criticism. We saw, too, how Gressmann stated that he himself believed in the existence of a compact, unified source concerning the succession to David's throne. On the other hand, it is hard to elicit such a view from his commentary on this material, where he seems rather to have divided the material into a number of more-or-less independent "Novellen" (such as II Sam 13-14 and 15-20)[49] and was duly criticised for this by Rost (see pp. 67, 83f.). For Gressmann, these narratives existed from the start in written form, whereas for Rost it was the succession story as a whole that was "without doubt transmitted in written form from the very beginning" (p. 4). Others had seen parts of the succession narative as once having had an independent existence,[50] and such a view found its most detailed exposition in the commentary, published in the same year as Rost's study, by Wilhelm Caspari; but his work, in many ways fresh and stimulating, in some ways eccentric, was overshadowed by Rost's thesis.[51] Rost, for his part, is remarkably reticent about our ability to penetrate the present well-unified structure of the succession story in a quest for older units of material.

Gunkel wrote little in detail on this story, though he does characterise the account of Absalom's revolt, in particular, as "history writing" (Geschichtsschreibung), and of this we shall say a little more below. But the direction of Gunkel's, and Gressmann's, form- and traditio-historical investigation of the pentateuchal narratives was to lead away from the idea of sharply defined literary sources with a clearly ascertainable theme and purpose, and thus to this extent was quite unlike what Rost was claiming for the succession story and other "blocks" within Samuel. Yet, for some scholars at least, the wheel has now come full circle with Rendtorff's argument that conventional source-criticism is basically incompatible with form- and traditio-historical criticism in pentateuchal studies, and with his creation of a model rather

more like that postulated by Rost for Samuel, with the
material bunching in its history around individual figures or
events - though still with a much greater traditio-historical
depth than anything Rost was able to claim for those
books.[52]

We may say, therefore, albeit with certain reservations in
matters of detail, that Rost's study helped significantly to
offer an exit from the impasse in the study of the historical
books which was well recognised by the 1920s. Here, then, we
have an important factor in the success of his work. To this
we must add the creative role played by his theses in the
work of several immensely influential Old Testament scholars, all of them concerned to move beyond a rigidly cir-
cumscribed and, in itself, rather sterile source-critical
treatment of the historical books, and all of them concerned
to explore the crucial role of the monarchy in Israel's history,
literature and religion.

First, there is Albrecht Alt. In his study of "The Formation
of the Israelite State in Palestine" (1930),[53] Alt expresses
his agreement with Rost regarding the ark narrative (p. 181
n.20); with his understanding of the story of David's rise (pp.
187f., 205f., 210 n.94, 211 n.99), without mention of Rost; and
with his delimitation and statement of theme in the
succession story - it "confines itself to the question of the
succession to the throne" (p. 206).[54] He is clear that while
the sources have their own purposes, and need to be handled
with a degree of caution, yet "in many cases we can take the
relevant details directly from the ancient text with full
confidence" (p. 207).

It is, I think, important to note that Alt's use of Rost's
work is for essentially _historical_ purposes. We may also
venture to say that this is the way most later students have
approached it. One can, perhaps, hardly blame historians for
attempting to make such use of it, as we find in the work of
Noth, Bright and Herrmann.[55] A textbook so widely influential in the English-speaking world as B. W. Anderson's
"The Living World of the Old Testament" pays only passing
attention to the literary character of the story before making
use of it as a straightforward historical source.[56] But it is
unwise to handle the literary questions so superficially, even
- no, especially - for the historian. Rost himself was rather
more circumspect in his assessment here than many who have
quoted his name and followed in his train (see pp. 103f.), and
as we have already stressed, his basic purpose was not to
reconstruct the political history of the early monarchy period
by means of this narrative.

An example or two may make my general point clearer. Alt ("The Formation," pp. 228ff.) makes historical use of the designations "Israel" and "Judah" in the narrative in his sketch of the political dynamics of the revolts of Absalom and Sheba. But the use of these terms in the story is in fact rather complex: what if the writer has other than purely historical reasons for designating the participants as he does? In a slightly different way, Rost himself may be suspected of confusing literary and historical arguments in his comments on the reasons why II Sam 6.16, 20-23 (in his view, part of the succession narrative) was incorporated into the ark narrative in II Sam 6 (see pp. 85, §4, 87f. - there is an uncharacteristic tenuousness in the argument here). Finally, we may note the comments of Herrmann on the "succession narrative":

> This group of chapters is centred on the question of the successor to David, even where that is not explicitly mentioned. The rebellions of Absalom (II Sam. 15-19) and Sheba (II Sam. 20) have their own significance in this context. These were the acute crises experienced in the heart of David's empire, crises which were decisive for its survival and which in the last resort could put in question the permanence of David's achievements.[57]

Might this, too, be regarded as a confusing of historical and literary arguments? We may well be able to make historical use of the narrative in tracing the steps which led eventually to the accession of Solomon, but this is very different from characterising the theme of the narrative as "the succession to David's throne." That could, as Rost argued, be seen as the theme of the story, but the literary investigation should not be short-circuited by taking over this or any other narrative as a ready-made historical source,[58] its "theme" commensurate with "historical reality." We shall offer some further comments on the issue of genre below.

A second influential scholar to make significant use of Rost's work is Martin Noth. Prior to his "History of Israel," Noth had drawn on Rost's discussion in his enormously important "Überlieferungsgeschichtliche Studien," published in 1943,[59] in which he expounded his theory of a "Deuteronomistic History" running from Deuteronomy to II Kings. The concept of a "Deuteronomistic History" was not in itself new: it is an idea whose roots reach back at least as far as Ewald. But the older exponents of the concept characteristically traced such a "history" from Genesis to II Kings, and saw it for the most part as composed initially by the interweaving of source strands through virtually the whole of its length.[60] Noth's theory was quite different: for him, no such extensive work existed, and the connected work which did exist was put together not by the interweaving of continuous strands but by the exilic Deuteronomist's own creative work in bringing together separated collections and blocks of tradition from Israel's earlier history. In this study, Noth takes a number of Rost's conclusions almost for granted (see pp. 54 and n.3, 55f. and nn.18-23,[61] 56f. and nn.30-1). Even more significantly, we may suggest that, through its extension to the historical books in general, Rost's model for the composition of Samuel, in terms of the linking of blocks of material concerning important persons or events, played a decisive role in Noth's concept, in a way that the older hypotheses could hardly have done.[62] Hints of this may be detected in Noth's work (see pp. 9f., 76), though I certainly do not wish to claim it as the only significant contribution to what has proved to be a fruitful theory.[63]

Thirdly, Rost's influence on the work of Gerhard von Rad should be noted, and here pride of place must be given to the essay "The Beginnings of Historical Writing in Ancient Israel."[64] Von Rad (who had, incidentally, succeeded Rost at Erlangen when the latter left for Berlin in 1929) accepts Rost's analysis of the limits and character of the succession story down to small details, with hardly a glance in the direction of those who had expressed problems with it. More significantly still, we have in the essay a clear and forceful attempt to define the genre of the succession story. We have here, von Rad claims, "the oldest specimen of ancient Israelite historical writing" (pp. 176, 192ff.). The material is not appropriately characterised as "saga" or "legend" (Sage)(p. 192); indeed, it is explicitly distinguished from the "hero sagas" (Heldensagen) of the Book of Judges (pp. 171-6); rather, it is "history writing" (Geschichtsschreibung). At the same time, von Rad offers some appreciation of the literary artistry of the story, and (against E. Meyer) expounds the theological dimension he discerns within it.

This is not the place to enter in detail into the complex issue of how such terms as "saga" or "legend" and "history writing" should be defined and used in critical study; it is well known that even the translation of such terms from one modern language into another is a thorny business.[65] But since the question of genre is one of great importance in the study of Old Testament traditions, and especially in view of the frequently firm and confident description of the succession story as "history writing," and its dominant use in historical study (as noted above), a few observations are in order.

Gunkel was able to describe the story of Absalom in II Sam 13-20 as "the most exquisite piece of early historical writing in Israel,"[66] and to distinguish this from the "Sagen" of Genesis. But Gunkel's criteria for making such distinctions[67] cannot always be applied to the material in a clear-cut and absolute way. To label a text as "history writing" on the basis of Gunkel's criteria does not necessarily express a judgement on its factual character, its correspondence with "what actually happened" in every detail. So, for instance, Gressmann could describe II Sam 13-14 and 15-20 as "history writing" (Geschichtsschreibung), without denying thereby the artistically developed character of these narratives.[68] Now it is precisely the degree and nature of such development which may illegitimately be passed over if we are too quick to label the succession story as "history writing." Are we perhaps to detect some apologetic role in von Rad's description of it in these terms?[69] Is this really an appropriate term to use for what we find in the succession story? Is there not the danger that we shall too easily put a straightjacket on the possibilities of interpretation if we insist on such a label with all the inherited baggage it carries with it? How far has other material in Samuel suffered as a consequence of applying to the succession story this label, which almost inevitably connotes for the modern reader a value-judgement? That the narrative is a brilliantly powerful piece can hardly be disputed; that it should be described as "history writing" cannot without more ado be presumed to be the case.

Von Rad's study is essentially an exposition of narrative character, rather than a properly historical analysis.[70] This is not to say that the latter would necessarily be more valuable (if we could carry it through); nor is it to assume that the question of historicity can automatically be determined by considering narrative technique; it is simply to plead for caution in applying potentially misleading classifications of genre.[71] And, we may add, if we find the label "history writing" inappropriate, we need not despair. We shall then be driven back again to "the whole problem of the relation of truth to fact and to fiction" which, as is well known,

has been hotly debated, especially since the post-Renaissance rise of historical critical method. The core of the problem is that there seems to be an inevitable element in reconstruction of events which tries to do justice to their many-faceted richness, and this can even lead to a historical novel expressing the truth of a person or period better than conventional history ... Any simple separation of fact from fiction is especially difficult when it is a matter of conveying a vivid character. How important is the verification of details when they are being used as part of a complex synthesis to portray an individual?[72]

IV

It may fairly be claimed that the work of these three great scholars has played a significant part in extending the influence of Rost's study. Its effect is felt, too, in many of the most widely used "Introductions" and commentaries. We need only note here the way Weiser draws on it in his comprehensive sketch of the formation of I and II Samuel,[73] and the extremely significant impact it has made on Hertzberg's commentary.[74] We may also recall once more the creative role it plays in von Rad's theological interpretation of the traditions of the early monarchy period. An associated problem, however, is that once it is operating at this level, a working hypothesis may almost imperceptibly come to be taken as an "assured result," with a consequent failure by scholars to test its literary and historical grounds; and this may breed complacency.[75]

There is one other possibly important factor contributing to the impact of Rost's work. This is its relationship to previous studies of II Sam 9-20, I Kings 1-2, not so much at the level of literary delimitation as at that of historical analysis.

We remember that Rost argues, though with a degree of caution, for the essentially historical character of the narrative. "The whole succession story," he feels justified in saying, "reveals itself to be a lively extract from an eventful period" (p. 103: "als lebensvoller Ausschnitt aus bewegter Zeit"). And yet the very artistry of the story necessarily leads to the question whether we are dealing with "real history" (wirkliche Geschichte) or "merely the play of fancy" (blosses Spiel der Phantasie), with "fact" (Wahrheit) or "fiction" (Dichtung). (We leave aside the question, touched on earlier, whether these are appropriate alternatives to set forward.) Rost, for his part, is clear as to where the answer lies: "On the one hand, it must be granted that everything gives an impression of probability and realism [Wahrscheinlichkeit und Wirklichkeit], so much so that one would most like to maintain that long stretches of the narrative come from immediate eye-witnesses"; and though, on the other hand, the possibility of a very high degree of artistic creation with no real relation to events cannot be excluded - and might well be suggested by the style and shape of the story - yet the author's use of a source (the Ammonite war report), and particularly his portrait of David, suggest that we have here a true reflection of what was historically the case. For "it can hardly be assumed that somebody would later have dared to expose David in this way without sound evidence" (p. 104).[76]

How much later might "later" be? As regards the time of composition, Rost says it is likely to have been the early years of Solomon's reign, given the story's failure to reflect the later division of the kingdom (does Rost really do justice here to the account of Sheba's revolt in II Sam 20?), and the atmosphere of peace and security suggested by the conclusion at I Kgs 2.46. (This latter is hardly in itself a convincing argument: accepting that the story concludes at this point, we should still need to ask whether there might not be literary and theological reasons for such a conclusion, not straightforwardly determined by the historical point at which the writer was working; one may compare the force of arguments from the presumed mood of optimism reflected in the Yahwist's work). Unlike many subsequent writers, Rost makes little use here of the argument that the story written "to Solomon's greater glory" is likely to come from that king's reign, using this description of the story, rather, in the course of discussing the author's identity (pp. 105f.).

But can we with any assurance claim that the portrayal of David in the story must be the work of a contemporary in close touch with the events which he faithfully recorded? There are, I suspect, various problems here, connected with the nature of the later "idealisation" of David and how far we may use this point (as often it is used) to support a "near-contemporary" date for the succession story.

And even if Rost is right to consider the succession theme as primary in the narrative, the isolation of the theme does not necessarily reveal the attitude of the narrative towards the events of which it speaks. Was Rost correct in thinking of the story as written to the glory of Solomon? This consideration in turn raises questions about original and redactional forms of the work, which have figured much more prominently in recent work than in Rost's study or in most of those scholars who preceded or followed him, as we shall indicate later.

For Rost's purposes, however, it is unnecessary to argue that we have a strictly accurate description of events:

> The most probable explanation is that real historical facts are related here, but in a strongly stylized dress ... For our purposes, it is sufficient to establish that this source is an historical narrative which rushes along with the excitement of a drama; it is based on actual events; it does not provide us simply with a poor imitation of reality but groups the events together around a theme, adopting them only so far and in such form as they are relevant to the basic questions of the story (p.104).

In the context of these observations, I want to suggest that an important factor in the influence of Rost's work is the way it has been used, often no doubt at second hand, and partly by laying undue emphasis on subsidiary points in the argument, as a support for the older views of the character and importance of the succession story.

The orthodoxy of the 18th and 19th centuries was reticent about delineating the sources of I and II Samuel. By and large, we see little attempt to move beyond the much older use of I Chr 29.29 by means of which parts of our canonical books were attributed to Samuel himself and other parts to Nathan and Gad, their work having been brought together perhaps by a later compiler - Ezra was sometimes suggested.[77] Hobbes and Spinoza had indeed noted indications of later date within the books, though without attempting any kind of source criticism; orthodoxy on the other hand stressed the role of prophets in the writing of the material, and the contemporary character of the writings as the work of participants in, or observers of, the affairs of the time. Thus the gap between the events and the recording of them was kept as short as possible. Even where the reasons postulated by the newer critics for source analysis were partly accepted, there may be detected a reluctance to admit any factual "error" within the sources, and a tendency to place even the compiler in close proximity in time to the events recorded.[78] But the idea that I and II Samuel comprised the records of the contemporary prophets, brought together by another prophetic writer soon after the division of the kingdom, was extremely common.[79]

With this approach we have to contrast the growth of a new and more radical kind of critical study, found in Eichhorn and his successors. Nevertheless, through all this complex development the general estimation of the character of the story of David in the second half of II Samuel remained remarkably constant. A recent writer has made the point nicely:

> Where else in the Bible can you find fourteen consecutive (almost!) chapters that emerged unscarred from the battles between the "critics" and the "conservatives" in the nineteenth and early twentieth centuries? Until recently, the critical consensus about II Samuel 9-20, I Kings 1-2 was embarrassingly similar to pre-critical, un-critical, or even "anti-critical" views of its character and origins.[80]

Thus the story of David's family, or "court history," as it was normally characterised, was commonly understood by the more critical scholars as the work of a contemporary or near-contemporary of the events and regarded as a close, objective portrayal of them.

A number of factors appear to have influenced this critical stance.

Again and again we find the notion of "objectivity" stressed in relation to this story in particular,[81] even where a disposition generally for or against David could be discerned; obviously this was a congenial emphasis for scholars in the later 19th and earlier 20th centuries. Not all, indeed, saw the story as the direct work of an eyewitness,[82] and some underlined the need to take seriously other ways of accounting for its vivid clarity,[83] but there was general agreement that here was "an historical source of the first rank," certainly linked more-or-less closely with eyewitness testimony.

Thus we find this characteristic of "objectivity" related on one side to the author's first-hand participation in events, and on the other to an assessment of the "authority" of the writing.[84] May we observe here the desire of a generation which laid so much store by "objective" ("scientific") historical writing for some such "objective" standing-ground within an Old Testament whose character as first-hand, objective testimony was at almost every other point open to question?[85] The complex of factors involved is well illustrated by, for example, William Sanday:

> In the art of narrative as such the Hebrew historian has no superior ... It is otherwise when we turn from the form of the narrative to its substance. Here there is a great variety, corresponding to the different degrees of nearness in which the historian stands to the events. Here too we may say that the Hebrew historian at his best is very good indeed. In a story like that of Absalom

we feel that we are being told the naked truth with the utmost clearness and impressiveness. The familiar tale awakes in us at this day the very same emotions which the scenes themselves awoke among those who witnessed them. The reason is that the document on which this part of the narrative is based is an excellent one, a pure transcript of nature, drawn from fresh and vivid recollection. [86]

Other related factors might include, I think, the "freshness" of the narrative style, which was often stressed; the apologetic value of the lack of the "miraculous" in the story, and the presumption that such a lack naturally suggests an early date; and perhaps to some extent, in the early 20th century, a reaction against the excesses of the exponents of "pan-Babylonianism" applied to the accounts of the early monarchy period. Each of these avenues could usefully be explored, along with the relationship between them and the characteristic circularity which can be detected in the discussions. Yet the influence of the older styles of argument continues to be felt, and it is quite likely that Rost's thesis has often appeared simply as a valuable support for them, without sufficient account being taken of the rather different shape of his discussion.

V

It now remains for us to indicate briefly the main outlines of study of the succession narrative since Rost's work, and we must begin by pointing out that no major point of his treatment has over the last two or three decades escaped serious criticism, a fact which is in itself a testimony to its immense influence. For clarity, we may distinguish different strands of criticism, though it will be apparent that at many points they are interrelated.

First, Rost's acceptance of the unity of II Sam 9-20 with I Kgs 1-2, and his precise definition of the narrative's extent, have been challenged.

As we have seen, the sort of position outlined in Eissfeldt's review continued to be held by Eissfeldt himself, and was advocated by some other scholars (most fully by Hölscher and, more recently, Schulte): namely that the "succession story" should not be separated too distinctly from the material which precedes and (to some extent) follows it. This has remained a minority position; and yet Eissfeldt's important observations on method should not be too readily discounted.

For one thing, they have the merit of keeping before us various connections between the succession story and other material in Samuel which have too frequently been overlooked.

The problem of accounting for the rather odd starting-point of the narrative as delineated by Rost, and some links of content with preceding chapters, have suggested that earlier material (as, for example, much of 2 Sam 2-4) may have formed part of the narrative of II Sam 9-20, I Kgs 1-2.[87] On the other hand the question has been raised whether some of the connections might not be due to later redactional linking, as Veijola (below), for example, has argued. Again, the issue is posed in a quite different way by those recent scholars who have stressed the connections in terms of narrative patterns and the use of "traditional" forms or motifs, whether this is conceived of either as evidence for the influence of oral traditional narrative forms or at the level of direct literary borrowing by the author of the "court history."[88]

At the other end of the narrative, a few scholars have questioned the grounds for seeing I Kgs 1-2 as an original continuation of II Sam 9-20.[89] Perhaps the most thorough-going recent attempt to sever the connection is that of J. W. Flanagan, who tries to demonstrate that an original "court-history" of David has at some later time been transformed into a "succession narrative" by the addition of I Kgs 1-2 and the narrative of David and Bathsheba, though his grounds for making such a separation seem to me unconvincing.[90]

In a more general way, recognition of the significant forms of continuity in the narratives of I and II Samuel may lead to a rather less well-defined picture of the origins and scope of the sources used,[91] though to see the books simply in terms of the grouping of smaller narrative units[92] may be a counsel of despair. At any rate, the attractive simplicity of Rost's approach seems to leave unresolved many literary issues, which in turn put question marks against his characterisation of II Sam 9-20, I Kgs 1-2 as a "succession narrative."

Secondly, there is the matter of the "Tendenz" of the story. Here we must note some doubts raised about Rost's view that when the question "Who shall sit on the throne of David after him?" is answered by the story in Solomon's favour, the author was not merely offering a description of events but also judging them affirmatively. In this opinion he has been followed by a multitude of scholars,[93] though we should not forget that an anti-Solomonic tendency had been discerned by some critics long before Rost expounded the opposite viewpoint[94] - and Rost perhaps failed to do justice to the features which led them to this view. In an influential paper in the Rost "Festschrift," L. Delekat accepts Rost's delimitation of the story, but finds a critical stance not only towards David and Solomon, but also towards the institution of kingship in general.[95] Nevertheless, within the story as we have it, it is difficult not to see expressions of a very positive kind concerning the two kings.

It is perhaps not surprising then, thirdly, that several attempts have been made to find a far greater degree of redactional work in the narrative than Rost, with the majority of scholars, has discerned. The most effective, to my mind, is that of Timo Veijola,[96] who argues that a narrative originally unfavourable to Solomon has been heavily edited by the Deuteronomists (within whose activity, following Smend and others, he finds different "layers"),[97] in order to change it into a theological legitimation of the Davidic dynasty. In a rather different way, E. Würthwein has concluded that the succession story (in his view II Sam 10-20, I Kgs 1-2) has been altered by redaction from a thoroughly "profane" narrative, critical of kingship in general, into one in which David is idealised and Solomon's kingship justified theologically.[98] I believe that much of this work has to be described as unconvincing.[99] Question-marks must be set against both the methods and conclusions even of so attractive and all-embracing a study as that of Veijola.[100]

A number of these queries stem from doubt as to whether proper account has been taken of the literary character of the story, and whether at points a too-historical reading (on whose dangers we have reflected above) has not "called the tune". This may bring us, fourthly, to note the concentration, in a torrent of recent studies, on the investigation of the succession story, or whatever we prefer to call it, as a story, and not simply as a source for political or religious history, or the spirituality of its author, or for ancient forms of propaganda. Such literary criticism may reveal something of the worth of engaging with the narrative in its own right.[101] The recognition that we are not necessarily dealing with "history writing" in any conventional modern sense shifts the whole range of the older questions put to the narrative - more sensitively by Rost than by many others - on to a different level; the older positivism has in this sense come apart at the seams. This is not in my view to deny the legitimacy of the older questions, but to assert that they take on a rather different character when placed in the context of these other issues. How are the historical and literary discussions to be related? Can they be related in any meaningful way? How appropriate, and how possible, is it to put historical questions to the succession story? And what is the shape of the questions the narrative in its turn puts to us, about humanity - and about God?

Even this brief sketch may be sufficient to show something of the creative and stimulating role played by Rost's study. As we have seen, not every point Rost made was new; not every point was properly handled; least of all dare we say that every question was correctly solved. But there is no need to try to underline once more the strengths of the work: it is of age and can speak for itself. We may come to criticise it, but if we are wise we shall come also, not to bury it, but to praise it.

E. Ball
St. John's College
Nottingham

ABBREVIATIONS

AJSL	American Journal of Semitic Languages and Literatures
ATD	Das Alte Testament Deutsch
BKAT	Biblischer Kommentar Altes Testament
BWANT	Beiträge zur Wissenschaft vom Alten und Neuen Testament
BZ	Biblische Zeitschrift
BZAW	Beihefte zur Zeitschrift für die Alttestamentliche Wissenschaft
EHAT	Exegetisches Handbuch zum Alten Testament
ET	English translation
ExpT	Expository Times
FRLANT	Forschungen zur Religion und Literatur des Alten und Neuen Testaments
HKAT	Handkommentar zum Alten Testament
IDB	Interpreter's Dictionary of the Bible
JSOT	Journal for the Study of the Old Testament
JSOTS	Journal for the Study of the Old Testament, Supplement Series
JPOS	Journal of the Palestine Oriental Society
KEH	Kurzgefasstes exegetisches Handbuch zum Alten Testament
KHCAT	Kurzer Hand-Commentar zum Alten Testament
OLZ	Orientalistische Literaturzeitung
OTL	Old Testament Library
RGG	Die Religion in Geschichte und Gegenwart
SAT	Die Schriften des Alten Testaments
SBLDS	Society of Biblical Literature, Dissertation Series
SBT	Studies in Biblical Theology
TLZ	Theologische Literaturzeitung
VT	Vetus Testamentum
WMANT	Wissenschaftliche Monographien zum Alten und Neuen Testament
ZAW	Zeitschrift für die Alttestamentliche Wissenschaft

NOTES TO THE INTRODUCTION

1   For a brief appreciation, see E. Kutsch: "Leonhard Rost (1896-1979)," ZAW 92, 1980, pp. 1f., and for details of the wide scope of his work see D. Kellermann: "Bibliographie Leonhard Rost" in the Rost Festschrift: F. Maass, ed.: Das Ferne und Nahe Wort, BZAW 105, Berlin 1967, pp. 265-75. His later publications included: Vermutungen über den Anlass für griechischen Übersetzung der Tora, Zürich 1970, and: Einleitung in die alttestamentlichen Apokryphen und Pseudepigraphen, Heidelberg 1971 (ET, Nashville 1976).

2   Die Überlieferung von der Thronnachfolge Davids, BWANT III/6, reprinted without change in: L. Rost: Das kleine Credo und andere Studien zum Alten Testament, Heidelberg 1965, pp. 119-253. Cf. also the summary in: E. Sellin/L. Rost: Einleitung in das Alte Testament, 9th edn., Heidelberg 1959, pp. 90f., where no obvious shift in Rost's views is apparent.

3   B. S. Childs: Introduction to the Old Testament as Scripture, London 1979, p. 270.

4   H. J. Stoebe: "Gedanken zur Heldensage in den Samuelbüchern" in: Das Ferne und Nahe Wort, p. 208. Cf. also Kutsch, art. cit.: p. 1.

5   C. Kuhl: TLZ 53, 1928, cols. 99f.

6   H. Gressmann: "Neue Bücher," ZAW 44, 1926, pp. 309f.

7   Kuhl appears later to have changed his mind on a number of these points, in favour of the essential correctness of Rost' views: The Old Testament. Its Origins and Composition, Edinburgh 1961 (ET from: Die Entstehung des Alten Testaments, [1953] 2nd edn. 1960, ed. G. Fohrer), pp. 129ff.

8   H. Gressmann: Die älteste Geschichtsschreibung und Prophetie Israels ... übersetzt, erklärt und mit Einleitungen versehen, SAT II/1, (1910) 2nd edn., Göttingen 1921, pp. XIV, 157ff. [ET: see Bibliog.]

9   H. M. Wiener: JPOS 7, 1927, pp. 135-41. Cf. Wiener: The Composition of Judges II 11 to I Kings II 46, Leipzig 1929.

10   O. Eissfeldt: OLZ 31, 1928, cols. 801-12.

11   See his: Die Komposition der Samuelisbücher, Leipzig 1931, and esp.: The Old Testament. An Introduction, Oxford 1965 (ET from 3rd German edn. 1964), pp. 132-43, 241-8, 268-81.

12   Eissfeldt: Introduction, p. 138.

13   Komposition. Cf. the review by K. Budde: OLZ 34, 1931, cols. 1056-62, who comments: "my disagreement does not lie basically in the acceptance of three independent source documents originally running through the material, but with the present attempt to identify them" (cols. 1061f.).

14   Thus, for example, Rost is not concerned to ask why the "ark narrative" is divided and placed as it is within I-II Samuel (see p. 123, n.48).

15   Among other scholars who, after Rost's work, have continued to postulate a continuation of the sources of the earlier historical books into Samuel and in some cases even into Kings, may be noted E. Auerbach: Wüste und gelobtes Land, I, Berlin 1932, pp. 22-33, G. Hölscher: Geschichtsschreibung in Israel. Untersuchungen zum Yahwisten und Elohisten, Lund 1952 (cf. his earlier works: "Das Buch der Könige, seine Quellen und sein Redaktion" in the Gunkel Festschrift: Eucharisterion, FRLANT 36, Göttingen 1923, I, pp. 158-213; Die Anfänge der hebräischen Geschichtsschreibung, Heidelberg 1942); C. A. Simpson: The Composition of the Book of Judges, Oxford 1957, p. 6. But the differences between such scholars' views should not be overlooked. H. H. Guthrie: God and History in

the Old Testament, London 1961, pp. 26-39, regards the succession story as "probably independent in origin," but as incorporated within the extensive "J document" which forms the basic nucleus of the narrative from Genesis to Kings. Cf. the tentative comments of D. N. Freedman: "Pentateuch," IDB, Nashville 1962, III, pp. 714f. Attention may again be drawn to the variety of opinion regarding the degree of independence of the succession story before its incorporation into the wider context, a pointer to the continuing significance of the questions raised by Eissfeldt. (The same may be said of the differing views on the compatibility of such views with Noth's understanding of the "Deuteronomistic History": see, e.g., Freedman: op.cit., pp. 716f.). H. Schulte: Die Entstehung der Geschichtsschreibung im Alten Israel, BZAW 128, Berlin 1972, is the most recent thoroughgoing exponent of the view that we may trace a Yahwistic work extending from Gen 2 into I Kings, composed around 900 B.C., and drawing on oral and written traditions, including an almost contemporary account of the events surrounding the accession of Solomon (pp. 174f.).

16   On this, cf. the well-known paper by W. K. Wimsatt and M. K. Beardsley: "The Intentional Fallacy" (1946), reprinted in: Wimsatt: The Verbal Icon. Studies in the Meaning of Poetry, London 1970, pp. 3-18, and with other studies on the same theme in: G. Newton-de Molina, ed.: On Literary Intention, Edinburgh 1976. But see already the comments of R. G. Moulton: The Literary Study of the Bible, London 1896, pp. 92f.

17   We have noted above Eissfeldt's identification of theme and content (OLZ 31, col. 805). But such terms need more precise definition, along with the related question of "motifs," since a proper consideration of these is in fact essential to the proper characterisation of a narrative work. Cf. the valuable discussion and references in: D. J. A. Clines: The Theme of the Pentateuch, JSOTS 10, Sheffield 1978, pp. 17-21 and notes. Thus, for instance, we might possible characterise the issue of the succession to David's throne as a significant motif in II Sam 9-20, I Kgs 1-2, without necessarily designating it (with Rost) as the theme of the work.

18   Cf. Eissfeldt: OLZ 31, cols. 810f., referring to the very limited role played in Rost's work by textual criticism in the narrower sense, and to the need for a proper view of the relationship between source- and textual-critical work.

19   As Rost partly admits, this has a fairly rough-and-ready character to it. So, for example, we may ask whether the consideration of vocabulary is not unduly confined; and it is hardly surprising, perhaps, that we discover links with the vocabulary of the cult, given the subject-matter of the text. A. F. Campbell: The Ark Narrative (1 Sam 4-6; 2 Sam 6). A Form-Critical and Traditio-Historical Study, SBLDS 16, Missoula 1975, p. 43, may be correct in criticising K.-D. Schunck's criticism of Rost, but we are still entitled to ask why Rost made the selection of vocabulary which he did.

20   P. D. Miller and J. J. M. Roberts: The Hand of the Lord: A Reassessment of the "Ark Narrative" of 1 Samuel, Baltimore & London 1977, p. 23.

21   Rost's view is accepted by, e.g., R. E. Clements: Prophecy and Covenant, SBT 1st Series 43, London 1965, pp. 56f., and more tentatively in: Abraham and David. Genesis XV and its Meaning for Israelite Tradition, SBT 2nd Series 5, London 1967, p. 53 n.18. See also the scholars on both sides of the argument noted by D. M. Gunn: The Story of King David. Genre and Interpretation, JSOTS 6, Sheffield 1978, p. 132 n.6, and Gunn's own critical comments on pp. 66f. and elsewhere. T. N. D. Mettinger offers a useful sketch of research on II Sam 7 as an introduction to his own discussion (King and Messiah. The Civil and Sacral Legitimation of Israel's

Kings, Coniectanea Biblica OT Series 8, Lund 1976, pp. 48-50).

22   A number of scholars prior to Rost had found in the Ammonite war report a separate source: so, e.g., B. Luther, in: E. Meyer: Die Israeliten und ihre Nachbarstämme, Halle 1906, pp. 184-6 [ET: see Bibliog. under Luther]; H. Gressmann: Älteste Geschichtsschreibung, p. 153 (see also Rost, p. 126 n.1); contrast (e.g.) A. Kuenen: Historisch-kritische Einleitung in die Bücher des alten Testaments hinsichtlich ihres Entstehung und Sammlung, I/2, Leipzig 1890, p. 50 n.9; K. Budde: Die Bücher Richter und Samuel, ihre Quellen und ihr Aufbau, Giessen 1890, p. 247; W. Nowack: Richter, Ruth u. Bücher Samuelis übersetzt und erklärt, HKAT I/4, Göttingen 1902, Sam. p. XXI; J. F. Stenning: "Samuel, I and II," Hastings' Dictionary of the Bible IV, Edinburgh 1902, p. 390. But Rost's discussion, which treats this report as an independent source taken up by the author of the succession story, circumvents the main problem felt by these scholars. I find unconvincing J. W. Flanagan's view that the war report is "more deeply embedded in the narrative that the David-Bathsheba-Uriah triangle" ("Court History or Succession Document? A Study of II Samuel 9-20 and I Kings 1-2," JBL 91, 1972, pp. 172-81, see p. 176).

23   K. Budde: Die Bücher Samuel, KHCAT 8, Tübingen & Leipzig 1902, p. XVII (not "the favourite text of the exegetes," as Rost, p. 65, has it).

24   C. Steuernagel: Lehrbuch der Einleitung in das alte Testament, Tübingen 1912. Cf. Rost, pp. 10, 67.

25   G. P. Ridout: Prose Compositional Techniques in the Succession Narrative (2 Sam 7, 9-20; 1 Kings 1-2), Diss., Graduate Theological Union 1971, offers a detailed and valuable analysis of the forms of composition in the narrative, making appreciative but not uncritical use of Rost's work. See also R. N. Whybray: The Succession Narrative. A study of II Sam 9-20 and I Kings 1 and 2, SBT 2nd Series 9, London 1968, pp. 19-47.

26   Rost suggests that an attribution to Ahimaaz (with Klostermann, and later R. H. Pfeiffer: Introduction to the Old Testament, 2nd edn., London 1952, pp. 356f., and others) is more feasible than regarding the story as the work of Abiathar or someone in his circle (after B. Duhm: Das Buch Jeremia, KHCAT 11, Tübingen & Leipzig 1901, p. 3; cf. K. Budde: Geschichte der althebräischen Litteratur, Die Litteraturen des Ostens 7, Leipzig 1906, pp. 38ff., and more recently E. Würthwein: Die Erzählung von der Thronfolge Davids - theologische oder politische Geschichtsschreibung? Theologische Studien 115, Zürich 1974, pp. 56f.), in view of its pro-Solomonic stance, though in the end he leaves the question open (pp. 105f.). Among the other suggested authors are Nathan or an associate (cf. Wiener: Composition; J. Gray: I & II Kings, OTL, 2nd edn., London 1970, pp. 19, 21f.), Jonathan ben Abiathar (e.g. Schulte: Entstehung, p. 175), and Hushai (cf. H. W. Hertzberg: I and II Samuel, OTL, London 1964 [ET from 2nd (rev.) German edn. 1960], p. 379, tentatively), while T. C. Vriezen ("De Compositie van de Samuel-Boeken" in: Orientalia Neerlandica, Leiden 1948, pp. 167-89; and still followed in: The Religion of Ancient Israel, London 1967 [ET from Dutch edn. 1963], pp. 79f.) conjures up Zabud (I Kgs 4.5). Quite apart from the inevitably speculative character of all such suggestions, there is the perhaps unconscious danger that having once determined a possible author in line with whatever "Tendenz" we discover in the narrative - whether pro- or anti-Solomon - this attribution then takes on a substantive confirmatory role in one's interpretation of the nature of the narrative. The same may be true in arguments about the contemporary, eye-witness character of the story, reached initially on circumstantial grounds (is there a hint of this in Gray: Kings, p. 17?).

27   C. Conroy: Absalom Absalom! Narrative and Language in 2 Sam 13-20, Analecta Biblica 81, Rome 1978, pp. 101-5, finds no evidence for the succession theme in II Sam 13-20.

28   Gunn: Story of King David, p. 81.

29   See the discussions of this material by J. Wellhausen: Die Composition des Hexateuchs und der historischen Bücher des Alten Testaments, Berlin, 3rd edn. 1899, pp. 246-55 ("Erste Geschichte Davids. 1 Sam 15-2 Sam 8") and: Prolegomena to the History of Israel, Edinburgh 1885 (ET from 2nd German edn. 1883), pp. 262f. For a survey of research on this material after Rost, cf. especially J. H. Grønbaek: Die Geschichte vom Aufstieg Davids (1 Sam. 15-2 Sam. 5). Tradition und Composition, Acta Theologica Danica 10, Copenhagen 1971, pp. 11-36, and his own magnificent work; see, among later works, J. Conrad, "Zum geschichtlichen Hintergrund der Darstellung von Davids Aufstieg," TLZ 97, 1972, cols. 321-32; H. J. Stoebe: Das erste Buch Samuelis, KAT VIII/1, Gütersloh 1973, pp. 58ff. and ad loc.; F. Schicklberger: "Die Davididen und das Nordreich. Beobachtungen zur sog. Geschichte vom Aufstieg Davids," BZ 18, 1974, pp. 255-63; Mettinger: King and Messiah, pp. 33-47; J. A. Soggin: "The narratives about the rise of David" in J. H. Hayes and J. M. Miller, eds.: Israelite and Judaean History, OTL, London 1977, pp. 333-5; F. Crüsemann: Der Widerstand gegen das Königtum, WMANT 49, Neukirchen-Vluyn 1978, pp. 128-42; P. K. McCarter: I Samuel, Anchor Bible 8, New York 1980, pp. 27-30 and ad loc. N. P. Lemche: "David's Rise," JSOT 10, 1978, pp. 2-25, is a significant discussion of the historical value of this narrative complex.

30   Campbell: Ark Narrative, p. 12; see his survey of previous work on the ark narrative, pp. 1-54. Cf. McCarter: I Samuel, pp. 23-6.

31   Cf. also, though differently, O. Kaiser: Introduction to the Old Testament. A Presentation of its Results and Problems, Oxford 1975 (ET from 2nd German edn. 1970 incl. rev. 1973), p. 155; G. von Rad: Old Testament Theology, I, Edinburgh 1962 (ET from 1st German edn. 1957 incl. rev. for 2nd edn.), p. 45.

32   P. D. Miller and J. J. M. Roberts: The Hand of the Lord. For the attempt to link parts of I Sam 2 with chs. 4-6, cf. already W. Caspari: Die Samuelbücher, KAT VII, Leipzig 1926, pp. 57ff.

33   Wellhausen: Composition des Hexateuchs, p. 254.

34   Cf. J. J. Stähelin: Kritische Untersuchungen über den Pentateuch, die Bücher Josua, Richter, Samuels und Könige, Berlin 1843, p. 135, and: Specielle Einleitung in die kanonischen Bücher des Alten Testaments, Elberfeld 1862, pp. 108, 110, and the reference to the strict connection between Samuel and Kings on p. 125. Stähelin refers back to his comments in A. Tholuck's Lit. Anzeiger, 1838, p. 526, for significant links of vocabulary between I Kgs 1-2 and the Books of Samuel, suggesting that these chapters do, in fact, belong with I-II Sam. With this view, cf., for example, S. Davidson: An Introduction to the Old Testament, Critical, Historical, and Theological, I, London 1862, p. 526; J. (F.) Bleek: An Introduction to the Old Testament, London 1869 (ET from 2nd German edn. 1865, ed. A. Kamphausen), p. 399. But such opinions need to be examined within the general context of developing views in the late 18th and early 19th centuries of the links (or otherwise) between Samuel and Kings. For the connection of I Kgs 1-2 with II Sam 11-20, see also O. Thenius: Die Bücher der Könige, KEH 9, 2nd edn., Leipzig 1873, p. 1. In his commentary on Samuel (see n.22) Thenius to some extent anticipates a "block-view" of the composition of the books, and seems to me to be more noteworthy than J. G. Eichhorn (see Stoebe: I Samuelis, p. 35) as a forerunner of Rost's views.

35   Besides the work of Steuernagel, we may refer to A. R. S. Kennedy's view: Samuel, Century Bible, Edinburgh n.d. [c.1904], pp. 20f., that II Sam 9-20 is "to all intents and purposes a literary unit," which finds its "continuation and probable close" in I Kgs 1-2, and whose connection with previous material in Samuel is left open (cf. pp. 8, 21, 233). Kennedy's attractive analysis of I-II Samuel has continued to find supporters (e.g., G. W. Anderson: A Critical Introduction to the Old Testament, London 1959, pp. 74-7).

36   So, for example, Stenning: "Samuel, I and II," p. 389; Budde: Geschichte, pp. 35, 39; B. Stade: "Samuel (Books)," Encyclopaedia Biblica, IV, London 1907, cols. 4278f.; S. R. Driver: An Introduction to the Literature of the Old Testament, (1891) 9th edn., Edinburgh 1913, pp. 182f.

37   J. A. Soggin: Introduction to the Old Testament, OTL, London 1980 (ET from 2nd [rev.] Italian edn. 1974, incl. further rev.), p. 192.

38   C. P. W. Gramberg: Kritische Geschichte der Religionsideen des alten Testaments, II, Berlin 1830, pp. 71-116. Cf. the conspectus of his source-division in: W. M. L. de Wette: Lehrbuch der historisch-kritischen Einleitung in die kanonischen und apokryphischen Bücher des Alten Testaments, 7th edn., Berlin 1852, p. 225. (Gramberg, it may be noted, holds II Sam 9-20 to be an uninterrupted section of his second source.)

      J. J. Stähelin: Untersuchungen, pp. 112ff.; Specielle Einleitung, pp. 66-117. Stähelin's views must, of course, be set within the context of his "supplementary" hypothesis regarding the sources of the Pentateuch.

      W. M. L. de Wette: Lehrbuch der historisch-kritischen Einleitung ..., neu bearbeitet von E. Schrader, 8th edn., Berlin 1869, pp. 325-61.

39   K. Budde: Richter und Samuel, 1890, and later commentaries on Judges and Samuel in KHCAT. Cf. also, e.g., C. Cornill: Introduction to the Canonical Books of the Old Testament, London 1907 (ET from 5th German edn. 1900), pp. 148-221, with references to earlier essays by this writer which antedate Budde's work; Nowack: Richter, Ruth und Samuelis, Jgs. pp. XII-XVI, Sam. pp. XIVff.; I. Benzinger: Jahvist und Elohist in den Königsbüchern, BWANT 27, Stuttgart 1921; R. Smend: "JE in den geschichtlichen Bücher des AT," ZAW 39, 1921, pp. 181-217. Such scholars, like their later followers, were not agreed as to where the sources ended. P. Dhorme: Les Livres de Samuel, Études Bibliques, Paris 1910, pp. 6-8 and ad loc., was one of the few who divided even the "succession story" into "J" and "E" components.

40   So, for example, in: Das Buch der Richter, KHCAT 7, Freiburg 1897, p. XIV. Cf. the comments of R. A. Carlson: David, the chosen King. a Traditio-historical Approach to the Second Book of Samuel, Uppsala 1964, pp. 42f. Budde speculated as to the possible role of Abiathar in composing not only the succession story but also earlier parts of Samuel belonging to the same source (Geschichte, pp. 38ff.). Contrast E. Sellin: Introduction to the Old Testament, London 1923 (ET from 3rd German edn. 1920), p. 115.

41   R. Kittel: "Die pentateuchische Urkunden in den Büchern Richter und Samuel," TSK 65, 1892, pp. 44-71. For later developments of Kittel's views see the successive editions of his History, and his notes on Samuel in: E. Kautzsch/A. Bertholet, eds.: Die heilige Schrift des Alten Testaments I, 4th edn., Tübingen 1922, pp. 407-92.

42   T. H. Robinson: "Karl Budde," ExpT 36, 1924/5, p. 300 (my stress).

43   G. von Rad: "The Form-Critical Problem of the Hexateuch" (ET from German edn. [BWANT IV/26] 1938) in: The Problem of the Hexateuch and Other Essays, Edinburgh 1966, pp. 1-78, see p. 1.

44   See W. Klatt: Hermann Gunkel, FRLANT 100, Göttingen 1969, p. 74.

45   H. Gressmann: "Die Aufgaben der alttestamentlichen Forschung," ZAW 42, 1924, pp. 2ff.

46   Cf. the discussions and further references in: D. A. Knight: Re-discovering the Traditions of Israel, SBLDS 9, Missoula, 2nd edn. 1975, pp. 64-8, 70-87.

47   H. Gunkel: "The 'Historical Movement' in the Study of Religion," ExpT 38, 1926/7, p. 533.

48   R. E. Clements: A Century of Old Testament Study, Guildford 1976, p. 40. Cf. the similar remarks by K. Koch: "Samuelisbücher," RGG 3rd edn., V, Tübingen 1959, col. 1359. Eissfeldt's comments (Introduction, pp. 270f.) seem to me more justified.

49   Gressmann: Älteste Geschichtsschreibung, pp. XIV, 163, 181. But he also speaks of I Kgs 1-2 as having strict connections with related sections in Samuel (p. 193).

50   See especially, B. Luther: "Die Novelle von Juda und Tamar und andere israelitische Novellen" in: Meyer: Die Israeliten, pp. 175-206, see pp. 188f. (for II Sam 20), pp. 189ff. (for II Sam 11-12), and pp. 195ff. (for II Sam 13-19) [ET: see Bibliog. under Luther].

51   Caspari: Die Samuelbücher, pp. 509ff. Among his earlier studies to which Rost refers cf. especially: "Literarische Art und historischer Wert von 2 Sam. 15-20," Theologische Studien und Kritiken 82, 1909, pp. 317-48 [ET: see Bibliog.]. For some discussion of Caspari's work, see R. A. Carlson: David, the Chosen King, pp. 182ff.

52   R. Rendtorff: Das überlieferungsgeschichliche Problem des Penta-teuch, BZAW 147, Berlin 1977. In spite of the great differences, the extent to which Rendtorff's questioning of our ability to delineate extensive "sources" in the Pentateuch is similar to (say) Eissfeldt's criticisms of Rost should not be overlooked.

53   A. Alt: "The Formation of the Israelite State in Palestine" in: Essays on Old Testament History and Religion, Oxford 1966, pp. 171-237 (ET from: Die Staatenbildung der Israeliten in Palästina, 1930, repr. in: Kleine Schrif-ten zur Geschichte des Volkes Israel, II, München 1964, pp. 1-65); reference here is to ET.

54   Cf. "Salomo", RGG 2nd edn., V, Tübingen 1931, cols. 85-7, where Alt follows Rost's delineation of the narrative, including II Sam 6.16, 20ff.

55   M. Noth: The History of Israel, 2nd edn., London 1960 (ET from 2nd German edn. 1954), pp. 165 and n.2, 179 and n.1, 191, 199 and n.1, 199ff., for Noth's use of Rost's work.

        J. Bright: A History of Israel, 2nd edn., London 1972, pp. 179, 202ff., 215 (these statements are unchanged in the 3rd edn. [1980]).

        S. Herrmann: A History of Israel in Old Testament Times, London 1975 (ET from German edn. 1973), pp. 32 and n.45, 141f. n.1, 149f. and n. 12, 157f. and n.33, 163ff.

56   B. W. Anderson: The Living World of the Old Testament, 3rd edn., London 1978, pp. 176, 184f., 189 (these statements are unchanged from the 1st edn. [1958]).

57   Herrmann: History, p. 163.

58   For a rather extreme example of the danger here, cf. B. D. Napier's comment that in the succession story "every detail is authentic and unimpeachable," rightly criticised by J. R. Porter: "Pre-Islamic Arabic Historical Traditions and the Early Historical Narratives of the Old Testament," JBL 87, 1968, p. 22 n.24. In the second edition of his work (Song of the Vineyard: A Guide Through the Old Testament, Philadelphia 1981, p. 128) Napier says, "in this remarkable biography even details appear to be authentic and unimpeachable."

59   The first part of this work has appeared in an English translation as The Deuteronomistic History, JSOTS 15, Sheffield 1981 (to which my references correspond).

60   See Noth: Deuteronomistic History, p. 12, and cf., e.g., Steuernagel: Einleitung, pp. 113, 338; J. Meinhold: Einführung in das Alte Testament, Giessen 1919, pp. 190ff.; Sellin: Introduction, pp. 124-6.

61   For Noth's later disagreement with Rost about II Sam 7, cf. his essay: "David and Israel in II Samuel VII" (ET from: "David und Israel in II Samuel, 7" in: Mélanges Bibliques ... André Robert, 1955, pp. 122-30) in: The Laws in the Pentateuch and Other Studies, Edinburgh 1966, pp. 250-9.

62   J. A. Bewer/E. G. Kraeling: The Literature of the Old Testament, 3rd edn., New York 1962, p. 73, ascribes the decline of the older source-critical views of the historical books to Noth's theory; but we may suggest once more that Rost's work forms an important foundation for this theory.

63   Eissfeldt: Introduction, pp. 241-8, has a valuable discussion of Noth's theory over against his own views; cf. his conceding of the possibility of Noth's view in: "The Hebrew Kingdom," Cambridge Ancient History II/2, 3rd edn., Cambridge 1975, ch. XXXIV, p. 537.

64   "The Beginnings of Historical Writing in Ancient Israel" (ET from: "Der Anfang der Geschichtsschreibung im Alten Israel," Archiv für Kulturgeschichte 32, 1944, pp. 1-42) in: The Problem of the Hexateuch, pp. 166-204. Cf. Old Testament Theology I, pp. 308ff.

65   Cf., e.g., J. A. Wilcoxen: "Narrative" in: J. H. Hayes, ed.: Old Testament Form Criticism, San Antonio 1974, pp. 57-98.

66   H. Gunkel: The Legends of Genesis (ET from the introduction to: Genesis, HKAT I/1, 1901), [Chicago 1901] New York 1964, p. 10. Cf. Gunkel, "Die Israelitische Literatur" in: P. Hinneberg, ed.: Die Kultur der Gegenwart I/7, Berlin 1906, pp. 73f.; "Geschichtsschreibung. I. Im AT," RGG 2nd edn., II, Tübingen 1928, cols. 1112-5, where he describes the old stories of David in II Samuel as "the most precious jewel of the older history writing" (1113).

67   See the summary in: Wilcoxen: "Narrative," p. 60.

68   Gressmann: Älteste Geschichtsschreibung, pp. XIV, 163, 181.

69   R. H. Pfeiffer: Introduction to the Old Testament, 2nd edn., London 1952, pp. 356-9, would perhaps exemplify such a tendency in another way.

70   Von Rad's work needs also to be considered in the context of his hypothesis of a "Solomonic enlightenment," which has been increasingly, and I think justly, criticised in recent years, at least in the way von Rad described its radically new and dramatic effects. Do we see something of the origins of his conception in Rost, p. 106? Conroy: Absalom Absalom, p. 23 n.16, says in criticism of von Rad at this point that in II Sam 13-20, I Kgs 1-2 "we have to do ... at least as much with the nature and technique of narrative as with a new theological outlook" (cf. p. 98 n.12). Von Rad was, of course, trying to investigate how the two were related.

71   Gunn: Story of King David, pp. 20f., makes some important points on these issues; cf. also Whybray: Succession Narrative, pp. 11ff., for an earlier statement of the problems in describing the story as "history writing." On Rost's comparatively brief and cautious discussion of this question (esp. pp. 103f.), see Carlson: David, the chosen King, p. 136, distinguishing Rost's grounds for the characterisation of the story as "history writing" from those of Gunkel and Gressmann.

72   D. F. Ford: "Barth's Interpretation of the Bible" in: S. W. Sykes, ed.: Karl Barth. Studies of his Theological Methods, Oxford 1979, pp. 80f.

73   A. Weiser: Introduction to the Old Testament, London 1961 (ET from 4th German edn. 1957, with minor rev.), pp. 157-70. (Weiser wrongly attributes to Rost the view that Abiathar was the author of the "court history of David," p. 165).

74   H. W. Hertzberg: I & II Samuel. In addition to the comments in the introduction (pp. 17-20), see, for instance, on the ark narrative, pp. 47, 62f., 296; on II Sam 7, pp. 283-8; on the story of David's rise, p. 296; on the Michal episode as part of the succession story, pp. 277, 296, 299; on the succession story proper, pp. 299, 375ff. But he regards II Sam 10.1-6a as an original part of 10.1-11.1 (p. 303), and wonders whether parts of II Sam 3-4 may not have belonged also to the succession story (pp. 297 n.a, 299, 376).

75   I think we may detect a hint of this in, for example, W. Brueggemann's treatment of Carlson's work ("David and His Theologian," Catholic Biblical Quarterly 30, 1968, p. 157 n.11).

76   For the character of Rost's argument here, cf. again Carlson: David, the chosen King, pp. 136f.

77   So, e.g., J. Priestley: Notes on All the Books of Scripture for the Use of the Pulpit and Private Families, I, Northumberland (!) 1803, p. 478.

78   As one example, note F. J. Falding: "Samuel, the Books of" in: P. Fairbairn, ed.: The Imperial Bible-Dictionary VI, London 1887, pp. 96-8.

79   Cf., e.g., K. F. Keil: Manual of Historico-Critical Introduction to the Canonical Scriptures of the Old Testament, Edinburgh 1869 (ET from German edn. 1853), pp. 245-50; A. F. Kirkpatrick: The First Book of Samuel, Cambridge Bible, 1st edn., Cambridge 1880, pp. 10-12 (contrast later editions) and so among "conservative" scholars down to E. J. Young: An Introduction to the Old Testament, London 1964, pp. 177f.

80   J. A. Wharton: "A Plausible Tale: Story and Theology in II Samuel 9-20, I Kings 1-2," Interpretation 35, 1981, p. 341.

81   Cf. Wellhausen: Composition, p. 259, and many others.

82   So, e.g., Kuenen: Einleitung I/2, pp. 49f., Nowack: Richter, Ruth und Samuelis, Sam. p. XXII.

83   Cf. especially Kuenen: Einleitung, I/2, p. 51: "The vividness of the portrayal is not so much the result of the author's personal sight, as of his gift for imagining himself in the frame of mind of the persons involved and at the scene of the events."

84   For one much more recent reflection of such a view, cf. R. K. Harrison: Introduction to the Old Testament, London 1970, p. 699: "The Davidic court history is unquestionably of the greatest value as a source, being nearly contemporary with the events described, and as such constitutes a thoroughly authoritative document" (my stress).

85   In this respect, study of the succession story in the 19th and early 20th centuries may illuminatingly be compared with critical study of the Gospel of Mark.

86   W. Sanday: Inspiration. Eight Lectures, London 1893, pp. 160f.

87   Cf., e.g., Gunn: Story of King David, pp. 65-84 for the inclusion of II Sam 2-4 within the story; see earlier R. Rendtorff, "Beobachtungen zur altisraelitischen Geschichtsschreibung anhand der Geschichte vom Aufstieg Davids," in H. W. Wolff, ed.: Probleme Biblischer Theologie, München 1971, pp. 432, 439; N. K. Gottwald: "Samuel, Books of," Encyclopaedia Judaica, 14, Jerusalem 1971, col. 794, and others.

88   See especially Gunn: Story of King David, pp. 38-62 (with reference to earlier papers), for the former view; for the latter see J. van Seters: "Problems in the Literary Analysis of the Court History of David," JSOT 1, 1976, pp. 22-9; "Oral Patterns or Literary Conventions in Biblical Narrative," Semeia 5, 1976, pp. 139-54, with response by Gunn, ibid., pp. 155-63. But perhaps we do not have to make a straight choice between these alternatives.

89   Cf. S. Mowinckel: "Israelite Historiography," Annual of the Swedish Theological Institute 2, 1963, pp. 10-14; Stoebe: I Samuelis, pp. 57f. We

should also observe here Martin Noth's later view (to me quite unconvincing) that, in a rather complex way, most of I Kgs 2 is supplemental to the original narrative (Könige, BKAT IX/1, Neukirchen-Vluyn 1968, pp. 8ff.

90   See VT 27, 1977, p. 269 n.4; I find unconvincing Flanagan's literary balancing of sections in II Sam 9-20 (cf. also Conroy: Absalom Absalom, p. 145), in addition to his argument for the secondary character of II Sam 11-12, in view of close literary and thematic relationships between this material and that which surrounds it - to say no more.

91   Cf. now especially P. R. Ackroyd: "The Succession Narrative (so-called)," Interpretation 35, 1981, pp. 383-96, together with his commentary: The Second Book of Samuel, Cambridge Bible Commentary on the New English Bible, Cambridge 1977, p. 10 and passim, and earlier comments in: ExpT 83, 1971/2, pp. 37f. R. A. Carlson: David, the chosen King, p. 43, argues that "the task of reconstructing a pre-Deuteronomic cycle of tradition in 1-2 Sam is so complicated as to be impossible" (this work is usefully surveyed in its Scandinavian context by Knight: Rediscovering, pp. 327-38). Cf. also J. R. Porter, in: G. W. Anderson, ed.: Tradition and Interpretation, Oxford 1979, pp. 151f. S. A. Cook: "Notes on the Composition of 2 Samuel," AJSL 16, 1899/1900, pp. 145-77, was almost alone among earlier critics in seeing a great deal of conscious redactional reshaping in II Sam 9-20, I Kgs 1-2, but he believed himself able to identify this with some accuracy on source-critical grounds.

92   M. Tsevat: "Samuel, I and II," IDB Suppl. Vol., Nashville 1976, p. 780.

93   So, e.g., von Rad: "Beginnings"; Weiser: Introduction, p. 165; Gray: Kings, pp. 18, 105. Cf., differently, P. K. McCarter: "'Plots, True or False': The Succession Narrative as Court Apologetic," Interpretation 35, 1981, pp. 355-67.

94   Cf. R. Kittel: Die Bücher der Könige, HKAT I/5, Göttingen 1900, p. 1; A. Šanda: Die Bücher der Könige, I, EHAT 9, Münster 1911, p. 50; et al.

95   Delekat: "Tendenz und Theologie der David-Salomo Erzählung" in: Das Ferne und Nahe Wort, pp. 26-36. See further on "Tendenz" (e.g.): Gunn: Story of King David, pp. 21-6 (and cf. subject index); McCarter: "Plots, True or False" (see above, n.93).

96   T. Veijola: Die Ewige Dynastie: David und die Entstehung seiner Dynastie nach der deuteronomistischen Darstellung, Helsinki 1975, pp. 16ff.

97   See the sketch in: R. Smend: Die Entstehung des Alten Testament, Stuttgart 1978, pp. 111-25.

98   Würthwein: Die Erzählung von der Thronfolge Davids, and cf. his commentary: Das Erste Buch der Könige, Kapitel 1-16, ATD 11/1, Göttingen 1977, pp. 8ff. Würthwein is less concerned than Veijola to identify the redactional elements as thoroughly "Deuteronomistic" and to trace connections with this redaction outside the succession story.

99   Other major attempts at redactional analysis include Mettinger: King and Messiah, pp. 27-32, and the immensely patient and detailed work of F. Langlamet: see "Pour ou contre Solomon? La rédaction prosalomonienne de I Rois, I-II," Revue Biblique 83, 1976, pp. 321-79, 481-528, and later papers.

100   Cf. my comments in: VT 27, p. 279; for criticism which to some degree coincides with my own detailed work, see Gunn: Story of King David, pp. 23ff., 115ff.; cf. Crüsemann, Widerstand, p. 129 n.5.

101   One good attempt at an overall literary interpretation is Gunn: Story of King David, pp. 87-111. A recent study of major proportions is J. P. Fokkelman: Narrative Art and Poetry in the Books of Samuel ... Vol. I: King David (II Sam 9-20 & I Kings 1-2), Studia Semitica Neerlandica 20, Assen 1981.

THE
SUCCESSION
TO·THE
THRONE·OF
DAVID

INTRODUCTION

he generally accepted result of literary-critical work on I and II Samuel has been the distribution of the individual narratives between two major sources running through the books, and called variously K and K^1 or J and E or whatever. Attempts to go beyond this and find subsidiary sources used within these major source strands have been rejected categorically by Budde,[1] acknowledged with varying degrees of reservation by others. Yet the wish to find major continuous sources here as in the Hexateuch and Book of Judges has often led, on the one hand, to the establishing of connections between quite unrelated components and, on the other hand, to the severing of parts which belong together.

Such divisions and connections have been facilitated by the fact that for the most part critics have assessed only a source's vocabulary and thought-content, whereas, apart from a few minor attempts, nobody has examined style, although here we have at our disposal an important aid to criticism. It is true that a person's vocabulary is restricted and all of us as individuals have our own favourite words which we use over and over again. But it is also the case that every now and again we exploit a word or expression which would normally be alien to us and, more to the point, might also happen to be another person's favourite word. And in the end we should not forget that where members of the same family, background or class are concerned, each individual's vocabulary may be extremely similar through accommodation to mutual influences. In the same way, narrators, writers, all have their own leading ideas which shape what they say and write. Yet here, too, it is possible for a group of people to share the same ideas just as it can happen that a person may emphasize different ideas at different times.

It is a different matter with someone's style. To be sure, a writer will use traditional forms and formulas, adopt conventional devices and niceties of style. But style is and will remain a person's most individual creation - which is always being fashioned anew, creatively producing singularity and stubborn idiosyncracy, the more singular and stubbornly idiosyncratic the writer's own nature.

Thus the investigation of a text's source derivation cannot do without an examination of style. Now clearly this is not to be done with general phrases. No, we must rather determine why the one account gives the impression of a simple, concise narrative while the other seems to offer an expansive, comfortably spun-out idyll. It must be shown how each account makes use of speech in the narrative; how, also, the one tells its story in one breath while the other likes to round off clearly each individual scene within the whole framework and so to string its narrative together scene by scene. Impressions and feelings must be raised to the level of sound knowledge. And indeed this is possible. The individual sources then stand out in sharp contrast to each other. No longer does the question of authorship have to do with lifeless stereotypes but with flesh-and-blood people, with living personalities.[2] We can look into their hearts and perceive their piety, nurtured in the same soil but in each person shaped somewhat differently. The portrait of a period then becomes richer, livelier and more realistic.

It is generally admitted that the so-called "story of David's family" or "story of the succession to the throne of David" challenges one to just this sort of examination. For here we have a lengthy and coherent text, little interspersed with unrelated material and without doubt transmitted in written form from the very beginning. Nonetheless, close inspection shows that it is not completely uniform, inasmuch as various more ancient sources are included within it or joined to it. These sources are in every respect individual, independent creations which, by means of more or less skilful transitional formulas, are attached to, or imbedded in, the larger narrative of the succession to David's throne.

Whether we should see here a lack of literary sensitivity on the part of the author, who is quite happy to borrow at length from other sources quite different in style, may remain an open question. It could be, rather, that we have here the first indication of a regard for copyright, or, alternatively, the author's desire to incorporate into his own narrative accounts known in wider circles, and so possibly enjoying a certain prestige, in order to give the impression of a history based on

4

original sources. For present purposes we may simply observe that to this peculiarity of Hebrew historiography, which, incidentally, bears a great similarity to later Islamic practice, we owe the preservation of very valuable sources - in which case we can well afford to overlook any lack in stylistic sensitivity. So, too, are we indebted to the writer of the succession story for linking his work with the end of the ark narrative, and for including both an oracle (in its present form much revised) concerning the future of the house of David and the account of the course of the Ammonite war, without being forced by his self-consciousness as a writer - as were perhaps Herodotus or Thucydides - to transmit this other material in his own words in order to retain the stylistic unity and uniformity of his work.[3]

In the following pages we shall first examine the characteristics of these subsidiary sources used by the author of the succession story and distinguish this material from its wider context. Then we will turn to establishing the characteristic features of the succession story itself. Needless to say, our investigation cannot be restricted to purely stylistic matters alone but must examine, in addition, not only how close is the writer to historical reality but also what theological outlook he has and what ideals of religious devotion he entertains - especially how he views God's intervention in human affairs.

Turning now to our investigation, we begin with the ark narrative.

Chapter One

THE ARK NARRATIVE

hile recognizing in I Sam 4.1b-6.21 (or 7.1) a closely-knit literary unity, Wellhausen keeps it quite separate from II Sam 6. Löhr agrees with this opinion, regarding I Sam 4-6 as an old narrative dealing with the fate of the ark, which was included in order to give some information about the conflict with the Philistines. II Sam 6, on the other hand, is to be counted as part of the David story proper. Nowack is of a similar opinion and regards I Sam 4.1-7.1 as an old source which he attributes to E. At the same time, he assigns II Sam 6 to his source S, along with II Sam 9-20.[1]

What all these attempts to analyse the ark narrative have in common is that they all propose dividing the text into discrete sections, that is, they allocate the chapters in I Samuel to one source and II Sam 6 to another separate source.

Budde, on the other hand, attempts to divide the narrative along its length (distributing the material between J and E) and in this he is in general agreement with Smith. Sellin's assessment is similar to Budde's, though he separates the text into two sources only in I Sam 4-6, attributing II Sam 6 to a single of the pair of narrative strands to be found in I Sam 4-6. He asks in conclusion, however, whether all narratives concentrating on the ark may not go back to more ancient material, "a history, which was specifically concerned with the ark."[2]

In the earlier editions of his history of Israel and in his treatment of the Books of Samuel in Kautzsch's Old Testament, Kittel advocates the idea of two layers within the ark narrative, in the sense that he regards I Sam 4 and 5 on the one hand and I Sam 6 and II Sam 6 on the other as being more closely related - a distinction which he later withdraws in the sixth edition of his history.[3]

Contrary to these attempts to divide the ark narrative into

various sources, or at least into various source strata, Steuernagel thinks it appropriate to assign the ark narrative to a single source (Sa), while accepting that the story in I Samuel is based on an older source used by Sa. Similarly, Gressmann appears to believe that both parts - both in I Samuel and in II Samuel - belong to a single source and, further, that they are closely connected with one another. In the process, however, he deletes large sections of the Massoretic text (I Sam 4.7a[b], 8, 15, 16b, 18b, 21b[b], 22; 5.2a, 3b, 4a; 6.3b[b], 5-13, 15, 17-7.1; II Sam 6.3b, 5b) which he regards as later additions from a parallel narrative.[4]

In the face of this abundance of highly divergent attempts to fit the ark narrative into specific sources, it seems justified to enquire into the reasons that have given rise to these various suggestions and, of necessity, to go beyond previous attempts.

In nearly every endeavour to split up the text - whether a solution to the problem is sought by dividing the text into sections or along its length or by some other method - the alternation between the names Kiriath-jearim and Baalat-judah and between Eleazar and Uzzah in I Sam 6 and II Sam 6 has played a decisive role.[5] Only Kittel (who, as already mentioned, divides I Sam 6 and II Sam 6 [L1] from I Sam 4 and 5 [L]) and Steuernagel do not regard this alternation as a basis for source division. While the latter does not go into the present problems, the former defends his point of view by maintaining that, according to Jos 15.9 (cf. 15.60; 18.14), Baalat-judah is another name for Kiriath-jearim: "[Baalat-judah] is without doubt the more ancient and, so to speak, sacred name for the place; so the same writer who uses Kiriath-jearim in I Sam 7.1 could equally use the other name." On Uzzah he remarks: "Probably the same as Eleazar."[6] In this context we could ask whether in I Sam 7.1 an original "Baalat-judah" may not have been changed into "Kiriath-jearim." This is supported by the fact that the LXX has totally misunderstood Baalat-judah in II Sam 6, a misunderstanding increased even more by a second translation which has then gone into the textus receptus. This seems to prove that the name Baalat-judah for Kiriath-jearim gradually went out of use and was finally no longer understood. Hence, though only after the two parts of our ark narrative were separated, Kiriath-jearim could have been substituted for Baalat-judah on the basis of the notice in Joshua, with Baale-judah in II Sam 6.2 escaping this fate because it was no longer construed as a place name.[7]

The alternation of Eleazar and Uzzah[8] could also be explained similarly - perhaps from the wish to give the priest in charge of the ark in I Sam 7.1 a theophoric name, which was not necessary in the case of the person conducting the ark in II Sam 6. It would also be possible to go back to the old explanation offered, for example by Keil:[9] given the time difference between both events, the ben Abinadab in II Sam 6 could be regarded as the grandson of Abinadab.

In any case, we do not have sufficient weight of evidence from the alternation in the place names and in the name of ben Abinadab to justify, on this basis alone, the division of the ark narrative into various sources. For looking at the Commentaries and Introductions also shows that additional factors play a role and are frequently decisive. Nowack is compelled to divide the text into sections because he considers 4.1 to 7.1 to be an independent ancient source which later had set before it a narrative of Samuel's boyhood. He needs II Sam 6, however, as an important part of his S-source - a source running continuously, with some extensive interpolations, from I Sam 9.1 to I Kgs 2 and depicting the history of the earlier monarchy. Löhr arrives at his divisions on the basis of similar considerations. For him I Sam 4.1b-7.1 is "an independent work of ancient character and historical value which was adapted into this text from an otherwise unknown source, probably of Ephraimite origin." On II Sam 6, he expressed his opinion to the effect that: "Chapters 5, 6 and 8 exhibit a good deal of valuable ancient material about David's government - but compiled by an editor." He summarizes the content as follows: "5.1, 17-25 ... 8.1. David becomes king of all Israel and meets his former overlords, the Philistines, in battle, with a happy outcome. 5.6-12. Occupation of Jerusalem. Transfer of the royal residence thither. 6. Solemn entrance of the ark into Jerusalem. 8.2-6, 7-14 (3.2-5, 5.13-16) 16-18. Accounts of David's further military activities, of his family and his most powerful officials." For Löhr as well, chapter 6 is indispensable to the structure of the narrative of David's rise to power.[10]

Anticipating later conclusions, we must provisionally make the following objections:

1. The narrative strand relating David's rise to power finishes at II Sam 5.10.[11] To it belong as a kind of epilogue the supplements vv. 13-16 (David's sons in Jerusalem), 17-25 (two battles with the Philistines) and, perhaps, also parts of chapter 8.[12]

2. Accordingly, II Sam 6 belongs as little to the original

narrative of David's rise as does I Sam 4-6.[13]

3. Rather, II Sam 6 is connected with I Sam 4-6 on account of the close association in vocabulary, style and range of religious ideas.[14]

4. The structure of the whole ark narrative also demands this conclusion, for only then does the purpose of the story stand out.[15]

5. Only then can we see that the aim of the narrative is to depict the fate of the ark from its removal from Shiloh until its installation in Jerusalem.[16]

Only by neglecting important considerations, therefore, can one postulate larger source connections and divide the unit I Sam 4-6 and II Sam 6 into two patently unequal sections in order to assign them to two separate narrative strands. This would mean regarding the one half as some kind of misplaced block of material, alien to its context, while attributing an inappropriate purpose to the other section and placing it in an unnecessary, even impossible, context.

Budde's endeavours are dominated by the desire to have just two sources in the Books of Samuel.[17] He thus divides I Sam 4-6 into two sources. The main bulk of the material in II Sam 6 is to be assigned to one of these sources, J, which is so little seen in I Sam; I Sam 4-6 on the other hand is mainly from E.[18] The determinative factor in his division is the consideration of J's structure: in Budde's opinion, this source described the development of the kingdom and was one of the sources compiled by the earliest editors, "forming the essence of all pre-exilic traditions." In view of what we have just said we need go no further into this question.[19] However, other factors also play a role and these require further consideration.

Budde bases his hypothesis primarily on the use of doublets[20] which he finds particularly numerous in I Sam 4, and not so much on the basis of the alternation in the divine name which proves to be an "unreliable guide" here.[21] He does not attempt to carry out a thorough separation of the sources,[22] probably because the material available is not sufficient to reconstruct two sources; rather one of them has to remain more or less fragmentary. This having been conceded, we should ask whether each doublet is not rather an explanatory gloss or an expansion:[23] for example, "in the field" alongside "in the ranks" (I Sam 4.2); "on the morrow" alongside "in the morning" (5.4); "Ashdod and its territory" alongside "them" (5.6); further 5.11b[b] alongside 11b[a]; "make" alongside "take" (6.7); "Beth-shemesh" alongside "on the way to its own territory" (6.9). Further doublets can be explained as later redaction, e.g., 6.3b[b] alongside 3b[a]; 6.5f. alongside 6.4. Others, such as the anaphora in 4.7-8 and the inclusio in v. 9, can be accounted for by the rules of Hebrew style; this is generally accepted in the first case,[24] but in the second example its importance for the structure of the speech must be more closely examined below.[25]

A further criterion advanced by Budde also influenced Kittel to combine I Sam 4-5 into one unit and I Sam 6 and II Sam 6 into another. This is the mention of field mice in I Sam 6. According to Budde,[26] they are to be attributed to one of his sources and regarded as a symbolic representation of the plague boils, which belong to the other fragmentary source. Kittel,[27] however, deletes the mention of the boils in I Sam 6 and retains only the mice, regarding the boils as a later addition from I Sam 5. Against Kittel's separation one can cite the close linguistic, stylistic and religious relationship between I Sam 4 and 5 on the one hand and I Sam 6 and II Sam 6 on the other.[28] What Nowack[29] remarked on this passage can be used to refute both men's hypotheses. We will show below that I Sam 6 has been revised considerably: the introduction of the plague can be ascribed to the work of one of these editors who was no longer aware of the symbolic significance of the mice. As has already been mentioned, Gressmann also thinks that the ark narrative - and especially I Sam 6 - has been extensively revised; he, like Steuernagel, defends the unity of the ark narrative.

Our deliberations so far have shown that it is not feasible to divide the ark narrative either into sections or along its length. The question of sources can only be solved by combining all narratives in which the ark has a central importance. Steuernagel and Gressmann take this course. In principle we will follow their procedure. But not all the time. Rather it will prove necessary to review the origin of certain passages. In doing this, we will come to numerous alternative conclusions. Our concurrence on certain basic features does not mean agreement on details. Without going into purely textual problems, we will now attempt to examine all parts of the ark narrative.

I Sam 4.1a either belongs to the preceding narrative or, what is more likely, is a redactional connecting passage. Samuel is not mentioned at all in the following narrative. The introductory sentence, which in LXX is placed in front of v. 16, is a connective and can be dispensed with.[30] "In the field" in v. 2 is a gloss. Against Gressmann, v. 7 should be retained.[31] The sentence beginning "For they said ..." gives the reason for their fear while "and they said, etc." depicts the consequence of this fear. V. 8 can also be retained.[32] Anaphora is very common in Semitic languages and the narrator could quite easily put his own views of God's activity in past history into the mouths of the Philistines. Anyway, God is so characteristically seen as being connected with the ark in vv. 7a[b] and 8 that is is scarcely possible to trace these verses back to a later emendation. The inclusio[33] in v. 9 is to be retained on the grounds of Hebrew speech style. We should also ask ourselves whether מְצַפֶּה in v. 13 simply means "waiting", just as an Arab can speak of "looking with his heart" in cases like this.[34] On the other hand, the reading מִצְפָּה has also much to speak for it since "Mizpah" is probably the next largest town in the southwest on the old north road.[35] It is usual to delete v. 15.[36] This is not supported by v. 14 which quite obviously states that although Eli can hear the uproar he is unable to see it or the cause of the commotion.[37] We should make some reference to the well-known fact that circumstantial information necessary for the continuation of the plot is often not inserted until much later when it becomes important. 16b should not be deleted simply because it is parallel to 16a. For it could be the author's intention to show the man's excitement by making him begin his statement twice. Nonetheless, the alternation between the two words for "I", אני and אנכי, is so conspicuous that it should not be viewed as authorial intention but rather as a later accretion from a variant text. This is further supported by the fact that 16b anticipates an idea in the following verse and weakens its impact. On the other hand, 18b is to be deleted as a later insertion on the basis of the scheme used for the judges. V. 19 profits from the deletion of the words from אל־הלקח to ואישה (that the ark of God was captured and that her father-in-law and her husband were dead), which presumably came from v. 21. In this latter verse, the last two words are an addition and should be deleted together with v. 22. This verse was attached only after the addition of the final words in v. 21 to correct the previous, now expanded, verse on account of the key word לקח (take, capture).[38]

Against Gressmann, v. 2a in chapter 5 can be retained, in 1 Sam 5 so far as לקח is interpreted as "take" and not as "capture." While 5.1 simply reports the transfer of the ark to Ashdod, v. 2 supplements this statement by relating that the ark was brought - perhaps after some deliberations - into the temple of Dagon. Extending the motif of the falling idol can quite plausibly be attributed to the first narrator with the result that, against Gressmann, vv. 3b and 4a can be retained. In v. 6 the words "Ashdod and its territory" should be deleted, with Gressmann. In v. 7, MT can be retained; but the last five words in v. 11 are to be deleted. They disturb the context and seem to have been added because of 5.6.

1 Sam. Chapter 6 presents greater difficulties. Here Gressmann deletes almost everything after v. 4. It will be shown that these deletions are not necessary to this full extent and are therefore not justified. Having recognized that the ark and the plague are causally related, the people have already decided that they want the ark to be sent back. The priests and diviners are thus questioned not about whether this should be done but about how it should be done. The answer comes in v. 3 which relates that the priests are certain of the prospect of a halt to the plague, as hoped for by the people. The end of v. 3 contradicts this however: firstly, the causal relationship - already recognized as a definite fact by both priests and people - is now no more than a possibility; secondly, the priests and diviners are depicted as being "in the know" in contradiction to the people who are not. The five golden models of the boils caused by the plague, in v. 4, have found their way in from chapter 5, after the symbolic significance of the mice has been forgotten. Further, the last word is to be deleted as a gloss on the previous "upon all of you." The passage vv. 5-9 should also be regarded as an expansion, for the following reasons:

1. The Philistines' last question to their priests and diviners concerned the nature of the guilt offering. The answer to this is given in 4b.
2. Vv. 3 and 9 take into account once more the possibility of another cause.
3. V. 6 asks, in a reproachful tone, why the Philistines have hardened their hearts; in other words, the possibility of keeping the ark is considered. This is contradicted by the end of the previous chapter and the beginning of this one.
4. The instructions for the procedures to be followed in returning the ark are a more detailed exposition anticipating v. 10.
5. As will be shown later, the speeches in the ark narrative are as a rule short, rarely lasting for more than one verse. The style is concise.

The last phrase in v. 11, "and the images of their boils," is an addition. Similarly v. 15 is the addition of a reader concerned about the rights of the Levites. Vv. 17 and 18 are to be deleted as additions by various hands. The LXX version of v. 19 should be preferred to MT. The "fifty thousand men" are a later elucidation of the "great slaughter."

In II Sam 6.1, ויסף עוד (and he again gathered) is used instead of the more usual ויאסף because of 5.22. The preposition in מבעלי יהודה (from Baale-judah) is proleptic: an emendation is not absolutely necessary. חדשה (new) without an article alongside העגלה (the cart) at the end of v. 3 is presumably an insertion by the same hand as ordered the new cart to be prepared in I Sam 6.5-9. In v. 4, ועזא הלך (and Uzzah walked) is to be inserted before עם ארון (with/alongside the ark) as the easiest correction of the corrupt text. In v. 5, the text of Chronicles is to be preferred in place of בכל־עצי ברושים (with cypress wood); similarly in v. 7 in place of the uncertain על־השל. V. 16 raises doubts on account of the rather awkward והיה which disturbs the flow of the narrative. It gives the impression of being an insertion. As will be shown later, we have here the beginning of the succession source which is dovetailed into the end of the ark narrative by means of the Michal scene and the preparatory statements in v. 16. V. 17 follows on immediately from v. 15. As far as content is concerned, 7.1-7 also belongs to the ark narrative and could once have formed its conclusion. But the passage is so different stylistically than one cannot simply explain away the differences by assuming that the passage was revised by another hand. Further, it has been closely connected with Nathan's prophecy (7.8ff.), which means that 7.1-7 can only be examined in connection with this promise.

Thus we see that the ark narrative comprises: I Sam 4.1b-18a, 19-21; 5.1-11b, 12; 6.1-3b, 4, 10-14, 16; 6.19-7.1; II Sam 6.1-15, 17-20a.

We now have the basis for further examination. This involves first dealing with the vocabulary and then studying the style. Following that, the structure of the narrative, its purpose, date of composition, historicity and the religious concepts it contains must all be considered.

Obviously, the present work cannot possibly describe the whole of the source's vocabulary like a concordance, although such a compilation would indeed show something of the special characteristics of the ark narrative. Rather, only a selection of important words occurring within the text in

question is provided here together with some related information concerning the occurrence of these words in other
contexts. This material may be found set out in the Appendix
at the end of the book.

Summing up we can take note of the following points:

1. The vocabulary of the ark narrative has relatively little
connection with that of the other sources of the Books of
Samuel.

2. Alongside words that occur frequently in the Elohistic
and Yahwistic writers, there are clearly a great number
which belong to the vocabulary of the Priestly source.

3. Particularly striking, however, are the connections with
the language of the prophets, Psalms and Job, i.e., the
language of religious poetry and of the cult.

4. By contrast, echoes of the books of Chronicles are quite
rare.

5. Accordingly it would seem that the ark narrative is a
special block within the Books of Samuel.

6. It has probably a close relationship to cultic or
prophetic circles.

The style of the ark narrative is relatively simple and
straightforward. The sentences are short, often consisting of
no more than subject, object and predicate or predicate,
subject and object. There are practically no subordinate
clauses such as relative and conditional clauses. Participial
constructions are also very rare. Similarly there are almost
none of the constructions with היה plus a temporal phrase or
an infinitive and a subsequent main clause which are so
favoured elsewhere (I Sam 4.18; 5.9 and 10). One looks in vain
for comparisons and metaphors. Admittedly, such features
are not so very common in Hebrew narrative style, but the
author likewise uses almost none of the other rhetorical
devices. Only in I Sam 4.7 and 8 is there an anaphora in the
repeated "Woe to us" - whether in fact by design or accident
remains an open question - and in v. 9 of the same chapter
there is an inclusio, though this is not formulated with
precision.

All this could give the impression that we have in front of
us a piece of rather unsophisticated prose. This, however, is
not the case, for the author is fully aware how to use the
little at his disposal to its full extent. The narrative comes
alive by changing the word order within the sentence, by
scrupulous choice of words, which gives us some idea of the
rich vocabulary at the author's command, and by the

exceedingly rare and therefore extremely impressive use of particles.[39] So it is not a matter of lack of literary sophistication and ability on the part of the author. Rather he eschews all rhetorical decoration and embellishment by conscious choice, achieving a simplicity which is deliberate but seemingly natural.

This impression is confirmed by looking at the speeches scattered throughout the narrative. These also use short, precise sentences. They rarely continue for more than a single sentence. Curiously, they consist almost exclusively of questions. The hearer or reader just cannot help being interested and naturally waits for the answer with increased anticipation. This usage is in keeping with the function of speeches to enliven the narrative and retain attention. They mostly occur in passages which are of radical importance for the progression of the narrative, or which are climaxes within the larger whole.

The elders of the defeated Israelites ask: "Why has Yahweh defeated us today before the Philistines? Let us () bring back the ark () of Yahweh from Shiloh! It should come among us and save us from the hand of our enemies!" In this way, the ark, which will form the central focus of the following narrative, is introduced for the first time in a speech. The ark comes and the Israelites surge jubilantly around it. The Philistines' questions about the cause of the noise and their anxious cries clearly express the importance of this event. What will the Philistines do? Another speech tells us that they have decided to risk another battle despite the appearance of the ark.[40] The second battle results in the total defeat of the Israelites. The messenger's speech vividly underlines the outcome and finishes in something of a climax with the loss of the ark. The speech of Phinehas' wife stresses that the loss is decisive.

The next speech is in chapter 5. The ark is in the hands of the Philistines, at first in the temple of Dagon in Ashdod. The idol falling and the plague in Ashdod occasions the wish: "The ark of the God of Israel should not remain with us; for his hand lies heavily upon us and our god." Here there could be a turning point in the narrative; the return of the ark becomes a distinct possibility. But first, the council of princes has to be consulted as to what should happen with the ark and they decide that it should be transferred to Gath. Then finally to Ekron. And this is where the turning point actually comes. Accordingly speeches are packed in here. First an assessment by the population of Ekron, then an agitated request to the council of princes. Subsequently, the opinion of the priests and diviners is sought and this turns into a dialogue of laconic brevity. The result is the return of the ark to Israel, which is accomplished without any hitch. It arrives in Beth-shemesh and here, after the sudden death of the 70 men causes another complication, there is yet another question: "Who can stand before Yahweh, this holy God, and to whom should the ark go up from us?" The answer follows in the request to the people of Kiriath-jearim to fetch the ark.

In II Sam 6 there is, for our present purposes, only one speech, again a question: "How can Yahweh's ark come to me?" This question appears once more in an important place. The mysterious death of Uzzah makes it seem doubtful whether it is Yahweh's wish that the ark should be brought to Jerusalem. The matter is left in abeyance for further deliberation. So this speech, too, stands at a turning point in the narrative. If 7.1-7 be also counted as part of the ark narrative, then there is yet another speech at the end of the complex when it is decided where to put the ark. But, as already indicated and as will be proven later, this is not a feasible conclusion.

Our investigations so far have shown that the narrator often weaves speeches into his narrative as a means of enlivening his story. He wants his characters not only to act but to speak as well. He therefore attempts to bring them closer to the listeners. As we have already seen, given the importance allotted to words, to speech, it is no wonder that the spoken word appears at climaxes in the narrative or at important turning points.

But this is not a sufficient appreciation of the function of speeches in Hebrew narrative art. The spoken word must also serve another purpose, namely to express moods. This is connected with a certain inability on the part of the narrator to describe emotions, which may be due to the lack of subtlety in the language - its insufficient provision of clearly distinguishable words for making finer discriminations. One could almost say that even our narrator is unable to do very much better than express emotions and feelings in general terms. Thus the Philistines are afraid (I Sam 4.7), and so is David (II Sam 6.9). Eli is scared (I Sam 4.13). The people of Beth-shemesh are glad (I Sam 6.13). David is sad about the death of Uzzah (II Sam 6.8). And even when it says that the people of Beth-shemesh "mourned," we are not sure whether that is describing an emotional state or whether it should really be thought of as an external mourning ritual, such as wailing or tearing at the seams of their clothes. However, when the children of Israel rejoice so that the earth echoes (I Sam 4.5), we certainly have a case in point where the depiction of externals substitutes for the description of emotions. Yet even if our narrator does not have the means to describe feelings and moods directly, he is still more than capable of compensating for this deficiency with speeches scattered throughout. These, over against simple actions, have the advantage of vividness, clarity and immediacy. We will now consider this second significance of the speeches within the narrative.

So much is contained in the words of the defeated Israelites (I Sam 4.3): disappointment concerning the defeat, gnawing uncertainty, not about the author of their downfall but about its cause; and in the middle of all these dark thoughts shines the first gleam of hope, stronger and stronger, until finally the bright light of certain salvation dawns. This change of mood has its culmination in the cry of rejoicing at the arrival of the ark. Again, what fear can be detected in the Philistines' question: "What is the meaning of the noise of this great tumult in the Hebrew camp?" The sober comment in v.7 that the Philistines were afraid is directly replaced by the terrible report: "God has come into the camp! " Now the Philistines are heard wailing aloud as if they were already lamenting over the bodies of those fallen in battle. "Woe is us! Woe is us! " Their complete helplessness is wonderfully expressed in the words: "It was not like this before! Who will help us?" They are totally at a loss what to do and the reason is given in the next verses: "That is the God who has smitten the Egyptians in manifold ways." But the shock is transformed into reckless despair. There is too much to be lost: the independence of their country and their personal freedom. So they decide to carry on the battle. The next speech is introduced in a way similar to the Philistine speeches we have just discussed. It arises from the same situation: the half-blind Eli hears the lamentation of the people of Shiloh and fraught with uneasiness and anxiety he asks: "What is the meaning of this uproar?" And now is imparted to him the messenger's answer. Through it deep anguish trembles, brought very finely to expression by the way in which the loss of the ark, the shrine, is left until the end, as if the messenger were shying away from telling the priest of the ark. Eli listens to the news in silence. It is too much, too shattering for him to find the right words or for him to air his anguish in wordless groans and weeping.[41] His daughter-in-

17

law also remains silent at first. She is as if in a coma. The events of the outside world no longer touch her. Not until faced with death can she find the words and give her son a name. He is to make people remember this national disaster and to keep reminding those around him of it, a living admonition.[42] With its gripping brevity, this speech reveals the mood of the people in double aspect - their high estimation of the ark, their mourning at its loss.

When the narrator has the people of Ashdod say: "The ark of the God of Israel should not remain among us, for his hand lies heavy upon us and upon Dagon our god," he uses this to depict their fear of the sinister visitor. Similarly, when he has them face the council of princes with the question, "What are we to do with the ark of the God of Israel?", he is expressing their helplessness, which is presumably connected with the fact that Ashdod, as a single partner in a federation, does not have the sole right to dispose of booty captured by the whole federation. The decision of the council of princes to send the ark to Gath bears all the signs of a compromise solution. It is noticeable how difficult it has become, in the mêlée of different opinions, for those in power to solve the problem in such a way as to offend no one and hurt nobody's feelings. No one wants to restore the ark to Israel, national pride forbids that. Perhaps they do not think the danger is so great. They do not want to offend the people of Ashdod, but they do want to allay their fear. Perhaps there was also some hope in these circles that the danger could be removed by shifting the ark to another place - as if they thought that the wrath of Yahweh was directed only against the people of Ashdod and not against the Philistines as a whole. This struggle between sense of honour and fear, disregard of danger and compliance with the federation, is expressed by the narrator with splendid brevity when relating the final decision. The fear of the sinister power of the ark increases to the point of horror with the people of Ekron crying out in their anxiety: "They have brought God's ark to me to kill me and my people." This frame of mind is so important to the author that he gives the people of Ekron a second speech in the form of the petition to the council of princes to send back the ark. Its conclusion is almost exactly the same as the first speech.

In chapter 6, the deliberations of the Philistines are pervaded throughout by a certain anxiety, but they provide us with insight into the speakers' outlook on life and into their social stratification more than into those emotions and

feelings which are our present interest. The shocked outcry
of the people of Beth-shemesh, on the other hand, again
shows us the use of speech to depict moods. One can almost
see the people standing there with their knees shaking and
their faces distorted in fear. The invitation to the inhabitants
of Kiriath-jearim also serves to express the horror of the
people of Beth-shemesh. To be sure, there is also something
here of the deliberations of the Gadarenes which comes to
expression in the proverb: discretion is the better part of
valour. We will later return to this point once more. The only
speech in II Sam 6 comes from the mouth of David. Once
again it is a cry of horror: "How shall the ark come to me?"
The shock of what has happened is coupled with anxiety about
what might yet happen, the fear of the terrifying, unpro-
pitious shrine and the god behind it. Perhaps this is further
increased by the humiliating sense of his own impurity and
impotence.

Summing up one can say that nearly all the speeches in our
narrative, besides having the purpose of making the description more interesting and accentuating the turning points
and climaxes, have also been chosen with the particular
purpose of expressing moods in the face of which the
narrator's vocabulary is inadequate. One should also note that
it is almost exclusively fear and horror that are revealed in
these speeches. The author glosses over joyful events and
happy moods without giving the participants anything to say.
One need only look at I Sam 5.5f., I Sam 6.13, II Sam 6.5 and
12ff. This is either because he intends, wishes, to create a
dark, sinister atmosphere over the whole narrative, or, less
probably, because of his lack of ability.[43]

We have now discovered two reasons for using speeches in
the stories. There is a third reason as well. The Hebrew narrator does not wish, or is unable, to depict either the external
appearance of a person or his way of thinking and acting.
Admittedly, he does try to do the first on occasion: the
messenger who brings the awful message of the defeat of the
Israelites to Shiloh has torn clothes and his head is covered
with dust. Eli is depicted as being a heavy man whose eyes
have lost their power of sight. David is wearing an ephod
when the ark is brought to Jerusalem. But this is all that our
narrator can summon up to characterize external appearance.
He makes no attempt at all to go further in revealing the way
they think and act. He is only able to hint occasionally at
some isolated characteristics, in which case he has to make
use of a speech.

We have thus determined a third task performed by the speeches and it arises out of the inability to describe a person's nature. The best example of this use is the speech of the priests and diviners in I Sam 6.3: "If you wish to get rid of the ark of the God of Israel, then do not send it away without recompense, but return him a guilt offering." It is the only speech in the ark narrative that contains a conditional clause. One might ask whether we have here an attempt to imitate juristic style in that the form of a legal judgement was chosen because of the speakers' station. Or could one perhaps go a step further? Might the narrator have chosen this form in order to hint at the dignity of their appearance and their sense of rank reflected thereby? One might even say that he wanted to show the oversubtlety of the priests, who do not say, "Send the ark away," but only, "If you wish to get rid of the ark, then do not send it away without recompense ..." - they are clever enough to leave open the possibility of a retraction.

We have already seen that the message from the people of Beth-shemesh to the inhabitants of Kiriath-jearim throws a side-light on their character. Here our interest is not the form and content, as in the previous case, but just the content. We detect a certain insincerity and dishonesty, mixed with too little brotherly love and too much selfishness. When the dying cry of Eli's daughter-in-law is "The glory has departed from Israel!", it is not just grief that forces this cry from her lips but her piety and a fervent love of her country. When the Philistines shout to each other, "Philistines, pull yourselves together and show that you are men, so that you will not be subjected to the Hebrews as they were subject to you! Be men and fight!", this seems to indicate great bravery, although the repetition of the call to be manly perhaps indicates that their courage had suffered a considerable blow.

The narrator makes very few attempts to describe the individual characters by means of speeches. This is perhaps due to the fact that only very few individuals say anything: Eli, the messenger, the wife of Phinehas, and David. It is much more common for groups of people to be given something to say: the elders of the Israelites, the Philistines, their princes, prophets and diviners, the people of Ashdod, Ekron, Beth-shemesh. We will return to this point later on in our discussion.

After this appreciation of the significance of speeches in the ark narrative in terms of these three aspects, we can now quickly deal with the mode of narration as a whole. What is most obvious is the vividness of the narrative: the whole situation can be characterized with a few strokes. This is also helped by the fact that the narrator only rarely describes the situation (for example, what the Benjaminite fugitive, Eli, or the fallen idol of Dagon looked like), but lets the listener experience something of the action. For instance, the Philistines and the Israelites make their camps, they form their battle positions, the Israelites are beaten and 3,000 of them are killed. Or, the Philistines fetch two cows and tether them to a cart, leaving their calves behind on the farm. They place the ark on the cart alongside the box with the guilt offering. David's companions at the solemn entry of the ark into Jerusalem do not just carry their instruments but they play them as well.

On all sides there is movement and life. And this life rolls on unstoppable and tireless like a film. The separate tableaux merge into one another almost seamlessly, without breaks and without pauses. Only every now and again is there a scene which is somewhat more self-contained, as, for example, the messenger scene or the birth of Ichabod. But even these are not sharply distinct from the general flow of the narrative but are carried along by it. A certain restlessness hangs over the narrative as it does the ark whose story it relates. This restlessness pushes the reader on towards the end - an end which cannot be reached until the ark has found a permanent place to stay. Nowhere is this urgency and disquiet expressed more clearly than at the beginning of chapter 4 which gallops on at full pace from one picture to another, without letting us rest anywhere. This is not incompatible with the fact that other sections of the story go into somewhat more detail (as has already been noticed in the cases of the messenger scene and the birth of Ichabod). Anyway, it is quite obvious that the detail in the description varies. While the beginning of chapter 4 is told highly succinctly, the Eli scene and the account of Ichabod's birth are a touch more expansive. In chapter 5, the fate of the ark in Ashdod and Ekron is described extensively, but in Gath it is only hinted at with a single verse. In chapter 6, there is a detailed account of the preparations for transporting the ark back to Israel and its final removal as far as Beth-shemesh; but the transfer to Kiriath-jearim and what happens to it there are related in a few short sentences. On the other hand, II Sam 6 gives quite a detailed description of the bringing of the ark to Jerusalem. After what we have already said, there should be no doubt that this alternation of terseness and detail was intended by the narrator. Perhaps it was a certain sense of rhythm that caused the author to do this; perhaps the wish to awaken interest and attentiveness by changing the pace - nothing is more fatal than uniformity. Perhaps - and this is the most probable suggestion - he wanted to show us by this very means which parts of the narrative were most important for the unfolding of the story.

All this leads us one step nearer to the question of the structure of the narrative.

The introduction is formed by the Israelites marching up to war to Eben-ezer where they make camp, while the Philistines camp opposite at Aphek. They meet in battle and the Israelites are beaten. The Israelite elders deliberate over the cause of their defeat and finally come up with the idea of bringing the ark from Shiloh. It is not clear whether this is because they believe they have angered Yahweh in not bringing the ark into battle, or because they think victory will be secured in some magical way by the presence of the ark. At this point we have the beginning of the narrative proper dealing with the fate of the ark. The arrival of the shrine in the camp presents the opportunity to stress the significance of this event to both sides. On the one hand, the joy of the Israelites is portrayed; on the other hand, in accordance with the law of action and reaction, the despair of the Philistines. Within the consistently single-stranded[44] narrative there is a transition which is skilfully effected by the report that the earth resounded with the rejoicing of the Israelites so that the Philistines had no option but to hear it. The Philistines join battle and the mention of their opponents provides the opportunity for the account once more to go over to the Israelites, whose renewed defeat culminates in the loss of the ark and the death of the two accompanying priests.

With this the climax of the first part is reached. The two subsequent stories, dealing with the death of Eli and the birth of Ichabod, serve only to show the effect of the loss of the ark on the Israelites. They do not produce a heightening of the story but should rather be regarded as a retarding force within the main stream of the narrative. Once more the transition is most adeptly effected through the flight of the Benjaminites who bring the news of the catastrophe to Shiloh. The scene culminates in the dialogue between the messenger and Eli. This account is related in a similar way to the description of the fear in the Philistine camp, but here the immediate consequence is the story of the birth of Ichabod.

We seem to be dealing with a quite definite format which our narrator uses in order that events, directly following each other but played out on different stages, may be linked and change of location effected. The catch-phrase at the end of chapter 4.21 - "because the ark of God has been captured" - appears to have a similar function. It is taken up again in chapter 5.1 and introduces the second major part of the narrative by shifting the story to the Philistine side.

The second part deals with the fate of the ark among the Philistines. The scenes are Ashdod, Gath and Ekron respectively, each one connected to the other by the removal of the ark. The first and the third are amplified, the second kept rather short. The order of the scenes reveals a certain heightening: at first the effect of the ark is restricted to the idol of Dagon, obviously a reason for horror and amazement but no cause for action. Not until the outbreak of the plague do they wish to be relieved of the ark. In Gath this sickness afflicts both great and small. Perhaps this indicates a worsening of the plague. In Ekron, they allow the ark to stay there temporarily, but only with lamentation. Here more than anywhere else we hear of the deadly effect of the plague.

Thus we reach the turning point in the narrative. This is shown by the introductory scene of the next section. The theme here is the return of the ark from the Philistines and its transfer to Jerusalem. The Philistines discuss how the ark should be sent back. This is followed by the account of the transportation of the ark to Beth-shemesh and the events there. The sudden death of the 70 people gives them cause to have the ark taken away by the people of Kiriath-jearim. It remains there until David takes it to Jerusalem. The third section now approaches its climax and conclusion. The solemn transfer of the ark is enacted in two stages, for the progress is interrupted and delayed by the death of Uzzah. The ceremonies are followed by a solemn sacrifice (II Sam 6.19).

Hence we can see that the narrative consists of an account of the fate of the ark from the time of its removal from Shiloh to the day on which it was installed in Jerusalem.

The narrator wants to show how it came about that the Shiloh cult symbol was brought to Jerusalem by way of the Philistine cities. The introduction tells us the reason why the ark was taken from Shiloh. The first major section relates the loss of the ark to the Philistines and demonstrates the importance of this loss for Israel through the examples of Eli and the wife of Phinehas. The second major section gives

information about the wanderings of the ark among the
Philistines and relates the damage it caused in Ashdod, Gath
and Ekron. The third section depicts the return of the ark,
what happened on the way, and its final installation in the
tent sanctuary in Jerusalem. All the individual scenes of the
story are organized around one common theme and, as has
already been shown, they are so closely connected together -
like links in a chain - that it seems impossible to delete a
single scene.

We must now ask whether the ark narrative is, or was,
really a complete and independent narrative devoted to the
subject of the ark.

This is contested by Budde,[45] although his work is restricted to the section in the first Book of Samuel. In his opinion,
the three chapters here were included to sketch the distress
caused by the Philistines and, against this background, to give
an even more favourable picture of Samuel. But while the
notion of inclusion to illustrate the Philistine domination is
one that could be conceded, it cannot be the case that the
story in its present form had this purpose. In fact, only in
chapter 4 is there an account of the Philistine oppression and
here it is only secondary inasmuch as the fate of the ark is
determined by the superiority of the Philistines. For this
reason Budde assumed that the section of the ark story in the
first Book of Samuel had been revised by deleting the original
accounts of the war.

However, the narrative by no means gives the impression
of being the result of deletion - no matter how well planned
this may have been. Its structure is far too systematic and it
is too closely integrated and interwoven for this. The revision
must have been carried out with the greatest skill - to say
the least - and would thus, in any case, count as an
independent work. No, it is rather improbable that a later
hand, some kind of chronicler, would have so revised a few
chapters in just such a book as I Samuel which echoes so
much with accounts of wars and battles.

Further, this view takes no account whatsoever of the
relationship with II Sam 6. As soon as II Sam 6 is joined with I
Sam 4-7.1, there is no longer any possibility of regarding the
narrative as being about the oppression of the Philistines.
Nor it is possible that an earlier form of this narrative served
this purpose. As already noted, the narrative gives the
impression of a planned, systematic structure and of close
internal unity, both in so far as no scene is dispensable and in
that there is no evidence of its gaining its present form by
major deletions.

Accordingly, if the content of I Sam 4-7.1 and II Sam 6 was always about the fate of the ark,[46] then we must ask whether both the beginning and the end of the narrative have been preserved intact.

We have already established that v. 1b would be perfectly acceptable as the introduction to a battle account. This does not mean that the battle scene is necessarily the beginning of the whole narrative. It is conceivable that our present ark narrative was merely an extract from a larger work about the ark dealing with its fortunes from the very beginning. The probability of such a work, however, is not very great. The prospective audience would have been too small and would most probably have been restricted to priests. Furthermore, the beginning of the narrative itself does not give the impression of being taken from a larger context. The ark forms the focus of the whole narrative but it is not mentioned until the end of v. 3. The preceding verses seem to be an introduction. This introduction itself has everything necessary to know for the further development of the whole narrative and makes no reference to anything mentioned previously.[47]

So at least it does not seem imperative to presuppose some preceding story. The material for this would most probably have been too scanty, above all, because the fortunes of the ark would have been too closely linked with those of its guardians. Under such conditions there is no compelling necessity to write the history of the cult object, whereas it is quite a different matter when it leads an independent existence separated from the tribal or national shrine. Then there is immediate interest in knowing the why and the how of this situation.

The beginning of the narrative is therefore in I Sam 4.1b. Its end could easily be in II Sam 7.1-7 as far as content is concerned, were there not so few points of contact in the style of this passage. Here Nathan proclaims it to be the will of God that the ark should always continue to remain in a tent. That would be a fitting end to the narrative. Yet there seems to be no original connection. (We shall deal with this question in the next chapter.)

If a link with II Sam 7 is not justified (as will be seen) then the conclusion must be in II Sam 6.20a. It is unlikely that the ark narrative was ever continued any further than this. In any case, there is nothing that has come down to us that could be regarded as a continuation. Furthermore the whole narrative works towards the tent of Yahweh in Jerusalem so that it is barely conceivable that a continuation of the narrative would have told about the ark being moved into a temple. There is also another reason why this latter assumption is unlikely: as already mentioned, the beginning of the succession story is to be found in 6.16, 20-23. We can only make a note of this at the moment; it will not be possible to draw the necessary conclusions until later.

Thus, to sum up: the ark narrative is to be regarded as an independent, self-contained source which has been preserved in its entirety. It relates the fate of the ark from its removal from Shiloh up until its installation in Jerusalem.[48]

A narrative such as we have here could have been the result of sheer pleasure in story-telling. Its origins could also be due to other factors and it could serve a specific purpose. This latter possibility does in fact seem to be the case. Without a doubt, we have here the ἱερὸς λόγος, the "cult legend" of the shrine of the ark in Jerusalem. The story served the purpose of explaining the significance of the ark to the visitors to the shrine, most particularly the pilgrims, an aim which could best be achieved by telling them of its miraculous past. It could also have been told in answer to questions arising from the members of the cultic community concerning the shrine. Perhaps the curious chest with the five golden mice was still in the treasury of the shrine and could be viewed for an appropriate consideration.[49] The visitors' thirst for knowledge would have been satisfied by this story. For that reason the ark is always the focus of the narrative and there is no attempt to fit its fate into the general passage of history of the period. This is also the reason why there is no sign of any chronological information apart from the statement that the ark was in the land of the Philistines for seven months. Political history comes to a halt before the gates of the sanctuary. It is only of interest in so far as it intrudes upon the separate existence of the sanctuary. The visitor to the cultic centre is not primarily interested in being told about the political events of the past but rather about the cultic history of this particular sanctuary.

Having thus established the purpose of the ark narrative by reference to the circumstances of its creation and the audience for whom it was intended, we are now in a position to see in which direction we should look for its author. Without doubt he must have belonged to the community of priests who looked after the ark. For they were the people to whom the visitors of the sanctuary could turn for information. It must have also been in their interest to preserve the

aura surrounding the ark and to increase the honour afforded
it. The narrative's sphere of interest also indicates a priestly
origin for the text. Apart from the central position occupied
by the ark, we should notice also that the names of Hophni,
Phinehas, Eli, Eleazer ben Abinadab, Uzzah, Ahio (? probably
וְאָחִיו) and Obed-edom are all mentioned as guardians of the
ark, while otherwise, with the exception of David, only
groups of people are mentioned; further, we notice that the
author reports the installation of the ark in the Temple of
Dagon, and mentions that it was the custom of the priests to
hop across the threshold of the temple; and that finally he
allows the priests and diviners a role in the returning of the
ark, albeit only an advisory and not decisive one. The word
usage also indicates priestly authorship: there are numerous
similarities with the language of the Psalms - the cult hymns
- and with the Priestly code (P), less so with the prophets -
the instructions of God through the "men of God."[50]
Therefore it seems unnecessary to look for a later author.
Indeed, there are other indications and grounds for believing
that to do so cannot be justified:[51]

1. The succession story, attributed by general agreement
to a contemporary or, at least, near contemporary, is dovetailed into the end of the ark narrative, thus presupposing
the latter.
2. The ark narrative, with its defence of the tent
sanctuary, can hardly be placed after the temple had been
completed, as it contains no polemic against the temple. In
addition, the ark tends to recede further and further into
the background in the later history of the cult.
3. The conception of God in the ark narrative is so
distinctive and so bound up with the ark itself that one is
forced to assign it to as early a period as possible.

Of course, we should not lay too great a stress on this last
point as concepts from earlier times are often preserved with
great tenacity in particular strata of society and handed
down from one generation to the next. But if we accept that
a priest wrote the narrative, then a conception of God such
as this in a later period could only be explained in terms of
extensive accommodation to popular views.

So we can conclude, therefore, that the ark narrative is the
ἱερὸς λόγος of the sanctuary of the ark of Jerusalem and
arose in priestly circles at the time of David or at the
beginning of Solomon's reign.

So far our study has been restricted in the main to the question of form: we now turn our attention to content.

The first question that demands an answer concerns the historicity of the events. The question has already been anticipated when we concluded that the whole of the writer's interest is devoted to the ark. In saying this, we recognize that it is not political history but cult history that we can expect to find in the ark narrative. That is everywhere apparent. And right from the very beginning of the narrative. The two battles reported here are no more than single events from the long and persistent struggle between the Philistines and the Israelites, but isolated events which, at least in the short term, resulted in more or less far-reaching political changes. It is hardly conceivable that the Philistines would not somehow have exploited such victories to bring parts of Israelite or Judaean territory under their yoke. Perhaps even Shiloh with its ancient sacred places was destroyed at this time. The narrator gives us no information about this. The loss of the ark monopolizes his interest - no more and no less. Even the lamentations of the people of Shiloh, the death of the aged Eli, and the demise of the wife of Phinehas[52] are used merely as means to demonstrate the gravity of the loss and not to express fear of the victors and the terrible fate of the conquered.

The same restriction of the narrative to what is important for the history of the cult can be seen throughout. It is most tangible in the account of the ceremonies surrounding the bringing of the ark into Jerusalem by David. The political changes that had taken place since the loss of the ark are irrelevant to the author. He gives no indication whatsoever of why it remained in Kiriath-jearim throughout Saul's reign and during the preceding period when Samuel was judge. Could it be that only David was successful in transforming the alliance with Kiriath-jearim,[53] one of the four Gibeonite cities, so that they became closer if not dependent? Whereas Saul, despite his attempts, was not able to achieve this aim?[54] Enough speculation! David brings the ark to Jerusalem. There is no reason to doubt this fact. Of course, it was above all an event of interest for the history of the cult. David deliberately identifies himself with the traditions of Ephraim and Shiloh, while choosing his capital as the cult centre for the northern Israelite ark. This is the political significance of the event, but, in accordance with his intentions, the narrator does not go into this. Similarly, he tells us nothing about the effect this act of David has in terms of the political and religious spheres.

Having established the author's intention to describe the origin and genesis of the ark cult in Jerusalem, i.e. to provide a "cult-history," we must now ask whether we are dealing with a "history" in the stricter sense. We should first point our how few of the participants are named: Eli, Hophni, Phinehas, Ichabod, Abinadab, Eleazer, Uzzah, Obed-edom, David. Apart from that he always speaks of groups of people: the Israelites and their elders, the Philistines with their princes, priests and diviners, the people of Ashdod, Gath, Ekron, Beth-shemesh and Kiriath-jearim. It must be granted that the author has succeeded in letting these people act and speak not just as crowds but as communities and confederations. This is not generally a characteristic of Hebrew narrators, as is shown, for example, by the succession story. Here the crowds remain crowds and the individual personalities stand out as active participants against this background. Communities and confederations have something timeless about them and this can easily be carried over into the narratives which recount events involving such groups. It is only possible to make an accurate chronological assessment of such inter-communal relationships when there is an exact date or when men appear who elsewhere step into the limelight of history. But there is no exact chronology in our narrative. This is shown most obviously by the beginning of I Sam 4. The narrator has no interest in the matter and makes not the slightest attempt to give a date. Only when the sons of Eli, Hophni and Phinehas, are named are we given names of men who can be understood to some extent in terms of history and thus given a rough date. And even if the length of the stay among the Philistines is given as seven months and the ark remains in Obed-edom's house for three months, these isolated pieces of information help us no further and prove nothing against our statement that the author is not interested in pinpointing the events historically. He gives no figure for the length of the stay in Kiriath-jearim and only the fact that it was David who brought the ark from the house of Abinadab to Jerusalem gives us any means of making an estimate - in particular, the time of the transfer of the ark to Jerusalem is more readily determined because this event unquestionably took place at the beginning of David's period of rule in Jerusalem.

Summing up, we can say that the narrator has no interest in fixing a definite chronology; he is simply not in the position to make the hearer or reader conscious of the long period of time covered by the narrative. This means that he is not an historiographer in the narrower sense of this word. Rather, we must describe him as the author of a legend which nevertheless comes very close to historical fact in many details and perhaps also in its overall picture of political and cultural relationships. The historical conditions seem, in general, to be depicted correctly - for example, the internal political situation in the Philistine pentapolis, the political position of Beth-shemesh and Kiriath-jearim, and David's behaviour. All the more so in that the other traditions do not contradict this picture. In consequence the legend gains a certain historical feasibility, though this is admittedly not a matter of probability, still less certainty.[55] Apart from accepting such a possibility there are no alternatives other than the risky paths of hypothesis.[56] To increase these hypotheses by yet another is not the purpose of this work.

A much more important question to be answered within the compass of the ark narrative is that of its underlying conception of God. This is all the more important inasmuch as it is then possible to gain an insight into the spiritual life and religious devotion of the early monarchic period. For the Philistines as for the narrator, Yahweh is the god of Israel (5.8 and 11) just as Dagon is the god of the Philistines or at least of the people of Ashdod. But unlike the Philistine god he is not worshipped through an image. His presence is symbolized by the ark. For the Philistines, indeed, the ark and God are the same thing, as is proven by their words: "God has come into the camp" (4.7). The same is perhaps also true of the people of Beth-shemesh (I Sam 6.20). But for our author[57] and the Israelites, things are different. Of course, even for them Yahweh is closely connected with the ark. They thought that in the ark they had a guarantee of his presence, though not in the sense that Yahweh acted in and through it exclusively: the elders ask "Why has Yahweh defeated us?" about the defeat Israel suffered when the ark was not there. Yahweh's relationship to the ark is to be seen, therefore, in terms of the ark being a symbol of his presence, in the sense that Yahweh requires that the respect due to himself be paid to this symbol. Yahweh's holiness is made known in this demand, for it is a holiness which extends also to that which is dedicated to him or to his service (I Sam 6.20). Yahweh is holy because he is the all-powerful, the one who excites fear and dread, not because he is the unpredictable one.[58] Otherwise the narrator could hardly make the elders ask why God had inflicted a defeat upon them; nor would he have taken the trouble to establish a causal connection between human disrespect or a mistake (even if well-intentioned) and divine intervention regarded as punishment. Thus the idea of retribution is in evidence here. In saying this we do not wish to deny that divine punishment could be regarded as excessive harshness bordering on ruthlessness. But the fact that it was regarded as punishment at all removes it from the realm of the unforeseeable and the arbitrary (note the text of II Sam 6.7 with the explanatory עַל; this should be supplemented from I Chr 13.10).

We have now already moved on to the question of the relationship between God and humankind. It is advisable to concentrate first on the divine aspect and to examine Yahweh's behaviour towards humankind. Yahweh does not look idly on people's actions and strivings. On the contrary, he often intervenes actively in the affairs of the individual and the community. Not only that, but even Dagon, the god of the Philistines, is not safe from his actions and is subject to his power. The narrator does not shy away from anthropomorphisms to characterize this immediacy of Yahweh. His hand lies heavy on a city (I Sam 5.6 and 8), he becomes incensed with anger (II Sam 6.7). Yahweh blesses the one who honours the ark, such as Obed-edom (II Sam 6.11f.), even to the extent of giving him material wealth. More often he has cause to intervene by punishing, destroying and annihilating. In previous times he had struck Egypt with a number of plagues. He is the one who defeats the Israelites before the Philistines: the latter withdraw into the background in contrast to Yahweh's actions. He afflicts the people of Ashdod, Gath and Ekron with the plague of boils. He strikes down the 70 people of Beth-shemesh. He kills Uzzah. A glance back over the material shows that Yahweh only once uses human mediation; otherwise he always acts directly and it is for this reason that his activity is so terrible and awe-inspiring.[59] Plagues which befall whole towns are attributed to Yahweh's intervention, and then sudden cases of death where people in the prime of their life succumb without any recognisable external cause.

If, then, in his behaviour towards humankind Yahweh has primarily awesome and mysterious characteristics, so the corresponding human attitude in the face of this is fear. Every expression of God's anger prompts the human question, whether the person affected has not earned this punishment through disrespectful behaviour towards God. So far extends this fear of Yahweh that people try to keep the symbol of his presence as distant as possible - as can be seen from the action of the people of Beth-shemesh (I Sam 6.20f.) and of David (II Sam 6.8f.). If this was the view of the Canaanites (?) and the Israelites towards Yahweh and his ark, we are hardly surprised that the narrator attributes the underlying feeling of fear, if not horror, to the Philistines, who seem to equate the ark with the deity (I Sam 4.7f., chapter 5 passim). But all this only characterizes one side of the emotional disposition of humankind towards God. The writer complements it by showing, on the one hand, how despite fear - or perhaps just because of that very distance it preserves - reverence, adoration, love and even joy in Yahweh the saving God can arise. The Israelites rejoice aloud at the arrival of the ark in their camp in the certainty that victory will then be on their side. The people of Beth-shemesh are glad when they see the cart with the ark rolling through the ripe fields. And David and his companions bring the ark from the house of Abinadab and later to Jerusalem with rejoicing and festive music. But much more convincing and compelling than this joy of the rejoicing crowds (which could anyway have something of the nature of a mass psychosis in it) is the depth of grief with which the aged Eli receives the news of the loss of the ark and the fact that the mother of Ichabod, apathetic to her newborn child, can only lament that the glory of Israel has departed. Here one feels the pulse of deep piety which is not only linked closely to the cult but which also seeks and finds communion with God in the cult.

So far we have dealt with the inward disposition of humankind towards God; now we must cast a glance at the outward expression of this attitude in the cult. It is self-evident that our writer, a priest (as has already been shown), and, moreover, one who was numbered among the community of priests of the ark, should speak of this. Here, too, we can achieve some clarification inasmuch as the cultic practices and ceremonies can be traced back in part to the basic feeling of fear and in part to that of joy. We have only one account of a ceremony among the Philistines - the consecration of the guilt offering to Yahweh. At least among the Philistines, the opinion was widespread that it was possible to appease the deity's anger at transgressions by consecrating expensive articles like the golden mice symbolising the plague. How far the writer would approve of this among the Israelites cannot be determined. David's procedure of making an offering after the first six steps of the procession is almost certainly an attempt to turn the God whose wrath he

fears to a favourable disposition. Out of fear, probably because of cultic uncleanliness, but perhaps also out of a sense
of human impotence in the face of divine power, David has
the ark brought to the house of the Gittite, Obed-edom, after
the death of Uzzah. On the other hand, it is joy that makes
the people of Beth-shemesh sacrifice the cows that had
drawn the cart with the ark. Joy makes David arrange a
sacrificial meal in which all those present can partake.

So we can say that our narrator sees Yahweh as the fearful
destroyer. The ark is regarded as a symbol of his presence,
but he is not restricted to it. Yahweh intervenes directly and
indirectly in the life of the individual and of the community -
and usually in a manner more likely to arouse terror than joy.
So a person's religious devotion is very much coloured by
fear, though joy can also be discerned alongside this. Cultic
observance, then, is reducible at the emotional level to basic
attitudes of fear and joy.

All that is left now is the question of how the narrator
depicts Yahweh's intervention within his story. A cursory
glance shows that he sometimes provides an indication of
Yahweh's actions within the account itself, and sometimes
puts the comment in the mouth of someone else. Thus he
reports of Ashdod, Gath and Ekron that Yahweh's hand lay
heavy upon them. Similarly, he gives his own view that
Yahweh struck down the 70 people of Beth-shemesh, carried
off Uzzah and blessed Obed-edom. On the other hand, he
leaves it to the elders of Israel to regard the first defeat
as being brought about by Yahweh and he has the Philistines
say that Yahweh struck Egypt with plagues. The people of
Ashdod say that the hand of the God of Israel bears heavily
upon them, and the people of Ekron cry that the ark will
kill them. The narrator is accordingly quite free with the way
in which he tells the listener of Yahweh's intervention. If we
can come to any conclusion now, it is that the narrator
himself sees God's activity everywhere and would like
everyone to share the same point of view. The devotional
purpose of his narrative determined that the supernatural
background of all that happens should be constantly
mentioned.

Summary

1. The ark narrative comprises: I Sam 4.1b-18a, 19-21;
5.1-11b^a, 12; 6.1-3b^a, 4, 10-14, 16; 6.19-7.1; II Sam 6.1-15,
17-20a.

2. Through its vocabulary and style it can be shown over

against its context to be independent and uniform, and through its structure to be self-contained and complete.

3. The narrative is to be regarded as the ἱερὸς λόγος of the sanctuary of the ark in Jerusalem, its author a member of the community of priests who took care of the ark during the latter part of David's reign or at the beginning of Solomon's reign.

4. As a cult legend it has only a limited interest in political events. It can lay a certain claim to historical reliability as regards the broad relationships and many of the individuals, but does not represent historical reality in every detail.

5. Yahweh appears as the all-powerful - but not arbitrary - God who normally brings ill fortune, but also salvation; accordingly, religious devotion is characterized by fear, but also by joyful adoration.

6. Yahweh's interventions are partly related by the narrator himself and partly placed as comment in the mouths of the active or passive participants.

Chapter Two

THE PROPHECY OF NATHAN, II SAMUEL 7

There is general agreement that II Samuel 7 in its present form is relatively late. The chapter is also quite often attributed to K1 or E, following the demonstration that there are only very minor traces of a Deuteronomistic revision to be found. Wellhausen places its composition in the time of Josiah, while Budde regards the narrator as being a forerunner of the Deuteronomist. Sellin thinks it was written in northern Israel around 800. Gressmann believes a writer had combined an old tradition with an originally poetic oracle which he converted into prose and to which he added a prayer of David. Kittel takes the present version of the chapter to be the work of an author near to D, indeed K^E, but thinks that 1a, 2-11b, 12, 14-17 belong to an earlier stratum. In Procksch's view the chapter was written in the 7th century, but preserves earlier fragments in 1-3, 4a, 5b, $11b^b$, 12, (14a?), 18f., 27a, which come from the larger historical work about David.[1]

We will have to bear in mind that the chapter is not uniform. This can be seen simply from the fact that v. 2 alone speaks of the ark which is not mentioned throughout the rest of the narrative. Further we should notice that in vv. 5ff. a house is to be built for Yahweh and in v. 13 for his name.[2] That there is a new start in v. 8 also gives us pause for thought. It is most appropriate to begin analysis at David's prayer (18-27), then to proceed to the prophecy of Nathan (8-17), and finally, we must examine vv. 1-7, which Gressmann isolated as a separate section. The core of David's prayer is in v. 27a: Yahweh had "uncovered his ear," saying to him, "I will build you a house." That is to say, David would not be like Saul, a king in his own person only, but he was to form the beginning of a dynasty. It is obvious that we are dealing here with a very ancient text. Quite apart from the almost word-for-word agreement of 7.11b, we are confronted with the same concept in 23.1ff., a divine revelation to David and a saying which can almost certainly be attributed to David himself (with Procksch and Gressmann).[3] Yet although it cannot be doubted that the content of the verse goes back to the time of David, we must still consider whether this is supported by its form. The strange expression, "to uncover (someone's) ear" is found only in the Books of Samuel, apart from one passage in the Book of Ruth (which has a consciously archaic style) and two occurrences in Job. In Samuel it belongs to an ancient stratum.[4] Similarly, there can be no objection to seeing the use of "Yahweh of hosts" as a name for God already in the early monarchic period, especially as it is alien to Deuteronomistic circles, as already noticed by Budde.[5] The Davidic period, therefore, cannot be excluded for verse 27 on grounds of either content or form.

We now have a firm basis for the further examination of this prayer, so let us turn to the beginning. The questions in v. 18 with their motif of submission remind one of the beginning of Jacob's prayer in Gen 33.11ff., an undoubtedly Yahwistic passage. There are also similar thoughts in David's answer to the men who come to arrange the wedding with Michal (I Sam 18.23), also in I Sam 18.18 with almost exactly the same words (again from the mouth of David), and, finally, in Saul's words in 9.21.[6] From this we can conclude that, at the very least, such ideas were not alien to the early monarchic period, i.e. to the time of David. If this verse can be assigned to an ancient source then the same is true for vv. 19 and 20 (in the latter case, compare II Sam 19.29b). Even v. 21, the text of which is admittedly not quite without error, seems to be old. There are considerable doubts, however, concerning the originality of vv. 22-24 as regards both content and form. While vv. 18-21 are spoken by a individual speaking in the first person singular, or alternatively, in the third person (the submissive style: "your servant"), in v. 22 the first person plural suddenly appears. Vv. 18-21 refer exclusively to David and his house; vv. 22-24 are reminiscent of Deuteronomistic thought. V. 22 maintains the uniqueness of Yahweh in a way that parallels Deut 4.35 et al., while 23 and 24 praise the mighty act of bringing the Israelites out of Egypt in much the same terms as Deut 4.34ff. Therefore, these verses must be attributed to a later reviser who wished to give the people of Israel a fitting place in this prayer. The date of this revision will be discussed later. V. 25 is closely connected to v. 21. David and his house are the focal point. In place of the first person plural we find once more the third person expression of humility as in vv. 18ff. There is no reason, either of form or content, to separate this verse from the ancient source. Whether v. 26 belongs to the older source or to a later revision cannot easily be determined. Neither form nor content speak against its inclusion in the old stratum, but v. 27 seems more readily to follow on from v. 25. Vv. 28 and 29 could be an old ending to the prayer: the language and the content do not seem out of place especially in the mouth of David. It is impossible to allocate this to a later source.

So we can sum up the results so far as follows: David's prayer consists of an old, basic source revised later. The older stratum includes vv. 18-21, 25 (26), 27-29. Vv. 22-24 belong to the later stratum.[7]

The old basic source presents a prayer which was supposed to have been spoken by David on the occasion of a revelation to him concerning the future of his dynasty. This prayer is spoken almost exclusively in the third person singular, in the Hebrew style of humility, and is self-contained. The style is uniform throughout the whole section. The abundance of particles is conspicuous and one notices a certain preference for infinitive constructions and subordinate clauses. These characteristics are most noticeable when compared with the simple language of the ark narrative. Sometimes the language does give the impression of formality, e.g.: "Who am I and what is my house?" "And what more can David say to you?" or "You have done all this greatness."

In this way the prayer has something rather vague or colourless about it which stands out strikingly against the single, concrete sentence so powerful in its brevity: "I will make you a house." In the face of this all embellishment takes second place. We can assume that prayer style had already adopted particular forms by the time of David. At least various parallels to our prayer indicate this. However, before it is possible to go into this, the structure of the present prayer must be established. By way of introduction, vv. 18-21 present a declaration of his own unworthiness for the mercies Yahweh has already shown him and for the new one that he has just received. V. 25 (26) is a transition: a petition for the realization of this promise of prosperity. V.27 contains the reason for the prayer: the promise is quoted. Vv. 28 and 29 bring it smoothly to a conclusion with a plea that the promise should be fulfilled. This shows that in itself the structure is well-rounded. It does not seem credible that we are dealing here with a totally spontaneous prayer; rather the likelihood is that certain forms have been observed, if not a fixed pattern. And we must go further than this. It is improbable that we have a word-for-word reproduction of David's actual prayer, but rather a more-or-less free exposition on the part of the author using particular forms.

This assumption is supported by comparison with other prayers. As already mentioned there is great similarity between the present prayer and that of Jacob in Gen 32.10ff. This relationship is not restricted to just a few phrases but encompasses the whole structure: v. 10 has the invocation of Yahweh in terms of an appeal to an earlier revelation made earlier; v. 11 has the motif of humility and submission; v. 12 contains the plea to be saved from Esau; v. 13 gives the basis for this petition citing Yahweh's promise. There is no invocation corresponding to v. 10 in David's prayer - this begins directly with the declaration of his own unworthiness (i.e. the second part of Jacob's prayer). In both prayers there now follows a petition: in Samuel a plea that the promise should be fulfilled, in Genesis that he should be saved from the hand of Esau. In both cases the petition has its basis in a revelation of Yahweh which is given in a quotation. The reprise-like conclusion of David's prayer with its renewed petition has no counterpart in Jacob's prayer. The common elements are the motif of humility, the petition, the appeal to a revelation from God which is quoted.[8] In the one case this pattern is preceded by an invocation of God, in the other one a repeat of the petition is added as a concluding reprise. The agreement is therefore quite extensive and within the body of the prayer it is complete. Obviously one has to admit that Jacob's prayer does reveal the actual situation from which it arose much more clearly. It is much more concrete, natural and vivid than the more abstract prayer of David, which is kept somewhat general. This could be due primarily to Jacob's more dramatic situation at that moment, but it could also show that there is no direct literary dependence here. At any rate, in view of the fact that this passage in Genesis is Yahwistic we can maintain that there was a specific prayer structure (among others, of course) in the early monarchic period, a type that can be recognized in Jacob's prayer and which appears again in David's. In that case, perhaps we have found a new argument which could possibly date the origin of David's prayer to the beginning of the monarchic period. Nevertheless, however welcome this conclusion may be, it should be regarded for the moment as secondary and we should carry on with our comparison with other prayers.

The most obvious choice for the next example is the extensive prayer of Solomon at the consecration of the temple. Here we are only interested in the beginning, vv. 23-26, and not in the main casuistic section. The invocation of Yahweh in vv. 23f. has been much revised by the Deuteronomist; it is followed by a plea that the promise to David be fulfilled and this is supported by quoting the divine oracle; the prayer then finishes with a plea that the promise be realized. So here there are: 1) the invocation of Yahweh, as in Jacob's prayer; 2) a petition and the divine oracle on which it is based, as in both; 3) the conclusion with a petition, as in David's prayer. The motif of humility does not appear at the beginning, but in general the same pattern can be recognized, even though this prayer is probably more recent. A comparison with I Chr 29.10ff. is of further interest. Here the introduction is formed by a hymn to God's power. The humility motif then follows in vv. 14ff., somewhat drawn out, and finally there is a petition. We have the invocation as in Jacob's and Solomon's prayers, the humility motif as in Jacob's and David's, and the final petition as in David's and Solomon's. Missing is the transitional petition, with the divine oracle on which it is based, a feature of all the other three prayers. The reason for its absence is the lack of such an oracle to which David could appeal here. The prayers used in comparison so far should suffice to show that there was a prayer pattern used in Judah and Israel from the early monarchic period till much later times, the characteristics of which can best be recognized in the prayers of David and of Jacob.[9]

So much for the more ancient stratum. Now to the interpolation in vv. 22-4. This later stratum is not uniform. Between vv. 22 and 23f. one can discern a break. While the first verse is a hymn to Yahweh's uniqueness, the latter two express joy concerning the special position of Israel in relation to this unique God. As already shown, we meet both of these ideas in Deuteronomy. It could, therefore, be a matter of Deuteronomistic interpolation of material which never existed independently. However it is also possible that the present formulation of the text is somewhat older than Deuteronomy 4. This would mean that we have here additions from a period and school of thought which later gave rise to the Deuteronomist.[10] One might point to the fact that the language of Deuteronomy is fuller and more sonorous than here and that one can find a series of typical phrases like "mighty hand" and "outstretched arm" in the Deuteronomy passage but not here in v. 23f. Throughout these verses we are faced with an intense nationalist feeling, religiously based, such as we find in the polemic of Jeremiah. And here there is no word of the house of David, but only of the people of Israel, whose election by God and delivery out of Israel are the subject of joyful thanks and praise, just as we find in Deutero-Isaiah. This interpolation gives the prayer quite a different sense. It is no longer a question of the preservation of the dynasty but rather of the continuation of the nation. This view is given further substance by the fact that the verses have been inserted immediately before the petition that Yahweh's words about David and his house should be confirmed. However in that case it is probable that these additions (contrary to what we said before) are not pre-Deuteronomic, but come from a time when the future of the nation was veiled in darkness and the people had to draw strength from the great traditions of the past in order not to lose faith in God and their own nation. Thus we come to the exilic period and in these verses, both in their manner of insertion and in their reshaping of the original sense, we have before us a document reflecting the religious feeling of those dark days of the Babylonian exile. And truly it is no trifling one. It speaks to us something of the spirit of Deutero-Isaiah, something of that defiant "Nevertheless" of faith which draws strength from the past to cope with the tragic present, a strength which allows hope for a future.

Summing up, therefore, we can maintain the following. The older stratum of the prayer has a pattern which can be shown to have existed from the early monarchic period. There is nothing which would exclude dating the prayer to the time of David - rather, there is much to be said for this time. The later stratum is not an independent tradition but consists simply of additions which probably came from the time of the Exile.

Having shown that the older account comes from the early monarchic period, we must now ask about its historicity. It can hardly be doubted that David somehow became convinced that his dynasty would endure. This is shown by the final words of the old king which Procksch declares, quite rightly, to be genuine.[11] Here, also, in the form of an oracle from the mouth of David, the writer speaks of a divine revelation afforded the speaker, according to which a lasting continuation of the dynasty is explained as the subject of a promise, a ברית, by Yahweh. Further reference can be made to I Kgs 2.24, where Solomon also knows something of a promise of this kind. Such a tradition[12] is not formed without cause. The only question is whether this revelation came directly to David (as one is tempted to believe from his prayer and his last words), or whether it was conveyed by Nathan, as indicated by 7.8-17. In any case we may uphold the historicity of a divine revelation even if it is not clear how it came about. The succession source could not have achieved its present form if a revelation of this kind to David had not lain before the narrator. Further, this revelation is merely a development of the one which granted David kingship over all Israel and which the Northern Israelites constantly re-called.[13]

All that is now left is the question of the religious content of the prayer. Naturally, only the older stratum is of interest here. Because of the brevity of the text the yield of basic theological views will hardly be great. Yahweh Sebaoth, the God of Israel, directs the fortunes of the petitioner. It behoves him to determine the events of the future, to carry them out and to bring them to fruition. God's revelations, his words, are truth. If he does turn a friendly face to humankind, then this is grace. As such is a divine revelation to be regarded which brings a prospect of future prosperity, or more properly, a fulfilment accomplished through God's intervention. Humankind is the servant and slave of Yahweh. Contact with the realm of God is a hazardous business (v. 27) and must be founded on some word of God, and it is the task of humankind to ask for the promise to be kept. Religious devotion is particularly strongly coloured by a sense of the enormous distance between God and humankind, expressed most clearly in the motif of submission and in the third person style of humility ("your servant"). This consciousness of personal unimportance greatly enhances the joy found in the grace of a revelation from God but it also hinders its conversion into intimacy. So, here we have a prayer of deep devotion before us, a wonderful witness to the power and individuality of religious life in the early monarchy, a royal prayer, worthy of David, whether it actually comes from him or whether it is an invention of the narrator who knew something of a prayer by David on the occasion of a divine promise.

The second section to be examined in chapter 7 is the prophecy of Nathan in vv. 8-17. This passage has a series of problems that make its interpretation difficult. That v. 13 is part of the original text has been maintained recently by Tiktin[14] alone, deleting instead 11b. There is much to be said against the retention of v. 13:

1. In 13b there is an uncommon polel of כין (establish) in place of a hiphil as in the parallel verse 12b.

2. The phrase "the throne of his kingdom" stands alongside "his kingdom" (end of v.12), whereas Chronicles has only "his throne."

3. The house is built for the "name" of Yahweh, whereas in 7.2 it is built for the ark and in 7.5-7 for Yahweh himself.

4. The building of the temple is made the duty of David's successor; this contradicts 7.4ff. where it is categorically forbidden for all time.

5. As already emphasized by Nowack and Löhr, 13a finds no mention in David's prayer of thanks, while 13b is parallel to 12b.[15]

The three last-mentioned points lose a little of their persuasive power given our intention to examine the prophecy separately from its present context. It is not feasible, therefore, to base our arguments against the originality of v. 13 on the surrounding passages. We can, however, readily do without these tools because there are others which are far more precise. If v.13 is excluded then the whole prophecy has nothing to do with the building of the temple but only with the future of the Davidic dynasty, the "sure house" (בית נאמן) which Yahweh will establish for him. Not a word in the whole text refers to the plan of David to build a temple. The whole passage then becomes uniform, dealing with a single idea: Yahweh intends to build a house for David. This raises another problem, which we can only mention here: is the connection with 7.1-7 original or not? Dependent on this decision is the question of whether one can maintain that there is a contrast here: "You are not to make a house for me, but I will make one for you." We will go into this later. For the time being we can register the conclusion that v. 13 does not belong in this context and should be deleted. We now have to ask ourselves whether Tiktin's suggestion to delete v. 11b and to place v. 11a in v. 7 after "all the people of Israel" does not present new problems for this conclusion. V. 11 is a well-known "crux interpretum" and there are numerous attempts to emend it. The view that v. 11b belongs to the original text is standard. Tiktin alone deletes the verse, for the following reasons:

1. The sudden change from the first to the third person is conspicuous.
2. There is no previous mention of a revelation from God.)
3. The thought contained comes too late after v. 10; here we are dealing finally with the people and no longer with David.
4. V. 12 connects to v. 10.

It must be admitted that v. 11b does stand out against its context on account of its form. Since the time of the Chronicler emendations have been employed in an attempt to help out here, yet without a real improvement. It does not seem absolutely necessary to reject the Massoretic text, especially since it is supported by the LXX. If, then, the verse is retained there are two possibilities: the first is that it is a direct reference back to v. 8, "thus says Yahweh" while the second, Tiktin's solution, is that v. 11 is alien to this context. If the latter alternative is upheld (as it must be, but for reasons other than Tiktin's) then there are still two more possibilities: v. 11 is either a later addition or an older version. Tiktin does not pose this question even though there is no way of getting round it in his case. If we think v. 11 is a later addition then its inclusion can be justified by reference to the prayer of David (cf. the original v. 27) and, of course, the influence of such passages as 23.5, I Kgs 8.25 etc. must also be taken into account. The glossator could not find in the prophecy of Nathan the basis for the oracle to which David refers. But where, then, does the third person come from? Would a later glossator really have been so inept as to include a saying in the third person in a speech of Yahweh in the first person, especially as the first person appears in the prayer of David lying before him? That is hardly credible. The suggestion of Procksch[17] that it comes from an older source has far greater probability. From the form of the words "And Yahweh declares to you, etc." we can see that this older version presented the prophecy of Nathan as a report of the revelation imparted to him. A glance at the books of Samuel and Kings shows that such a shaping as this for a prophetic speech was not uncommon - so there is no formal objection to the verse. A further question, then, is whether still more fragments from this older tradition exist in the section vv. 8-17. Vv. 8-11a do not come into consideration because of their form, nor likewise vv. 12-15. In these passages Yahweh speaks in the first person in the style of commissioning a messenger. V. 16, however, should perhaps be added, since:[18]

1. The form of the verse presents no difficulties.

2. The house of David, the dynasty, is the focus of attention as in 11b, whereas in the intervening verses there is mention of the "seed" (זרע), the descendents, amongst whom is intended here perhaps just the particular wearer of the crown, or, as is the intention of the glossator in v. 13, simply Solomon. It should be noted that in vv. 12 and 14ff. there is nothing that says that this "seed" will rule for ever; on the other hand, v. 16 speaks of the "house of David" (בית דוד) continuing for ever.

3. Finally, we can detect a difference between v. 11b and v. 16 on the one hand, and v. 12 and v. 14 on the other: the former proclaim David's salvation and the latter only deal with the "seed" of David. We gain the impression that the version in vv. 11b and 16 is the more all-embracing and goes further than 12 and 14f. - both in the number of people who are included in the promise and in the length of time envisaged.

Consequently, 11b and 16 are both to be regarded as a fragment of an earlier version of Nathan's prophecy.[19] In terms of content it offers assurances that David's house will be an everlasting dynasty; in terms of form, it is an incomplete report by Nathan - the beginning and perhaps other parts of the speech are lacking - concerning a revelation afforded to him about the future of the house of David.

Thus, in the passage 8-17, v. 13 should be regarded as a later gloss, whereas vv. 11b and 16 are an older stratum.

Now we must investigate the relationship of the remainder of the prophecy of Nathan to the older stratum. Vv. 8ff. form the point of departure. Apart from a few minor emendations, the main problems are in vv. 9 and 10. Are we dealing, in these verses, with waw-consecutives with the perfect or perfects with waw-copula? In other words, does the change to the future take place as early as in v. 9b as suggested by Klostermann (from ואכרתה "and I will cut off ..."), Budde, Nowack and Kittel (from ועשיתי "and I will make ..."), or later in v. 11b, or, as Tiktin suggests, in v. 12.[20] The answer to this question is dependent on grammatical factors and on the content. That ואכרתה is waw-consecutive with the imperfect ("and I [have] cut off") is disputed only by Klostermann,[21] and he is certainly wrong. This allowed, there is, on the other hand, no support for interpreting the subsequent perfects as perfect consecutive (and so future in tense). We can add to that the fact that perfects with the waw-copula are not so very rare in Hebrew, even in older

44

texts;[22] so there remains at least the grammatical possibility of regarding the waw as a waw-copula. An examination of the content gets us further. Almost everyone sees as the central idea: You are not to build a house for me, but rather I shall build one for you. This is only possible, of course, if vv. 1-7 are included; otherwise we are simply left with the much simpler motif: I will establish a house for you! This thought is expressed and developed in vv. 11b and 12ff., and clearly in the sense that it involves enduring continuation of the dynasty (11b and 16) or a particularly close relationship between Yahweh and all David's descendants (or perhaps just Solomon?) (vv. 12 and 14f.). If these are really the contents of the prophecy then this means that in future God intends to effect the preservation of the dynasty rather than the further rise of David or of the people of Israel. The hand of Yahweh in external affairs is replaced by his hand in internal affairs; the people's aggrandisement is succeeded by their mainten-ance. In his own person, David had reached the climax of his career, just as the people of Israel had reached their greatest possible extent and their greatest standing. Yahweh no longer wishes to increase the kingdom but wants to preserve it, to be a guarantor of its achievement. If this is so then the vv. 8ff. must look back into the past and so the promise becomes all the more multifaceted. The enemies have been routed, Yahweh has made David a name as one of the great of the earth. The people of Israel have found their place in the sun from which no enemy will ever oust them. Such a survey of past events is a common feature of prophetic oracles; thus on formal grounds as well it presents what we might expect.

Having decided, therefore, to accept the view that the sense in vv. 8ff. is perfective, we are now once more faced with the problem of whether these verses form a single unit with 12 and 14ff. and, further, whether they are uniform within themselves. There are no stylistic variations. That can be seen from the text. Throughout we find the same, elevated language with its preference for words and phrases belonging to poetry. There is a certain amount of rhythm throughout the whole, so much so that it is possible to produce metric verses in places (cf. vv. 12 and 14). Even a kind of "formation dance"[23] of repeated ideas can be discerned here and there. In terms of style, therefore, there are no doubts about the unity of the passage. From the formal point of view, too, the literary type of the prophetic oracle given in the shape of a message is consistent throughout. Finally, there remains only the question of whether vv. 8ff. and 12 and 14f. constitute a single unit in terms of content. This we cannot answer with absolute certainty. V. 8 speaks of the call of David and his appointment as "prince" (נגיד); v. 9 shows what Yahweh had done for David up to this point; vv. 10 and 11a[24] report the same for the people of Israel; v. 12 announces to David the appointment of a successor from among his descendants; vv. 14 and 15 depict the particularly close connection between Yahweh and David's successor. As can be seen, v. 10 does not fit into this pattern. While the rest of the oracle has to do with David and his house, here suddenly it is about the people of Israel. One might be tempted, therefore, to view v. 10 as a later addition on the pattern of II Sam 7.22-24. But closer inspection shows that v. 10 can be retained, not just for stylistic and formal reasons but also for reasons of content. The enumeration of the favours shown by Yahweh towards David would be incomplete it there were no mention of the people, whose state of prosperity depends in ancient Hebrew thought upon the favourable attitude of Yahweh towards the royal household,[25] and bears witness, therefore, to the divine favour towards David. V. 10 is thus to be regarded simply as a subsidiary item in the list of favours shown towards David. As for the future, it is only necessary to proclaim that God's favour towards David's house will continue and the salvation of the people is thereby presupposed. A particular assurance on this score is, accordingly, unnecessary. We can conclude that it is possible to retain v. 10.

In vv. 8-17 there are fragments of an old tradition in 11b and 16, then a later stratum in 8-11a, 12, 14, 15 and 17,[26] and finally another interpolation in v. 13. We must now investigate the relationship of these various strata to one another. It is probable that v. 13 was not introduced until the first and second strata had been put together. The dependence of 11b and 16, on the one hand, and 12, on the other, is self-evident. Much more important is the question of whether the first and second strata come from two independent sources or whether the first is so worked into the second that the second forms a sort of commentary on the first. The latter view, which up until now has only been hinted at, is more probable, for the following reasons:

1. After the review in vv. 8-10 of the previous favours shown by Yahweh, we expect a forceful transition to the future granting of salvation. If 11b is deleted then the transition in v. 12 is achieved by a dull, half-causal, half-conditional כי. Instead of a main clause, we have a subordinate clause.

2. The pronouncement for the future would have been without a forceful ending as well as a definite beginning if v. 16 (which is part of the older stratum) had not always formed the conclusion.

To come to a conclusion about the integration of the older stratum into the revision on the basis of its position between vv. 1-7 and vv. 18-29 would seem inadvisable. The most that could be concluded thereby is that the place of 11b and 16 here is very ancient, but not that 8-10, 12 and 14f. belonged here, as these verses speak only of the "seed" and not of the "house of David." We are thus left with just the two reasons mentioned above for believing that 11b and 16 are no purely alien elements but rather indispensible fragments of an earlier prophetic oracle which were embedded in a different context. So we can agree with Tiktin that 11b should not be attributed to the author of 8-11a, 12 and 14f. But, in contrast to him, we maintain that the verse was included by the more recent author in his revision. This conclusion is affected neither by the change from first to third person - the reviser was not prepared to change the old form - nor by the lack of a previous mention of an oracle of God - it is unnecessary to assume the existence of an earlier oracle of God on this subject, since the perfect והגיד (has declared) can also express the irrevocability of the current proclamation of salvation. Further, the argument that the passage comes too late after v. 10, as the context is no longer dealing with David but with the people, can be countered by the fact that v. 12 also speaks not about the people, but about the seed of David. Finally, as already shown, the possibility that v. 12 makes a better connection with v. 10 is also rather questionable.

In conclusion, we can say that in vv. 8-17 one cannot speak of various sources but rather of various strata lying one on top of the other.

The next task is to try to determine the age of the strata. Vv. 11b and 16 seem to be the earliest fragments: "and Yahweh declares to you that Yahweh will raise for you a house and your house will endure and your kingdom last for ever before Yahweh. Your throne will be established for ever." The content of this oracle of Yahweh holds out the prospect of the enduring continuation of David's dynasty. That such an oracle can be ascribed to the time of David has already been shown when we were dealing with David's prayer. It is, of course, only a possibility that 11b and 16 come from the early monarchic period, not a necessity. But as there are no decisive indications to the contrary, the assumption that these verses originated in the time of David is the most likely possibility.[27]

This raises a burning question, which has been kept back intentionally until now: does the oldest stratum in 8-17 belong with the oldest parts of 18-29 or not? The answer depends on the interpretation of v. 27. Does v. 27 mean that David is the immediate recipient of the oracle of Yahweh (as is perhaps indicated by the expression "uncover the ear" and perhaps also II Sam 23.1ff.)? If so, this prayer of David could only have been preceded by an account of the king receiving the oracle from God. Vv. 11b and 16 do not give the impression of being taken from such an account. They seem far more, as already remarked, to represent a report of an oracle of God to Nathan about the future of the Davidic dynasty from the mouth of Nathan himself. If this is so then we have here two parallel traditions which have been combined in such a way that the account of David receiving the oracle of God has been ousted by a similar one dealing with Nathan delivering an equivalent oracle.[28] This assumption is unnecessary if, as is quite conceivable, David did not mention in his prayer the name of the mediator of the proclamation of salvation. Further problems would then be caused, however, by the form of 11b and 24, so it seems simpler to accept the explanation of parallel accounts. Nevertheless, this does not mean excluding the possibility that both traditions are very old and not so far removed from the events reported. There is a suspicion of mutual influence (cf. vv. 16 and 26; 11b and 27). Yet this process seems to have come to an end before the two traditions were joined together. Otherwise we would expect a total assimilation of 11b to 27. When the two were joined together can no longer be ascertained. In any case, v. 18a presupposes it. On the other hand, there is no trace of the second stratum in 18b-29, nor is there any sign of the third stratum in 8-17. And, of course, the addition of 22-24 has just as little influence on 8-17. Whether this indicates that both these traditions were joined together after the insertions and revisions had been finished must remain an open question.

At this point we should try to determine the age of the second stratum. In it, in the form of a message-commission to Nathan, there is a divine directive concerning the intimate relationship of Yahweh to David and to his dynasty both in the past and in the future. The continuance of the dynasty plays no role here, but Yahweh's attitude to it does. Up until now Yahweh has always given David his help so that he and Israel have now reached a position where they enjoy the greatest respect and peace. This state of prosperity is to be preserved for the future. Moreover, the connection between Yahweh and David's descendants is to become still closer through Yahweh's adoption of David's successor as his son. The value of this relationship is particularly evident when he makes a transgression. Yahweh will, to be sure, punish him, but only through the blows of men. It should never come to a repudiation as in Saul's case. These are ideas which, in my opinion, can only be explained completely in a single situation - the time immediately after the fall of the northern kingdom. The Ephraimite royal house had been rejected like Saul before it, Saul the Benjaminite, whose support had come from the northern tribes. The Asyrian hordes thundered towards Jerusalem. The former transgressions of the Davidides were being visited upon it. But, as Isaiah, the man of faith, proclaimed, Jerusalem itself and the dynasty remained - though severely punished - still intact. With the blows of men was the house of David to be chastened but Yahweh would never let his mercy go from it: its continuance remained assured. The author of this stratum seems to have been a contemporary of Isaiah. He looked for strength to face the problems of the present and found it in the prophetic oracles of the past, revising the prophecy of Nathan in accordance with the needs of his time.[29]

The third stratum is represented by v. 13. It defends Solomon's building of the temple and has the purpose of stressing the importance of the temple in Jerusalem. There is no reason to dispute the usual assessment of this interpolation (which is presupposed in I Kgs 8.15ff.) as part of a Deuteronomistic revision.

Accordingly, there are three different periods that have worked upon the prophecy of Nathan. The content and the form of the prophecy were changed. But what remained common to all the strata was the certainty that through the mouth of his prophet, Nathan, Yahweh let his servant, David, have a glimpse into the future of his house. There can be no doubt that there must be some historical basis for this tradition. Support for this conclusion can be found in the independent, parallel traditions in the prayer of David, in the last words of David and in I Kgs 2.24 (though this last passage is not totally independent). Whether, of course, this revelation occurred soon after the conquest of Jerusalem and after the solemn installation of the sanctuary of the ark, or whether it must be assigned to the last years of David's life, is a question which can hardly be solved. In any case, both suggestions can equally well be defended. However, it will be shown later that a tradition about a revelation of Yahweh to David always existed at this place in the context from early on, whether the motivation for this was chronological or, as is more likely, literary.

All that remains now is to examine the theological outlook underlying the section and finally to sketch a picture of the religious devotion to be inferred from the individual strata. Given the brevity of the text the yield will be very small. The theological position held in common is that Yahweh directs the fortunes of humankind and can choose the recipient of his favours out of his own boundless plenitude of power and through his own free will. He can also make his intentions and plans known to people who stand particularly close to him - the prophets, whose task it is to act as mediators and to pass these revelations on to others. From vv. 8-17 we learn nothing of how these revelations come about.

Out of this basic theological outlook arises a different piety in each of the strata. The oldest stratum can only speak simply and plainly about the effusive favour shown to David through Yahweh securing the continuance of his dynasty for all time. The future of the Davidic house is dealt with in short, powerful sentences so that no room is left for any doubt, for any objection or reservation. Only people who have an unbroken, complete confidence in their God, who know that they are led and sustained by him, can be addressed thus; it would never occur to them that Yahweh could withdraw his favour from them. The pledge of Yahweh's favour is the unreserved continuance of their present place of honour.

The writer of the second stratum contemplates the past: David's rise and the peace brought to Israel are miracles in his eyes. But God's work goes on. No longer directed outwardly - the house of David is not to collect new honours; the powerful position of his people will not be increased by further conquests. Yahweh's future activity is for the inner life; the inner relationship with the king is to be deepened. Yahweh wants to be his father, to adopt him as his son. With fatherly care, he wishes to punish the transgressions of the son - but not to reject him. Religious devotion is turned inwards. Stark reality has brought this change about. The proud structure of the Davidic kingdom had fallen into disarray. The larger northern kingdom lay in ruins. The northern tribes were languishing in exile. The Assyrian armies thundered through the southern kingdom, destroying the last remnants of its former prosperity. As if by a miracle, Jerusalem alone was saved, the centre of the reconstruction. The house of David did not have to share the fate of the northern dynasty. It was not rejected like the North. In this the author recognizes Yahweh's mercy, the love of a father towards his son. It is not the guarantee of external honour which is decisive for him, but the certainty of an intimate relationship with Yahweh. As a consequence, he reworks the old prophecy of Nathan to form a confession of his own interpretation of the contemporary situation and thus provides a comfort and encouragement for the king and his people. It is a quiet, strong piety which we find here, tried and tested in need and suffering. Hanging over the whole account is a deep longing for quiet and peace, both external and internal, the result perhaps of a fatigue and a feeling of being worn down.[30]

The third layer (i.e. v. 13) is the deposit of quite a different piety, from the period of Josiah. The inner relationship to God strives after possibilities of practical application. The cult provides one opportunity. Its focal point is the temple in Jerusalem. It had been built by Solomon. But now this fact is taken as presupposed in the prophecy of Nathan and so it is related closely to David, the founder of the dynasty. The temple had become so important for our writer/reviser, so determinative for his own religious devotion, that he could not but think that the permission to build a temple for Yahweh was a matter worthy of a prophetic prediction. For him the granting of it was the essence of all divine favour. His piety was very strongly orientated towards the cult.

Finally, when we cast another glance at David's prayer, we can compare the ancient core of our first stratum. By contrast, the extra vv. 22-24 take us a step further in the history of Israelite religion, to the time of the Exile.[31] The house of David was in ruins. The prophecy of its lasting for ever had come to nothing. This caused the re-interpretation to refer to the people. God had to fulfil his promises and if not through the ruling family, then through the people. Here we find the beginning of the collective interpretation such as is still found over and over again, especially in Jewish commentaries. Religious devotion clings to the old promises and tries to understand and evaluate them in the light of the changed situation, to make new coins from old metal.

Thus Nathan's prophecy and David's prayer give us a rich impression of the religious trends in Israel through the changing eras. Going through the history of Israelite piety using our text provides us with surprising insights. Alongside the naïve, child-like trust of the Davidic period we find the inward religious devotion of the time of Isaiah, tested by misery and suffering. Then in the time of Josiah, it was made more outward-going, so that finally, under the yoke of exile, the old sources were sought again and these, in their new form, relevant to the contemporary trials, were extolled as a spring of fresh water.

The final section of the chapter to be examined is vv. 1-7. Gressmann has already dealt with this passage on the basis of style and content, but he failed to notice that 7.1-7 is itself not uniform. After v. 4 there is a clear hiatus. Vv. 1-4a tells of David's decision, enthusiastically supported by Nathan, to build a home for the ark; then a new scene is introduced by the words, "And it came to pass that night." This scene has been replaced by the account of Yahweh's instructions to Nathan to stop David from building the temple. This latter section then goes straight into Nathan's prophecy with no interruption. The fact that vv. 4a and 4b do not belong directly together is perhaps reflected by the fact that the Massoretic text leaves a gap between the two. In any case, further consideration shows that the repeated "and it came to pass" hardly indicates an extremely adept author. But this fact alone would not necessarily mean that the two sections should be kept separate. The problems lie in quite a different area. If Nathan agrees with David's plan in vv. 1-4a without any reservation, then his change of opinion could be brought about by a revelation to him and, as a consequence, David could be persuaded by him to give up his idea. That would be possible. But is it not also possible that there was an account here of David himself receiving the revelation, without any mention of Nathan, and, consequently, that 4a formed the introduction to an account of such a revelation from Yahweh to David (as already noted, this is presupposed in 7.27 and 23.1ff.)? The possibility cannot be dismissed that in vv. 5-7 we still have fragments of this old revelation later attributed by another hand to Nathan. It is only in this way that we can explain a series of conspicuous correspondences with this section which, on the other hand, must be set against considerable differences.

But before pursuing these questions further, the relationship of both parts of the passage in question to the ark narrative must be examined; for, as far as content is concerned, 7.1-7 forms a kind of conclusion to the ark narrative. In

7.1-4a, at least, the ark is expressly mentioned and David makes the decision to build a home for it. This would have meant that the ark came to rest after its long wanderings and the process, now associated primarily with Solomon, whereby the ark receded into the seclusion of the holy of holies, removed from the sight of the people, could be placed somewhat earlier. The building of the temple (which according to 7.4bff. is for Yahweh and not for his cultic symbol) is delayed by God's intervention.[32] And so the ark remains in the tent sanctuary till the ostentatious Solomon builds the temple. In the place of permanent rest for the ark there is peace for the whole of David's reign. Since 7.1-7 (or perhaps only 7.1-4a?) deals with the ark, we are justified in regarding it as a continuation of the ark narrative as far as content is concerned. A comparison of style, however, prevents us from concluding thence that the two belong to one and the same source. Too much weight should not be laid on the fact that David is called simply "David" in II Sam 6 and "the king" in II Sam 7.1-7, for even within the succession story the two names change, sometimes every paragraph and sometimes every sentence, without any apparent motive. What is more important is that in the whole of the ark narrative there are only three constructions with היה as an auxiliary verb (I Sam 4.18; 5.9 and 10), whereas this short passage has two of them (7.1 and 4a). Final infinitives are rare in the ark narrative (I Sam 4.13 and 15 and 19; 5.10; 6.13; II Sam 6.2 and 10). In the second part of this small passage, on the other hand, there are two (7.5 and 7) and, further, an infinitive construction representing a subsidiary clause (v. 6). In contrast to the laconic, almost breathless, style of the ark source, one can detect here (in both sections: 7.1-4a, 4b-7) a certain expansiveness and comfortable leisureliness which seems closest to the style of the insertion in I Sam 6.5ff., though, to be sure, there is not enough similarity to warrant assuming the same hand.

Despite the fact that both sections are connected with the ark narrative in terms of content, it is not possible to show that 7.1-4a and 4b-7 belong to the same source. Consequently we must now investigate whether they can be fitted into other sources. For 4b-7 there seems to be an obvious connection with 8-17. In both passages the revelation is clothed in the form of a messenger-commission and 8-17 runs on from 4b-7 without interruption. The phrase "to my servant, to David" in 7.5 finds a close parallel in 7.8; similarly the word "judges" in combination with "I commanded [appointed]" in

7.7 appears again, the same word and combination, in 7.11a. So there does not seem to be anything in the way of combining 7.4b-7 with 7.8-17. However, as Gressmann has already pointed out, the first section is concerned with a practical, contemporary problem and the second is a promise from Yahweh for the future consisting of independent fragments. This would still be no reason for dividing them if there were strong reasons for the reverse. But there are none, especially if v. 13 is deleted. Then we are left with no other option than a loose concatenation through the word "house." Furthermore the style in 7.8ff. moves along with more refined phrases and richer forms than 7.4b-7. Thus the possibility already mentioned, that we are dealing in 7.4b-7 with an ancient substratum, seems to gain new strength. This substratum was clothed by the author of the second stratum of 7.8-17 in the form of a messenger-commission and was added to the revision of the old Nathan prophecy because of the word "house." This would also be matched by the fact that one phrase in the prophecy of Nathan, "and I have been with you" (7.9), echoes "for Yahweh is with you" (7.3), while no other connections between 7.1-4a and 7.8ff. can be found.

The following picture of the relationships between the sources in 7.1-7 emerges: the section can be split into two parts, 7.1-4a and 7.4b-7. The first part belongs neither to the ark narrative (despite the similarities in content) nor to the second layer in vv. 8-17 (although it seems to have been used here). The second part should be placed with the second stratum in vv. 8-17 because of its form and idioms. The style, however, is somewhat different, due, it would seem, to the fact that it goes back to an earlier source which was perhaps once a continuation of 7.1-4a and formed a revelation to David (see above). It is now a question of whether 7.1-4a and the presumed ancient source of 4b-7 can be connected with the older stratum in vv. 8-17 or in vv. 18ff. As the oldest stratum in vv. 8-17 is only one and a half verses long, the material is too small to permit tangible results. Even if we are correct in assuming that 4a was followed by an account of a direct revelation to David forbidding the building of the temple, it would still be possible for the same narrator to add an account of a revelation to Nathan that David's dynasty would last for ever - perhaps motivated by the fact that both mention a "house." But if עָשָׂה בַיִת (make a house) in 11b is original (and there is no reason to doubt this and to change it into בָּנָה בַיִת (build a house), especially in view of I Kgs 2.24), then it is difficult to think it was the same author, unless one

54

assumes that he used בנה on purpose for the act of building itself and עשׂה for God's bestowal. As will be shown shortly, because the connections of 7.1-4a with 7.18ff are far closer and because 7.18ff. does not belong with 7.11b, 16, it seems advisable to try to establish contacts with 7.18ff. if we are to look for them anywhere. For here as well we find the phrase "build a house" (בנה בית) and the first person singular pronoun אנכי (7.2, 18). The style also reveals a certain similarity in its much more measured and solemn mode of expression compared with the rich expressiveness of 7.8ff. Further, 7.27 seems to presuppose a direct revelation from Yahweh, similar to the one which needs to follow on from v. 4a. We should note, of course, that there must have been two separate revelations, the first of which only rejected David's plan to build a temple while the second would have assured David's dynasty of eternal duration. David's prayer would then have referred only to the second revelation. This revelation would have been added to the first as an independent promise because of the catch-word "house." We are thus well into the question of the origin of the present form of chapter 7.

Our deliberations so far reveal the following development. In 7.11b, 16, are preserved fragments of an ancient report of a prophecy to Nathan promising the future continuation of the Davidic dynasty. Nathan passes on this promise to the king. In 7.1-4a (4b-7), there is a story relating David's plan to build a temple, approved of by Nathan, but later turned down because of a revelation from Yahweh to David. An old source within David's prayer does not seem to be far removed from this fragment (7.1-4a (4b-7)), all the more so since it also presupposes a direct revelation from Yahweh to David concerning the future of the dynasty. A later hand transformed the old report (of 7.11, 16) into a promise to Nathan clothed in the form of a messenger-commission; this was then combined with the revelation from Yahweh (which must have once come after 7.4a), again in the form of a messenger-commission. In doing so the writer suppressed the account, assumed by 7.27, of a direct revelation to David concerning the future of the dynasty, but left David's prayer intact. Later hands added v. 13 and vv. 22-24. It must be admitted that these hypotheses assume very complicated processes. But it would be difficult to surmount the problems of this chapter by simpler means.

We must still cast a glance at the historicity of the event related in 7.1-7. We can agree with Kittel[33] in saying that the essence of the story can be considered to be old and historical, and this despite the relatively late exterior in which it is clothed and our dismissal of a connection with the ark narrative source and the succession source. It is most likely that this event took place soon after the ark was transferred to Jerusalem.

The theological yield of the passage is restricted. Of greatest interest is its admission that a prophet can make a mistake - even though we should note that Nathan is giving only his personal opinion in v. 3, whereas in 7.4ff. he is proclaiming the word of God. This theme is developed, but with a somewhat different bias, in Jer 28. Here the prophet begins to doubt the truth of a divine oracle to him because of the definite opposition of Hananiah, but afterwards he receives confirmation of his prophecy.

From the religious point of view, it is interesting that the decision concerning an undertaking so important to the cult as the building of a temple should have been reached only during a private conversation between the prophet and the king, without it being deemed necessary to make some prior enquiry into the wishes of the deity so as to avoid subsequent reproof. Thus later correction is avoided. 7.1-7 is also of importance for the history of Israelite piety in so far as we gain an insight into the internal conflict within the Israelite community concerning the structuring of the cult according to the Canaanite/Phoenician/Egyptian pattern.

The intervention of Yahweh in 7.4b-7 is depicted by the author as an actual occurrence. The revelation is not direct, but the prophet acts as mediator.

Finally, in summing up the contribution of the whole chapter for our knowledge of the theology and religious devotion of the early monarchic period, we can consider the original version of 7.1-7 (though this is hard to distinguish), together with verses 11b and 16, and 18-21, 25 (26), 27-29. All three sections of the chapter agree that Yahweh is the all-powerful God of Israel, the lord of history and of their fortunes, and can reveal himself to certain favoured individuals, the king (?) and the prophets, for example, and can give them guide-lines for their behaviour and insights into the future. It is particularly stressed in David's prayer that these revelations and the attainment of worldly power and might are purely acts of grace on Yahweh's part. It is the task of humankind to submit to Yahweh's will and to thank him for his instructions and promises with a joyful heart. This thanks is expressed externally in prayer and in a mode of living fit for Yahweh.

Chapter Three

THE ACCOUNT OF THE AMMONITE WAR

ollowing the precedent of Winckler, a series of scholars (Kittel, Cook, Gressmann, Sievers) has found a separate source in II Sam 10ff. encompassing II Sam 10.1-11.1 and 12.26-31.[1] Budde, Nowack (who nonetheless attributes 10.15-19a to a redactor, following Winckler), Sellin(?), and Steuernagel, on the other hand, reject this quite firmly.[2] It is appropriate to start our examination of this question with the section 12.26-31. The passage is uniform, the style is consistently succinct, unpretentious, simple and clear, yet fresh and vivid. The action rushes along, with the change in the leadership of the operation skilfully achieved through the commissioning of the messengers. The narration is adroit and has a concrete effect. There are no mental leaps and so this passage must be entire within itself. However a fragment can also be entire within itself - and this passage can be seen to be such. It starts abruptly with Joab's battles at Rabbah of the Ammonites and then tells of David taking the city and of how the prisoners were treated, finishing with David going back to Jerusalem. The account has a natural ending, therefore, which could hardly be a mere caesura; but the beginning, which must have said something about the background to the conquest, is missing and has to be looked for in the preceding narrative. Thus our immediate task is to investigate the relationship of the passage to its context, both forwards and backwards. We must determine, first, whether the narrative finishes properly or only breaks off at 12.31; second, whether what immediately precedes provides the necessary beginning or whether it should be looked for elsewhere.

As already mentioned, v. 31 is, as far as content is concerned, the end of a story about the conquest of Rabbah of the Ammonites by David and thus of a report concerning this king's Ammonite wars, since the conquest of this city put an end to the national independence of the Ammonites for some time. Accordingly, a continuation would only be possible if the Ammonite wars were conceived of as constituting an episode in the life of David and were connected loosely (to a greater or lesser extent) with further David narratives. That is in fact the case: the subsequent Tamar narrative is attached, quite superficially of course, by means of a purely temporal (and not causal) ויהי אחרי כן (and it came to pass after this). Anyway, we can see that some time or other the connection was made. In saying this, however, we do not mean that 12.26-31 and 13.1ff. come from the same pen: it it quite possible that 12.31 was at some time felt to be a temporary break within a larger context and treated as such, but that originally it had been the end of an independent account.

This last hypothesis is necessitated by the totally different styles. From 13.1 onwards, we find a comfortably expansive narrative which loves to go into detail. The emotional rhythm has to do with more than just the kind of material. In the one passage there is the irresistible thrust forward of the report in short, powerful sentences, reminding us of the style of Assyrian royal inscriptions; in the other, the numerous adverbial phrases arouse the feeling of relaxed sauntering and lingering, as is familiar from many of the narratives in the Old Testament and from Egyptian novellen. In the one, the plot surges along with closely interwoven events; in the other, there is a loose series of scenes seeming like so many resting points and having, in part, a lyric atmosphere, as for instance in the dialogue between Amnon and his friend and in the king's visit to the sick man. The stern reality of boldly marching troops leaves a stamp of harshness throughout the one, while the other has feeling and softness, even in its style. The one is content to use a short sentence to express what is happening; the other dissects the action into its various phases and spreads it out into separate sentences. In the one, the account achieves its effect simply through the gravity of the events themselves; in the other, one has the impression of skilful stage-management which, to say the least, is not shy about trying to create effects. This difference cannot be attributed to the difference in the material alone. It is, in my view, based on the fact that there are two authors here. This point will be discussed again later. For now it is sufficient to note that 13.1 could not originally have been the continuation of 12.26ff. As there is also no other suitable continuation in the rest of II Samuel, 12.31 must be regarded as the conclusion of an independent source dealing with the Ammonite wars.

What about some connection with the previous material? If we are to find some association with what immediately precedes, then we must go back to 11.1 with Kittel, Gressmann, Cook, Sievers and others.[3] That there are strong ties to 11.1 cannot be denied. The progression of thought is quite smooth. There is extensive stylistic similarity. This brings us to the question of whether 11.2-12.25 is an interpolation or not. For the moment, we can ignore the doubtful place of the Nathan pericope in this passage and restrict our analysis to what remains after this section has been removed. There is a similarity in the content here with 12.26-31, inasmuch as 12.26ff. tells of the war between King David and the Ammonites and 11.2ff. takes place during a war. That, however, is the most that can be said in favour of their unity. For we do not know if the war during which the Uriah story was played out was the Ammonite war of 12.26ff. With the exception of 12.9, we have no indication of who David's opponents were, let alone the name of the city besieged. That is very striking. Further, the transition in 12.25-26 is so sudden and abrupt that it is hardly possible to believe that one writer could have written both verses, the one after the other, at one and the same time. Then there is the stylistic distinction which permits us to find the same authors in 11.2ff. and 13.1ff., but not in 11.2ff. and 12.26-31. (Cf. what was said above on the relationship between 12.26ff. and 13.1ff.) We can see that 12.26-31 is unconnected, or at least only loosely connected, with the material around it.

The question now remaining to be asked is whether the passage is in any way connected with 10.1-11.1. To answer this it is necessary to investigate the unity of 10.1-11.1 itself. The originality of 10.15-19a has been disputed by Winckler, H. P. Smith and Nowack on historical-critical grounds, but this surely has no justification. V. 14b, which is used to support this argument, loses its importance if vv. 15-19a are regarded as a second phase in the same war, where the troops are led not by Joab but by David. The term "beyond the river" need not be looked at from the Babylonian point of view. Finally the style of the passage is no different from that of the surrounding verses. That could be put down to assimilation if there were further evidence against an original connection, but as this is not the case it seems unnecessary to delete the doubtful verses. On the other hand, it is questionable whether 10.1-6 belong to the same

Ammonite source. Not, that is, for reasons of content, for there is nothing in these verses which contradicts what follows. On the contrary, they form an introduction that is indispensible for the rest of the narrative, telling the causes of the Ammonite war. If these verses were eliminated, the remainder would hang very much in the air. But for stylistic reasons this step is unavoidable. The style of 10.1-6a is much more closely related to that of 11.2ff. and 13.1ff. than to that of 10.1-6bff. Of course, we should not lay too much weight on the connecting formula ויהי אחרי כן (and it came to pass after this) in 10.1 (which we have already met in 13.1), but we should note: a) the unfolding of an action in terms of three parts in v. 3; b) the comfortable expansiveness with which are depicted first David's decision to send a legation to Hanun and then the dispatch of the messengers and their arrival in Ammon; c) the somewhat superfluous explanatory clause, "for the men were greatly shamed"; d) the parallel structure of David's speech in v. 2 and, still more, the speech of the Ammonite lords in v. 3. Later we will go further into some of these aspects which can be regarded as stylistically characteristic of the succession source. For now we can point out that there is hardly a perceptible gap between chapter 9 and 10.1-6a.[4] On the other hand, there is a distinct change in style in 10.6b. Instead of the comfortable expansiveness there is now an urgent brevity, concise expression instead of an abundance of words; and the cameos - one might almost describe them as intimate - in 10.1-6a give way to a description of restless action in broad outline. And this even though in both cases they are dealing with international relations. Accordingly, despite the close unity of content, 10.1-6a must be assigned to a different source from that of 10.6bff.[5] What we are witnessing can be explained as the substitution of a more detailed account for the beginning of the Ammonite source - a substitution made by the writer who inserted 11.2ff. and adopted the report along with it into his story of the succession to David's throne. We will return to this last statement later. We must still decide whether, over and above the unity of content between 10.6b-11.1 and 12.26-31 and their smooth fit, there are stylistic points of contact. This must be answered in the affirmative. In both sections there is brevity, succinctness and impetus. Both make the most sparing use of speech at a decisive point in the narrative and in both cases in the same form: a statement followed immediately by a demand (10.11f. and 12.27f.).

If, therefore, the unity of 10.6b-11.1 and 12.26-31 can no

longer be doubted, we must now ask whether we have here an independent source. No reasons of content tell against this as there is no reference beyond the Ammonite battles, which come to an end with the destruction of Rabbah of the Ammonites. The whole structure works towards this crowning conclusion. The original beginning, which was detached and replaced by another introduction, will hardly have contained a more detailed background to the dispute - it was probably significantly shorter. Thus we could well have a very short, independent source here. This conclusion is supported by the fact that the vocabulary of the passages in question shows certain peculiarities. Thus one of the favourite words of the account is ערך (arrange or set in order), both with and without מלחמה (battle) and לקראת (to meet) (10.8, 9, 10, 17; elsewhere only in I Sam 4.2 and 17.2, 8). The characteristic use of ראה in the sense of "recognize" is also typical. צור, "besiege", only occurs in 11.1 and in I Sam 20.15. The brevity of the source, its form and its content suggest that it is a campaign report, such as might have been intended to be preserved in the state archives. This gives us the time of David as the most likely date of authorship, presumably soon after the events depicted. Comparison with Assyrian inscriptions shows a remarkable objectivity in this particular account: the achievements of Joab are praised just as much as those of David; indeed, Joab appears here almost as the great war-hero who wins the decisive battles, leaving only the final taste of success to his master. Perhaps one might even go further and say that the narrator's sympathies lie more with Joab than with David. Note the loving care with which Joab is described as the clever general, staunch soldier and true servant of his master! By comparison, the figure of David remains colourless. The events here are related in a manner that inspires confidence and they should be assigned to the beginning of David's rule over the whole of Israel.[6]

Information about theological outlook and the religious devotion of the period can only be inferred from Joab's speech to Abishai. According to 10.12b Yahweh is the supreme governor of human fortunes and, if "cities of our God" in 12a is correct, he has a most intimate relationship with Israel.[7] It is, however, characteristic of the religious feeling attributed to Joab that first the challenge to his brother and himself to be strong is recounted, and only then is Yahweh mentioned as the disposer of their fortunes. It is a manly piety, as we would expect from a soldier, who wishes and intends to do everything himself to achieve success, but who humbly leaves the final decision to Yahweh Sebaoth.

Summing up, we can say:

1. The account of the Ammonite wars is shown to be an independent source incorporating 10.6-11.1, 12.26-31.

2. The beginning of the account has been replaced by a more detailed introduction coming from the author of the interpolated passage 11.2ff., the same person who wrote the succession source.

3. Apart from this the source has been preserved in full.

4. The style is simple, concise and terse; the action pushes continually forward; there are speeches only at decisive points.

5. The account is entitled to be treated as trustworthy and is very close to the events; it seems to have been a war report intended for the state archives.

6. Its contribution to a description of the theological climate of the early monarchic period is meagre; however, the figure of Joab provides us with an interesting picture of a devout person.

REVIEW

ur previous discussion has dealt with three major sections of the Books of Samuel. Of these, the first and the last (the ark narrative and the account of David's wars with the Ammonites) are in literary-critical terms relatively simple, easily distinguishable units, which have been preserved tolerably intact. II Sam 7 presents greater difficulty. It falls into three parts, the first, 7.1-7, stubbornly resisting all attempts at source division, the other two each containing an old source (which in each case is probably independent of the other) overlaid by more recent strata - two layers in the case of vv. 8-17, one in the case of vv. 18-29. These make a significant contribution to the history of Israelite piety. Here we are only interested in the more ancient strata of this chapter, which, like the ark narrative and the account of the Ammonite war, go back to the time of David or at least to that of Solomon. What is important for us is to try to look into the hearts of these authors and so gain an insight into the extraordinary abundance of independent writers in the early monarchic period - writers who are very sharply differentiated, not only by their mode of representation but, above all, by their peculiarities of style.

First we come to the writer of the ark narrative. Earlier we looked for him among the community of priests of the ark in Jerusalem. The whole content of his narrative points this way, especially the attention paid to cultic issues. He is a skilful narrator who has command of a simple, popular style and who can obtain great effects by the simplest of means. He is particularly dextrous at linking the individual scenes and settings, allowing them to flow into each other. Further, the author has an interest in the history of his shrine. He follows up everything and is not satisfied simply with the obvious and the ready-to-hand. At the same time, in so far as he is able, he cultivates an objective style. He does not pass over Israel's dishonourable defeats; indeed, he could hardly do this anyway because against this dark background Yahweh's works stand out all the more clearly and add to the glory of his ark - which, of course, is the author's main aim.

As he himself sees Yahweh's intervention in everything, whether for better or for worse, so he would like to lead others to the same certainty of faith. His own faith is significantly shaped by Yahweh's incomprehensible power and holiness, before which mortals tremble and shudder, and less so by his saving mercy, which noticeably remains in the background.

It is more difficult to characterize the writers of the oldest strata in chapter 7, if only because their work is restricted to the transmission to posterity of an oracle or a prayer. We can deduce, however, a great interest in the well-being of the Davidic house and an attentiveness to the hidden powers working within history. We can further guess that both these men were close to the king himself. At most we might think that the one or the other source was written by a prophet like Nathan, for example, but hardly by a priest, who would certainly not have failed to remind people of his own office.

The question is much simpler with regard to the account of the Ammonite war. Here it is quite clear that it was a soldier who wrote the report, perhaps even a general - whether Joab or Abishai or some other is an open question. He describes the most important phases of the war, mentioning in particular clever tactical manoeuvres. In any case, we can see that he knows how to depict scenes involving large groups of people and to report the events soberly and with welcome clarity. Of course, there is lacking to some extent a tightly-knit structure and a sense of definite purpose in the narrative. We only notice something of this right at the end, after seeing that the separate events have often been placed very loosely alongside each other. He is clear-headed and a capable soldier but hardly a skilful writer, still less one angling for effects. Only in one speech do we learn something of the inner life of the narrator, who subscribes to a kind of synergism in relation to the gaining of worldly success inasmuch as he allows individual ability precedence over divine assistance. This could also indicate a man of war. In any case, of the authors we have dealt with here he is the most reticent about his religious views.

These three or four writers we have looked at so far are joined by the greatest, the author of the story of the succession to the throne. It is with him and his work that the following chapter is concerned.

Chapter Four

THE SUCCESSION STORY

aving first investigated the subsidiary sources a-
vailable to the author of the succession story and
put to use by him, we now turn to the succession
story itself. Budde is of the opinion that no such
sources are to be positively identified in the two
major source strands which constitute (as he sees it) the
Books of Samuel.[1] Our choice of subject, as well as the
previous discussion, makes it quite clear, however, that his
view finds no support here. Indeed, we are entitled to ask
whether the "exegetes' favourite text" - the story of David's
family, or succession story - was itself an independent
source, and, if need be, to give an affirmative answer to that
possibility.

If Budde is unable to find any traces of editing, whether
distinctions in language usage, actual inconsistencies within
either of his two sources, or independent variant traditions
that would be evidence for a source division, we for our part
have only to point out, for example, the fundamental
difference between II Sam 21.1-14 and II Sam 9 - both passages which he allocates to the J source. In 21.1-14 David
consults Yahweh (just as in I Sam 30.8, etc.) whereas in II Sam
9-20 it is only at 16.23 that there is any mention of consulting
Yahweh and here it is equated with consulting Ahithophel. In
21.1-14 David knows which of Saul's family are alive and
where they are living, including Meribaal, whereas in chapter
9 he must ask whether there is any Saulide alive at all. His
retainers can find only Saul's servant, Ziba, and it is from him
that they gain further information. In 21.1-14, David spares
Meribaal for Jonathan's sake and in chapter 9 he endows him
with his father's property for the same reason. On the other
hand, reference is made in 21.7 to an oath that David had
made previously, whereas there is no mention of this in
chapter 9 and Meribaal is spared simply for the sake of his

65

father. In view of this, the (admittedly somewhat unlikely) possibility does arise that the writer of II Sam 9 knew nothing of David's oath. In II Sam 9-20, the writer himself only twice makes the connection between the divine will and events on earth a matter of personal comment; otherwise he leaves it to the characters in the story to point out these associations. In 21.1-14, on the other hand, the writer himself stresses these relationships. We can thus note at least some inconsistencies in the content of Budde's J-source which seem hardly to support his point of view.

Like Budde, Nowack regards chapters 9-20 as only a part of a larger whole - to which, indeed, 21.1-14 does not belong - and he supports his view by noting that there are accounts also before II Sam 9 which measure up to the family story in graphic descriptiveness.[2] That point must be conceded; but whereas prior to II Sam 9 we find such descriptiveness only sporadically and disjointedly along with quite different religious outlooks (cf. what was said above about the consultation of Yahweh), in II Sam 9-20 it is everywhere present and a feature of the material's coherence. We shall return later in greater detail to this point. For the present we confirm that the view of Budde and Nowack is not altogether satisfactory. The same is true for Sellin who indeed recognizes that there was no original literary unity but finally posits only a single narrator, who impartially connects all the material and imbues it with a single idiom and outlook on life.[3]

So it is not surprising that repeated attempts have been made to locate a special source in the second part of II Samuel. When Klostermann[4] starts this source at chapter 13 (the birth of Solomon) and finishes it in I Kgs 9, it is only because he is influenced by the idea of finding a unit dealing with the rise of Solomon to power and by the desire to prove that Ahimaaz ben Zadok is the author. Closer analysis, however, shows that - quite apart from the formal similarity - 16.1ff. and 19.25ff. are very closly connected with chapter 9, so that unless we accept that they belong together it is difficult, to say the least, to arrive at a correct understanding of 16.1ff. and 19.25ff. Moreover Solomon's birth is so involved with the rest of the narrative that it would seem impossible not to include chapters (10) 11f. as well. If, then, the source is to be traced back at least to II Sam 9, at the other end there is little likelihood of finding it any later than I Kgs 2. Considerations of form and content stand in the way. Here the fast-moving narrative of consecutive events turns into a description of the riches, wisdom, reputation and buildings of Solomon. On the other hand, 2.46 provides a good conclusion which the further story of Solomon seeks only to fill out. Klostermann's attempt at defining a new source should be rejected because he takes too little account of the previous material and too much of what comes subsequently.

Steuernagel[5] identifies one unified source in II Sam 9-20 and I Kgs 1-2, with the exception of some short insertions in II Samuel and a larger one in I Kgs 2. He describes the source as the story of David's family. He rejects the extension of the source back to include parts of II Sam 5, 6 and 7. We can agree with him in the case of chapter 5 but not in the cases of chapters 6 and 7. What we can only assert here - though it can be shown later to be at least probable - is that 6.16 and 6.20ff., which have been shown above not to belong to the ark narrative, should be regarded as the beginning of the succession story. Its end, as Steuernagel argues, is to be sought in I Kgs 2.

Caspari and Gressmann have both identified a series of independent narratives and novellen within the succession story - in particular an Amnon-Tamar novelle and an Absalom novelle.[6] It must be admitted that both of these novellen should be credited with a certain amount of independence in so far as in each of them a different character is, or seems to be, the centre of interest. Against this we should note that no peculiarities of language[7] or style can be discerned and that in terms of content the threads are interwoven. So the most likely solution is that we should recognize just one author, in which case the somewhat unlikely possibility exists that we should attribute the present form of the whole text to a final redaction by this same writer. Perhaps he had originally depicted only part of the whole action (for example, the Absalom revolt), then enlarged this narrative into an exposition of all the conflicts surrounding the succession to David. But just one look at the uniform style or the structure of the succession story proves that there is a unifying plan underlying the whole text which does not owe its origins to the industrious hands of some editor. To pursue this point somewhat further will be our next task. For then we can work backwards to reach some conclusion about the extent of the source, which, if it is to be properly established, must be supported finally by the investigation of the stylistic characteristics and religious conceptions.

Here, as is often the case, it might be a better strategy to start from the end and then work backwards to the beginning. The reason is that I Kgs 1 by itself (chapter 2 is only added as a concluding reverberation) can provide us with information about the writer's wishes and intentions. We discover a lively scene, an abundance of finely detailed characters: the hoary king, feeble in his old age, whose lack of body-warmth is the reason for the beautiful Abishag of Shunem being appointed as his maid; the haughty Adonijah, like Absalom handsome and strong-willed, trying prematurely to acquire for himself what he believes to be his; then the court prophet Nathan in his rather remarkable role which remains peculiar enough even if one accepts that David did make a promise to Bathsheba; further, the not especially distinguished figure of Bathsheba herself, together with Solomon, her favourite and Nathan's; and finally, the loving description of Jonathan ben Abiathar. The plot has much tension in it; it spurs its readers on and makes them hold their breath. And set in this framework - one could almost say with brutal insistence and frantic monotony - we have the insistent question: "Who shall sit upon the throne of my lord the king, and who shall reign after him?" Nathan's conversation with Bathsheba and their talk with David, David's order to Zadok, Nathan and Benaiah, and finally Jonathan's report to those banqueting around Adonijah's table, all centre on this question in agitated excitement. The whole action of the drama revolves around these disquieting words. The whole chapter is dominated by them - and not only the whole chapter, but, as will be shown later, the whole work. This chapter, therefore, is the key to understanding the whole work.

We can now turn to investigating this assertion. The chapter is not a self-contained narrative. It points forwards and also looks back for connections. Quite apart from the fact that I Kgs 1 is without any appropriate ending, the Adonijah episode in vv. 30ff. simply cries out for some continuation. A narrative so artistically structured could hardly have ended with this scene. V. 52 contains a crucial moment of excitement. This is not stilled by the short "Go to your house" of v. 53, for this is a command which fails to resolve matters clearly and gives too much the impression of being open-ended to effect reassurance. I Kgs 2.13-25 continues the story and shows how the second of Solomon's alternatives in v. 52 is horribly realized. This passage must certainly be taken together with I Kgs 1, though that is not to say that it must have been directly connected originally.

From the beginning of chapter 1 we know that Abishag is "a very beautiful maiden," and it is expressly stated that David did not approach her, a fact which obviously refers to an episode beyond this scene where it will be of some significance. Here in chapter 2, as in chapter 1, Adonijah seems not to be following an especially transparent plan. As 2.13ff. shows, he does not repudiate completely his claim to the throne and demands Abishag, though whether as compensation or as a means to the furthering of his plans remains an open question. In the end Bathsheba is, here in chapter 2 as in chapter 1, a not especially distinguished lady; she lends an all-too-ready ear to commissions, apparently quite happily, because she herself does not possess the requisite acumen and insight.[8] We know already from 1.7 that Joab and Abiathar are on Adonijah's side and this is taken up in 2.22. Benaiah, who here appears as a willing servant of Solomon, had already proclaimed his enthusiastic support for the young king in 1.36. 2.13ff. clearly refers to Adonijah's claim to the throne in 1.5ff. Perhaps the repetition of "sat on his throne" (v. 19) and "caused me to sit on the throne" (v. 24) can also be regarded as a conscious echo of chapter 1. Nevertheless, there would still be the possibility of regarding 2.13ff. as a later accretion despite all these connections, were it not for the abrupt and unsatisfactory end to chapter 1, which so desperately needs a continuation. Solomon's fate depends on that of Adonijah. Solomon cannot feel safe on his throne as long as his powerful rival is still alive. Thus there are strong reasons of content ("internal" grounds) for concluding that chapters 1 and 2.13ff. belong together. And this conclusion, moreover, is not contradicted by the way the material is presented ("external" grounds) as will be shown by our later analysis of the style.

If, then, 2.13-25 is regarded as a continuation of chapter 1, we must next ask whether with these verses we have actually reached the end of the narrative. That could be the case. Adonijah, in whom the opposition to Solomon was united and who provided its spearhead, is no more. Solomon can now feel safe on his throne. However, there are still two powerful men in the government, former allies of Adonijah, who are not to be ignored, at least not in Solomon's view (cf. 2.22) - Abiathar and Joab. Quite apart from the importance that they acquire in the course of the whole narrative (as we will see later and is already apparent from chapter 1) one can appreciate why we are told something of Solomon's action against them. First in vv. 26f. there is a report of Abiathar being dismissed from office. In consideration of his respected position and his loyal service to David, Solomon is satisfied to exile him for life to Anathoth. (Verse 27b should be regarded as a later addition which takes up I Sam 2.27ff.). There are no stylistic doubts about this additional passage, even less about vv. 28ff. which relates the death of Joab.

Joab's flight to the sanctuary must have confirmed the king's assumption that Adonijah's request concealed a conspiracy against him. Whether this assumption was justified remains an open question. At the order of the king Benaiah carries out the gory task of execution at the sanctuary altar. There is a certain difficulty with vv. 31bff. In my opinion the reference to the mutinous murdering of Abner and Amasa provides a justification not of the need to kill Joab but only of the propriety of carrying out the sentence within the sacred confines. The decision to kill him is already mentioned in v. 29 and would indeed have been carried out by Benaiah had Joab left the protection of the sanctuary. But Joab is not prepared to do so. It seems that it was possible to execute someone guilty of premeditated murder even if he was under the protection of the sanctuary (Ex 21.12ff. and Dt 19.11ff. could be interpreted in this way). On the other hand, such action would not, without further ado, have been permissible for a crime such as high treason. Perhaps it is for some such legal considerations that Solomon refers to the two unexpiated murders. Thus these verses, which do not diverge in style, can be retained.

Even though for internal, content reasons it is necessary that 2.13-25 be added to chapter 1, and at least arguably the case with vv. 26 and 27, as also vv. 28-35, the same is not true of the remainder of the chapter. It also cannot be argued that this passage is an absolutely essential part of the structure of chapters 1ff. Nevertheless there can be no doubt that it does in fact belong to the same source. The style requires this conclusion and furthermore, as we shall show, so does the whole conception of the succession story, especially of course II Sam 16.5ff. and 19.16ff. Here again Benaiah is the willing tool of his master who utters a conditional death-sentence, just as in 1.52ff., only to carry out the execution ruthlessly when the condition is broken. In 2.46 there follows the words "So the kingdom was established in the hand of Solomon," the great last chord, the final stroke that allows the reader and the listener to breathe again. For in this statement is the answer to the question in chapter 1: Who shall sit on the throne of David?

We have now managed to distinguish a single connected narrative in I Kgs 1 and 2.13-46. Beginning with an episode from the life of the aging David, the narrator depicts the attempts of Adonijah to make himself successor to the throne, Nathan's support for his favourite, Solomon, and the latter's accession to the throne and the final elimination of all his enemies, finishing with the Shimei scene. In the structure of all this just one thing is lacking: mention of the death of David. This is provided by 2:1-12, David's last testament. This passage seems to have been revised several times, particularly at the beginning, with the result that the task of carrying out an accurate analysis is impossible. It can be divided into an introduction (vv. 1-4), David's three instructions (vv. 5f., 7, 8f.) and a conclusion (vv. 10ff.). The introduction is obviously Deuteronomistic work[9] and, as such, dependent on the older passages II Sam 7.12 and 14f., whose content (but not idiom) it reflects. Perhaps a characteristic distinction should be noted here. In II Sam 7.12 and 14ff. it is wandering from the right path that is regarded as the exception; but here in I Kgs 2 it is the other way round, the exception is keeping the law. This shows the change in the times. The intercourse between God and humankind changes from being a relationship of trust (like that between father and son) to a way of conduct that is precisely regulated by legal requirements. Whereas in II Sam 7 the emphasis is on God, here it is on the human individual keeping the current law for practical considerations, for reasons of "wisdom." These are ideas that we meet in Deuteronomy and in the wisdom literature.

If the passage can be shown to be Deuteronomistic, then the only question that remains is whether there is any more ancient material in it. This may perhaps be the case in vv. 1 and 2, for the ideas, especially in the second verse, are not alien to the Davidic period as is shown by a glance at II Sam 12.23 and 14.14. But this suggestion cannot be proved conclusively even if the subsequent three instructions could be shown to contain old material. This question now requires some more attention.

The three instructions form a stylistic unity and should therefore be treated as such. For pointers to later composition we should note the following. In chapter 1 David is depicted as a decrepit old man and one could not credit him with the mental agility which is presupposed here. Against that it could be urged that David in chapter 1 does not really appear so decrepit as to be incapable of giving such orders, especially when one considers that despite growing weakness in mental faculties, some particular recollections can be tenaciously retained, as here the recollection of a grievous

71

sorrow and a gratefully experienced joy; and likewise, with encroaching old age, inhibitions which would otherwise stand in the way of totally instinctive behaviour, can fall away.

Much more important is another reason which could speak for a later addition. The executions of Joab and Shimei do not follow directly from the justification which David's testament offers. Joab is punished by Solomon for his support of Adonijah and it is only in order to justify killing him at the altar that Solomon fastens on to the two unexpiated murders of Abner and Amasa, which David offered as grounds for killing him. In Shimei's case no reason for the conditional death-sentence is given until the sentence is actually carried out, when reference is made to, among other things, the insult offered David. If one further considers that there is no mention at all of rewarding Barzillai's descendents then it is clear that there are serious doubts about whether the testament originally belonged to the main narrative. In that case it should be noticed that earlier we found the theme of the source to be the question of the succession; accordingly, all the narrator's interest is devoted to the difficulties which Solomon had to contend with in establishing his sovereignty. So we should not be surprised that the fulfilment of the instruction concerning Barzillai's sons is not mentioned. If David's reasons are only mentioned in passing, as the death sentences are carried out, we should remember that David has left everything in Solomon's hands, for him to find appropriate ways to punish them both, and thus in no way prescribes the means by which this should be achieved nor the justification for the sentence.

In the light of this, it is possible to regard 2.5-9 as ancient material which was incorporated in an appropriate position in the succession story by the narrator. And the possibility becomes more likely when one considers that Solomon's action against Shimei lacks any justification. Could it be that as one of the heads of Saul's clan he had rallied to Adonijah's party and so become involved in the downfall of this pretender to the throne? That is hardly probable, for Solomon would surely have made short work of him in that case. Or might he have exploited the weakness of the aging David in order to carry out ambitious plans of his own with the support of the Benjaminites and the northern Israelites? That again seems hardly likely. There is only one way through - assuming one does not prefer simply to admit to not knowing the answer - and that is to allow that Solomon was entrusted by David in some way with the punishment of this man.

Thus, especially as there are no stylistic objections, we must regard the retention of the testament in I Kgs 2.5-9 as being at least a possibility. And in that case an introduction is also necessary - perhaps provided by vv. 1 and 2, though it is also possible that the original has been completely replaced by another from a Deuteronomistic hand.

The final part of the section, vv. 10-12, is a report of David's death. Such a notice is imperative here, otherwise 2.13ff. would make no sense at important points. Whether the report in the present text is original is uncertain. Verse 11 does arouse some suspicion because of its similarity with the other chronological formulas in the Books of Kings. Hardly anything, however, can be said against vv. 10 and 12.

Thus far, then, we have definitely established the following passages as parts of the succession source: I Kings 1; I Kgs 2.(1f.), 5-10, 12-27a, 28-46.

The next task is to pursue the source in I Kgs 1 back to its beginning. We have determined that the theme of chapter 1 is the question of David's successor. The unusual emphasis with which this theme is taken up again and again brought us earlier to the conclusion that this is the theme not just of one single chapter but of a larger complex which is summed up and completed in striking fashion in I Kgs 1.

Such a complex may have presented either the story of the hero's background or else the story of the background to the succession; on the other hand it may have performed both tasks together. The latter alternative is preferable here, for II Sam 13-20 tells a story of the background to the succession, while II Sam 11 and 12 tell such a story of the one who was to succeed.

The latter story is closely connected with the account of the Ammonite wars. Earlier we decided that this was a campaign report, very close to the events. Its beginning appears to have been replaced by the author of 11.2ff., so that, after excluding the war report, 10.1-5, 11.2-12.25 remains. 10.1-5 tells about the cause of the Ammonite wars; 11.2ff. of how David, while remaining behind in Jerusalem, committed adultery with Bathsheba, the wife of Uriah the Hittite, and of the consequences of this action - David's vain attempts to conceal the act, the removal of the troublesome husband, Nathan's rebuke, the death of the child despite David's tears and finally the birth of Solomon, of whom it is stated: "And Yahweh loved him." The whole narrative provides a self-

73

contained story of Solomon's background, which could not have existed without the framework of the Ammonite war report to which it is connected.

Some critics have reservations ·concerning the Nathan scene: some object to individual verses, e.g. Wellhausen, Smith, Klostermann, Budde (who assigns the whole narrative to his E-source) and Sievers; others have doubts about the whole narrative, e.g. Kittel, Schwally, Gressmann and (most comprehensively) Cook. It must be granted that the pericope is not uniform. That is shown by the fact that the threat has two forms, one beginning in v. 7b and one in v. 11, to which are joined yet a third one in v. 14.

For a start, we will ignore the third threat; even so the first two (vv. 7bff. and vv. 11f.) are so different in content that it is not feasible that they could belong together. While the first emanates from the fact of Uriah's death at the hands of the Ammonites and foretells that the house of David will be continually ravished by the sword, the second stresses the secret act of adultery and threatens David, and him alone, with public punishment. The first oracle therefore appears to be the more far-reaching and thus the less precisely defined. It is clear that both threats are hardly possible alongside each other. So Kittel deletes the second as belonging to a redactor.

In order to check this procedure one could start either with the parable or with the fulfilment of the prophecy. The parable tells of a rich man who, in order to keep his own flock, takes the only sheep of a poor man in order to serve it to a guest whom he must entertain. As is shown by just a glance at the example given by the wise woman of Tekoa (II Sam 14), it is not necessary for a parable to be applicable to the actual situation in all its details. The comparison is rather unsatisfactory in II Sam 14 and the same is true in chapter 12. Of course, the counterparts to the rich man and the poor one with his single sheep readily present themselves, but the necessity of preparing a meal for the guest can only be set over against David's unrestrained sensual compulsion, both, of course, leading to covetousness. Here, though, we are less concerned with how far the comparison corresponds to the actual situation and with what we find in it, than with the question of how far it serves the narrator's purposes and with what aim it may be intended by him.

It is obvious here that the parable is only interested in the poor man in so far as he is the owner of the sheep - there is not the slightest hint about his condition otherwise. That must mean that the emphasis is on the rich man's action of robbing the lamb rather than on the suffering of the poor man. Thus the king's judgement concentrates on the rich man's robbery. Now if it is Uriah's death by the sword which is in the foreground in vv. 7bff., then on this assessment the parable has no sufficient point of reference, neither in its wording nor in the basic idea which it embodies. And this is decisive, for in II Sam 14 the parable chosen bears little resemblance to the actual conditions but clings fast to the basic idea, namely the necessity in certain circumstances of stopping a blood feud in order to preserve a line weakened by fratricide. Hence it is hardly probable that in II Sam 12 the same narrator could have handled the basic idea of that parable so cavalierly. As a consequence we will have to delete vv. 7b-10.

How is the second threat-speech to be dealt with? One cannot deny that it is closer to the parable's basic idea. Just like the robbery of the sheep by the rich man in the parable, the theft of the woman is the centre of attention here and it is this which provides the reason for the threat of retaliation in accordance with the "jus talionis."

Thus we can conclude from our analysis of the two threats in the parable speech that we must delete the first one and may possibly retain the second.

The next task will be to ask whether in the course of the narrative the conditions of one or other of the threats are met. From this no conclusions can be drawn, of course, about the threat speech that was actually made, but we can certainly come to a conclusion about the one that was most likely incorporated by the narrator. On this point it is necessary, however, to anticipate some of the points which we will be attempting to prove later and to take account of the whole of the succession source as it turns out in its final extent.

It seems obvious that the quite precise formulation of the second threat-speech is fulfilled to the very letter in II Sam 16.21ff. and so the impression arises that II Sam 12.11ff. was written with Absalom's actions in mind. But the question still remains of whether the passage in chapter 12 stems from the author of II Sam 16.21 or from a later one. The latter alternative would be imperative if II Sam 12.1-15a were a later addition; in this case the second threat-speech would function as a means of providing a connection with the larger context. The same would also be true, though, if both speeches were alien to the original narrative. We will come back to this question later. For the present, it is initially a matter of establishing that the second threat-speech does have an exact fulfilment within the succession story and can thus be shown to be possibly original.

The same cannot be said with certainty about the first one. It is true that in the further course of the succession story the sword does frequently cause havoc within the house of David. Amnon, Absalom, Adonijah, all fall prey to the sword. But in the very story that directly follows the Nathan pericope, namely the death of Bathsheba's child, there is no mention of it. Even though the later story of the house of David tells of no few violent deaths, these are not in such profusion as to warrant saying that the sword never departed from the house of David. Consequently, on the basis of the further course of events - and indeed that applies to the later fortunes of the Davidic dynasty as well as to events within the compass of the succession story itself - the second threat-speech should be preferred.

This conclusion has, however, a somewhat provisional air about it inasmuch as the dialogue between David and Nathan which immediately follows both these threat-speeches has not been taken into account. Taking it into view, the picture shifts once more.

The first threat-speech has been shown already to be a later insertion. Now its deletion is confirmed. But more than that, the second threat-speech begins to look distinctly shaky and it must go also. In v. 13 David admits his mistake and for this he receives forgiveness in Yahweh's name from Nathan and is released from the death sentence which the king has passed on himself. In its place he is told (v. 14) that the only punishment will be the death of the child of Bathsheba. This death-threat is justified by reference to the fact that David has flouted Yahweh by his actions. As Wellhausen has already made clear, faced with this verse it seems hardly conceivable that just previously, and quite separately, there should be pronounced two other, much more serious, punishments. This all the more so when both the other threats do actually come about, more or less, in spite of the "save that ..." (אפס כי).

So it seems likely that not only the first threat-speech - as shown already - but also the second should be regarded as a later addition. The structure of the whole piece achieves unity and force in this way. Instead of long-winded speeches, which at such moments rather weaken the impact because they provide the opportunity for retorts and excuses, the parable and the blazing judgement of the king are followed by

the short, crushing, "You are the man." Now the king sees his
guilt before him and confesses it, whereupon Nathan can
promise him forgiveness and the cancellation of the death
sentence he has pronounced against him, although he must
tell him that the child will die as punishment, a development
which is described more fully in the following narrative.

Yet, this said, even though the possibility and perhaps even
the necessity of deleting both the threat-speeches in 7bff.
and 11f. has been shown, it is still to be explained how these
sentences could have been added. There can be no doubt that
the words of prophets were often revised and extended. Thus
it is quite understandable here that the short statement,
"You are the man," should be expanded first with one and
then with another divine oracle, in order to compensate for
the lack of such an oracle. Further, the thought that David's
adultery was the source of all the later misfortune suffered
by his house might also have played a part here. Thus, one of
the compilers saw one consequence of this guilt in the action
of Absalom after his entry into Jerusalem when, on
Ahithophel's advice, he approached his father's concubines.
This insertion is all the more comprehensible as it is more in
line with the parable. Another, however, quite rightly saw a
divine curse in the grisly fate which made the house of David
tear itself to pieces in internecine struggles - a curse which
struck the household of the very person who had brought the
sword upon himself.[10] In this way, connections which had
at best been simply hinted at were retraced and made more
obvious. To be sure, this was done not without a certain skill;
but nevertheless, the additions were unnecessary and ex-
traneous to the original context.

It is difficult to judge when the insertions were made. All
that is certain is that they were not Deuteronomistic. Further, the first threat-speech presupposes a tradition of an
annointing of David preceding the meeting with Saul,[11]
provided that - and this is highly likely - the events in 7bf.
are listed in proper chronological order.[12]

We can thus see that the Nathan pericope in chapter 12
includes vv. 1-7a, 13-15a.[13] Thereby the uniformity and the
original shape of the pericope is re-established, though
nothing yet proves it to be an indispensible part of the
succession source. This is primarily disputed because the
whole pericope can be separated from its present context
without any difficulty. That fact must be acknowledged.
Then, especially if 11.27b is deleted, the section 11.2-12.25
comprises the story of David's adultery, the subsequent

murder of the unfaithful wife's husband, the death of the child born from the adultery and, in conclusion, the birth of Solomon. All of this is related without any word of judgement. Indeed, one can very much doubt whether the death of the child is to be understood as the result of Yahweh's intervention and punishment - even if 12.15b is retained - rather than as a chance occurrence which was only seen as an act of Yahweh because of the suddenness of the illness - like every other surprise illness and every sudden death. In that case, however, the possibility presents itself that the description of the illness and death of the child should be regarded as a loosely appended scene, unnecessarily detailed for the David-Bathsheba story - all the more so since it contributes no climax.

It is not easy to see why, of all things, the death of this child is of such importance for it to be related with such expansiveness. However, the situation is quite different if the Nathan pericope is included within the complex discussed above. The moral force then comes into its own. The reader's outrage concerning David's behaviour finds expression and achieves thereby its catharsis. We note that even King David cannot go against the holy moral law with impunity. So, as least from the point of view of folk psychology, this scene is not easily dispensed with.

However, the Nathan pericope is necessary not simply for the way it deepens the moral content but, at least as much, for its contribution to the structure of the whole section - the reason being, that it is not until Nathan is brought into this otherwise loosely attached story of the death of the child that it becomes an important part of the whole narrative. Nathan's appearance provides, first, a definite end to the adultery story and, second, tension and a forward momentum. Excitement is created, the listener and reader are aroused. Will Nathan's prophecy be fulfilled? The scene appropriately rounds off the whole section with David's struggle for the life of the doomed child.

Yet it also goes beyond this in referring to the birth of Solomon, the future successor to the throne. One could object that the Nathan pericope cannot be original for the very reason that it has a moral dimension to it and the following scene of the child's death shows no signs of moral considerations in David's behaviour. But how should David's inner repentance be manifested? Perhaps through his first doing proper penance on the death of the child and once more expressly demonstrating that the loss of the young life was a result of his own transgression (which seems to be the point of חטא, "sin," in v. 13)? He could have done that. But he had no good reason. His transgressions are forgiven in v. 13, albeit with the warning that the child of Bathsheba would die. Yet thereby the death of the child is to some extent a pledge for the total forgiveness granted.

So when David at first pleads for the life of the baby he does so thinking that Yahweh might have mercy on him and let the child live. He hopes thus, by means of his self-castigation, to be able to ward off the remainder of his punishment also. But he does not succeed. The life is lost - death knocks at the door. David's sins are atoned for. This means that the writer can explicitly testify concerning Solomon: "And Yahweh loved him." In responding to his courtiers' astonished questioning, David says simply that the death was unavoidable and thereby gives his reason for regarding all further fasting as worthless. It is an answer which reveals much more than just simple resignation: it reveals the recognition of God's unwavering justice. Only submission is fitting for David.

The dogmatic view that the pericope should be deleted because Nathan has in it a quite different role from that in I Kgs 1 is hardly convincing. Of course it must be admitted that Nathan seems all too entangled in worldly affairs to bring any great credit upon his vocation as prophet. But other prophets have also intervened with a greater or lesser force in the progress of history and in doing so have shown themselves to be at least as much "party men" as Nathan is here - a fact which did not detract from their prophetic activity and the respect given them as prophets. In I Kgs 1, Nathan confronts and warns the king exactly as here in 12.1ff. On that occasion he is safeguarding an oath extracted from the king in a moment of weakness, while here he is upholding justice and morality. The difference is not as great as has been maintained, once the original Nathan story in II Sam 12.1 has been restored (and this is absolutely imperative). Further, the use of a parable is by no means something alien to the narrator of the succession story, as is shown by reading II Sam 14. On the contrary, this seems to demonstrate that the narrator was fond of parables[14] and was quick to make use of them at every available opportunity.

Thus, in conclusion, we can add II Sam 11.2-12.7a, 13-25 to those passages which we have already identified as being the work of the narrator of the succession story. This background story of the future successor is embedded in an account of the Ammonite wars (10.6-11.1; 12.26-31) which already lay to hand and to which he added a somewhat more detailed introduction (10.1-5).

So far, with I Kgs 1 as our point of departure, we have dealt with the question of the successor's background story. This was located in II Sam 10-12. Now we must ask to what extent the writer has provided a story of the background to the succession. This question is all the more imperative since in I Kgs 1ff. there is allusion to a whole series of people and events that must somehow or other have been touched upon previously but do not appear within the story of the successor. There is, for example, Absalom, who is mentioned as the eldest brother of Adonijah in a way which presupposes earlier mention. Then there are Barzillai, Shimei, Joab, Amasa and Abner whose activities or deaths must have been related in some way or other - assuming there to be no overwhelmingly weighty reasons against this, as in the case of Abner. The same is true of the promise to David, alluded to in I Kgs 2.24. None of these questions is answered by the story of the successor's background; this narrative merely provides detailed information about the man himself, his mother and the prophet Nathan. Will the background story to the succession give us the answers we are looking for?

Starting from the material in I Kgs 1 (and with the exception of the appendices in II Sam 21-24 which belong to various different sources), we find a major narrative complex dealing undoubtedly with the question of the succession: the story of Absalom's revolt and of the rebellion of Sheba ben Bichri, that is to say, chapters 15-20. There is no doubt that these chapters are closely related to I Kgs 1 and 2. Evidence for this comes not only from the same style; a series of other observations also make this conclusion necessary, as for example, the fact that in II Sam 15.1 the display of pomp by the budding successor is depicted with almost the same words as in I Kgs 1.5. Further, it is here that we learn the answer to the question of Amasa's murder by Joab and that we hear about this warrior's harsh ruthlessness and get to know about Barzillai's willingness to help and about Shimei's bitter and pitiful curse. If all this leaves us in no doubt as to the material belonging together, then all that remains to be examined now is whether chapters 15-20 are uniform and completely self-contained. This task can best be fulfilled by looking at the structure.

The section in question begins with a description of Absalom's show of pomp as the future successor to the throne. The question of whether this is a proper beginning, prefaced perhaps by 14.25-27, as Caspari suggests,[15] or whether we only have a segment of a larger complex, can be left in abeyance for the time being. The portrait of Absalom's splendour is closely followed by a description of his attempts to win the hearts of the people. And now scenes come one after the other in rapid succession without a break: the request to David to be allowed to go to Hebron to fulfil a vow, the preparation of the conspiracy, the sacrifice, the proclamation as king, David's flight from Jerusalem leaving behind the ten concubines, David's order to Ittai the Gittite to go back, the dispatch of the priests with the ark back to the city, the meeting with Hushai the Archite and with Ziba the servant of Meribaal, Shimei's curse, Absalom's arrival in Jerusalem, Ahithophel's advice concerning the concubines and the pursuit of David, Hushai the Archite's treacherous opposition to Ahithophel, the dispatch of the priests with a message to David, Ahithophel's suicide, David's arrival in Mahanaim, Barzillai's, Shobi's and Machir's readiness to help, the preparations for combat, the battle, the death of Absalom, the negotiations for David's return, the meeting with Shimei and Meribaal, his farewell to Barzillai, the conflict between the northern and southern tribes, Sheba's revolt, the murder of Amasa, the encircling of Sheba and his death.

Each of the scenes occupies a fixed place within the whole structure, none is superfluous; yet at the same time none provides a key to the understanding of the whole. We can thus speak of a coherent unit here; we cannnot, however, regard it as being fully self-contained. For much of it is a continuation of a strand starting somewhere previous to 15.1 - and only with this beginning is an understanding possible - while a great deal is only partially carried through and calls for a conclusion in an appropriate direction. Chapters 15-20 seem in no way to form a self-contained narrative. For on the face of it, there is lacking any well-wrought start and finish.

Even Caspari, who regards these chapters as an independent narrative about Absalom's revolt, admits that there is no introduction. Accordingly he places 14.25-27 at the beginning and thinks of 15.1-6 as a further exposition. Even then there are still very great problems which require another explanation. Already in 15.8 there is an indication that Absalom had lived previously in Geshur, which poses the question of the reasons for this stay. So, too, the Ziba scene in 16.1ff is incomprehensible for anyone who does not know the story in chapter 9. On the other hand, however, it is not exactly explicable why the introduction should have mentioned the three sons and the daughter of Absalom who play no further role in the action. So it seems hardly feasible to agree with Caspari and Gressmann and regard 14.25-27 or 15.1 as the beginning of a separate narrative.

It is equally unlikely that 20.22 could form the end of a story of Absalom's revolt, the first reason being that the main characters in the story are Absalom and David. Absalom is prematurely removed from the scene by his death. His opponent, David, has won and maintained his position even in the final aftermath of the uprising. The end of such a story would have to contain some indication of David victoriously emerging from all these troubles with his throne secure. Instead of this David at the conclusion recedes further - and finally completely - behind the figure of Joab. In no way is something like this acceptable, even in the case of an anti-climactic conclusion or epilogue, as in I Kgs 2, for example. Second, a sentence like 19.23 absolutely demands some sort of continuation. Even the fact that Shimei is not punished on the day of victory is sufficient indication that the penalty will somehow be exacted.

All these factors mean that it is unlikely that chapters 15-20 ever formed an independent narrative. Rather, when we consider what has already been established, namely that I Kgs 1-2 in many cases picks up strands which begin in chapters 15-20, or at least can be traced in this section (e.g., Barzillai's help, Shimei's flight, Joab's killing Amasa), and, further, that similar events are related in similar phrases (e.g., Adonjah's imitation of Absalom's show of pomp); and when we add to this the fact that II Sam 20 provides no satisfactory conclusion, then the most likely solution is that II Sam 15-20 constitutes a story which is preliminary to I Kgs 1-2; that is to say, it is the story of the background to the succession. That II Sam 15-20 complies completely with this theme cannot be disputed, nor, for that matter, that I Kgs 1 may be connected to II Sam 20.22 without any difficulty. Accordingly, II Sam 15-20 is a section of material joined to a larger complex in at least this one direction.

But the question of the beginning of the story still has no answer. It cannot lie in the Bathsheba narrative, which we have already identified as the background story of the successor to the throne. Further, we learn nothing of David's relationship to Meribaal and Ziba and nothing, either, about Absalom's stay in Geshur. On the contrary, we learn about the latter in II Sam 14 and about the former in II Sam 9.

82

The latter chapter reports how David gives back to Meribaal, Jonathan's crippled son, the family inheritance, how he has it managed by Ziba, Saul's servant, and how he invites Meribaal to the royal table as a daily guest. Given that we have thereby solved all the problems arising from 16.1ff. and 19.25ff., we cannot avoid attributing this chapter to the story of the background to the succession, especially since the invitation to Meribaal to eat at court was at the same time meant to secure the position of David and his dynasty. Further, chapter 9 introduces Meribaal and Ziba according to the best rules of Hebrew narrative art so that this in itself is evidence for the beginning of a narrative strand continued in 16.1ff. and 19.25ff.

II Sam 14, where we read about the reason for Absalom's sojourn in Geshur, is itself closely connected with II Sam 13. Both chapters tell of Amnon's crime against his half-sister Tamar, the sister of Absalom, of Absalom's revenge, his flight to Geshur, his recall thanks to the intervention of Joab and his reconciliation with the king. There can be no doubt that we have a coherent unit here. (14.25-27 will probably have to be deleted, although it must be admitted that a storyteller can make up for something which he was not able to include earlier by putting it in at a later and not exactly appropriate stage; but this addition would have to be necessitated in some way by the subsequent narrative, and in the present case this cannot be asserted.)

The view of Caspari, Gressmann and Luther, is that chapters 13 and 14 form an independent Tamar novelle. This, however, is not feasible, although it must be admitted that the crime against Tamar reverberates in its repercussions through to the last sentence. Still, a Tamar novelle could finish with the murder of Amnon or at most, as a final, falling cadence, might relate the flight of the murderer and the arrival at court of the rumours of the murder, but it is not easy to understand how a Tamar novelle could be concerned with the recall and rehabilitation of the murderer. Here the crime against Tamar is no longer in the foreground but now it is Absalom's murder of Amnon, his half-brother - admittedly the result of Amnon's crime - which determines the further progress of the story; moreover, the narrator could have taken the offended honour of Absalom's sister into consideration, if only as a mitigating circumstance, but he does not even do this. Thus the second part of the story is no longer to do with Tamar, but only with Absalom.

It seems barely credible that the second part should have

been written because of the first part - it is far too powerful
to form an epilogue. Rather it is more probable that the
opposite is the case, i.e., that we have a preliminary story of
Absalom, which obviously had to begin with Amnon's crime
against Tamar, since the later developments can only be
explained in the light of these events; for his opposition to his
father David starts at this point and subsequently it will lead
to the revolt. That even the character of Absalom is the
same here as in the account of the revolt, need only be
mentioned here.

So we cannot talk of chapters 13-14 as being an independent Tamar novelle; rather, what is narrated here is the story
of Absalom's background. The question then arises as to
whether this narrative has its own ending or whether it is not
rather linked intimately with what follows, namely the
account of the revolt. This seems all the more likely for two
reasons: first, there is no real beginning at 15.1 and this
cannot be compensated for even by prefacing it with
14.15-27; second, the account in chapters 15ff. refers to
events related in chapters 13f. Furthermore, one could take
the view that chapter 14 does not end satisfactorily with the
reconciliation of David and Absalom. Of course this reconciliation does indeed mean an end to a stage in Absalom's
life. The period of rejection is past. But could a story dealing
with a royal prince have finished thus? Could it have been
satisfactory to show that he was reconciled once more with
his father without saying if and how this reconciliation worked out? This really does not seem possible, especially as in
15.1ff. the further stage in Absalom's life is described with
quite precise reference to what has preceded. In the face of
this we are forced to regard chapters 13-14 as an introduction to a further narration of Absalom's story, especially
since even chapters 13-14 form part of the background to the
succession question in that the murdered Amnon, as the
eldest son of David, would at least have had a stronger claim
to the throne than Absalom.

Accordingly, we have so far shown the extent of the
succession source to be as follows:

I Kgs 1 and 2 contains the conclusion, Solomon's accession
to the throne.
II Sam 10-12 recounts the background story of the
successor himself; this is embedded in an account of
David's wars with the Ammonites.
II Sam 9 and 13.1-20.22 presents the story of the
background to the succession.

Thus the whole complex of II Sam 9-20 and I Kgs 1 and 2, normally designated the "family story" or "succession story," is shown to be closely interwoven as regards content. However, as already indicated in the introduction, we must go beyond these limits and look for a beginning even further back than II Sam 9. Various considerations demand this:

1. Solomon, in talking with Bathsheba in I Kgs 2.24, alludes to a revelation to David from Yahweh which has a distinct similarity - even in the wording - to II Sam 7.11b;[16] and so we must assume that our writer had some knowledge of this oracle preserved here only as a fragment.

2. If, as we said above, the theme of the succession story really lies in the question in I Kgs 1.13, "Who shall sit on David's throne?", then we must ask whether II Sam 6.16 and 20ff. should not also be taken as part of the succession story. In the Michal scene it is expressly stated that Michal, Saul's daughter and so the connecting link with the deposed family of Saul, remained childless. This eliminated her as queen mother in the question of the succession.

3. The fact that we can discern in 9.1ff. the beginning of the Meribaal strand of the background story to the succession, hardly justifies regarding this scene as the beginning of the whole succession source; had this latter been the case there would undoubtedly have been in this scene some clear indication of the main theme, be it ever so slight.

4. Further, it should also be taken into consideration that, as already demonstrated, II Sam 6.16 and 20ff. belong with the ark narrative, as regards content, only in so far as this scene takes place on the day the ark was brought into Jerusalem; at any rate, we should not expect it to be taken up into a sanctuary legend.

These deliberations lead us to include both 6.16 and 20ff., and parts of II Sam 7 as well, in the succession source. It must be allowed that the news of the childnessness of the natural queen mother does fit very well at the beginning of a narrative dealing with the succession to David's throne. Thereby the question of who will occupy David's throne is for the present answered negatively, so that the possibility of complication arises in a way that is familiar to us from, for example, the seventh book of Herodotus' historical work or from the beginning of Xenophon's Anabasis. It must further be allowed that the structure of the whole complex can only gain if this negative answer is immediately followed by the proposition, Yahweh will make David a house; he will found a dynasty. It will be shown later that our writer has great skill and a predeliction for such effects based on antithesis, so that at any rate we have no need to reject this possibility out of hand.

However, there now arises a series of difficulties. First, those of the most serious kind. Whereas in 6.16 and 20ff. we are dealing with a single, unified scene, homogeneous in content, chapter 7 is, as has already been proven, a "mixtum compositum" of extremely diverse components, making critical analysis very difficult. Of course, we are only concerned here with the oldest strata - but such material was in fact found both in David's prayer and in Nathan's prophecy. We concluded that two separate reports of the one and the same event, differing in certain details, were handed down. The wording of I Kgs 2.24 makes it likely that our writer knew (or had himself written?) an account containing II Sam 7.11b. If we were right to think that this verse probably belonged to an account by Nathan of a revelation made to him concerning the future of the Davidic dynasty, then the prophet's further appearance in the story of the succession is ensured. Nathan's portrayal here is similar to that in II Sam 12 - as a prophet, as one who executes God's commissions. Further, it was shown above that verse 11b belongs closely with verse 16, so that what goes for 11b goes for 16 as well. The writer certainly did not have before him more than this old source in vv. 11b and 16, for, as already observed, 11b and 16 constitute a somewhat different account from that of 7.18-29[17]. Adoption of the one excludes the other. Further, 7.4b-7 cannot be reconciled with vv. 11b and 16 because of its form. There is no question of including 7.1-4a because it is probable that originally the opening words in v. 4a, "And there came to pass that night" were followed by a direct revelation by Yahweh to David which in terms of content appears to have had nothing to do with what follows.

So now we should first try to reconstruct the original connections between 6.16 and 20ff. and chapter 7. The conclusion of II Sam 6 presents the Michal episode. It finishes effectively with the words: "And Michal had no children until the day of her death." This meant that the continuance of the dynasty over all Israel was endangered, for David's sons so far were only sons of the king of Judah. Michal, the daughter of Saul, and thus an important political link between David and the northern tribes, remained childless. Accordingly, we can see that the narrator has well prepared us for a revelation which, like the one to Abraham, assured David that his dynasty would be established.[18] No further transition is necessary. But how, then, to account for the insertion of 7.1-7, as it stands? It would seem that there had been some old tradition ascribing what Solomon had carried out to a previous plan of David's. First, 7.1-4a was inserted and was followed by a direct revelation from David. A second step took place when this revelation was deleted and its content put into the mouth of Nathan who is to be thought of as the speaker. In the process the two revelations were moulded into a single unit, which indeed the catch-word "house" positively invited.

For the time being, then, we can regard the contents of the succession source as including: II Sam 6.16 and 20ff; 7.11b and 16; 9.1-10.5 (10.6-11.1); 11.2-12.7a; 12.13-25 (26-31); 13.1-14.24; 14.28-18.17; 18.19-20.22; I Kgs 1-2.1; 2.5-10; 2.12-27a; 2.28-46 .

In our previous discussions it was tacitly assumed that II Sam 6.16 and 20ff., the beginning of our source, were fitted like a cog into the already extant ark narrative. This contention must now be looked at once more. First we must reiterate the results so far:

1. The only thing that 6.16 and 20ff. have in common with the ark narrative is that these verses describe an event which happened during and after the transfer of the ark to Jerusalem. They therefore have no place in a ἱερὸς λόγος of the ark.
2. 6.16 and 20ff. belong rather to the succession source whose theme makes a negative appearance here.
3. II Sam 6.19 is the ending of the ark narrative which includes I Sam 4.1b-7.1 and II Sam 6.
4. II Sam 10.6-11.1 and 12.26-31 show that the author of the succession source also incorporated into his narrative, unaltered, sources which already had a fixed form, as long as they provided him with an appropriate framework or support for his own work.

This granted, it does not seem out of the question for the author to have used not only the account of the Ammonite wars - we can leave aside II Sam 7.11b and 16 because of the paucity of material and uncertainty about the author - but also the ark narrative. As already shown, it is very probable that the ark narrative comes from the time of David or at least from the time of Solomon, so that a process of this kind is at all events possible. Against it could be argued that the character and the religious horizons of both narratives are far too different for us to be able to posit their association.

The far-reaching differences cannot be denied. The one is a cult legend; it constantly places the greatest emphasis on Yahweh's acts of intervention; and the author was probably a priest of the ark sanctuary. The other is a narrative of important internal political events; it shies away from stressing Yahweh's action and makes only scant reference to the divine background of events involving God; the author was a man from the royal court.

How is it that the one, without hesitation, joins his work on to the very different work of the other and proceeds to continue it? Is it perhaps that we appreciate the difference more markedly? Or are there other lines of connection, some relationship in common? For a few of these questions an answer is not possible. To some others we will come back later. But a few should be answered at this point.

The possibility has to be conceded that the narrator of the succession story, because of his position as a member of the royal court (whether of David or Solomon can remain open), was well informed about the history of the royal house, and was presented with the chance of getting to know about a story of the origins of the ark, already fixed in one form or another. In that case, if such a story were extant, it could not have been kept secret and witheld from him.

It should also be taken into consideration that as the writer concentrated on the succession to David as his theme, he could hardly avoid dealing with the figure of Michal. It is further probable that the infertility of Saul's daughter was very early connected with her behaviour towards David on the day the ark was brought into Jerusalem, and not by our narrator in the first place, but by the people. But then it was necessary for the writer to give an account of this event with the full details of its repercussions. Why should he go to a lot of trouble himself when there already lay before him such a fine portrayal of the events as given in the ark narrative, especially if this account was slowly acquiring a certain authority? Perhaps it was precisely because there was a recognized account that he was not prepared to set a version of his own over against it, even though he himself had a different view on some things. By joining his story to one that was already noted and honoured, would he not also give his work a share in the prestige of the older one?[19]

But whatever may have been the reasons which motivated the narrator in his efforts, it is certain that he used the ark narrative as a point of departure, a convenient way into his own story (so, too, his use of the Ammonite war report), and thus provided us with one of the oldest examples of this literary method, so widely employed in Israel, of making use of older material.

But if we take the narrator's method in dealing with the Ammonite war report, a new question arises. In this case, he used the older account as a framework into which he inserted his own narrative, but in turn he incorporated this merely as a building block in his larger narrative. Could he not have acted in the same way also in the case of the ark narrative? Might it not be possible that he simply tore the ark narrative in two and then inserted what seemed necessary and important to him in the gap? This idea is attractive and should not be rejected out of hand. Most of all we must ask what could have been inserted here.

The narrative's theme is the question: "Who will sit on David's throne?" The story of the successor's background is provided in one complete unit in chapters 10-12. According to our previous results the story of the background to the succession begins with the statement that Michal remained childless; it then tells of a divine revelation to David assuring the permanency of his dynasty and finishes with the story of the various struggles surrounding the succession. The whole complex could only be preceded by the statement that David was king of Judah and Israel and perhaps by a list of his other wives and their children. On the other hand, the questions posed by our writer did not require as a preface an account of David's rise from shepherd boy in Bethlehem to king of Judah and Israel. But was it even really necessary for the narrator to mention first that David had been king of Judah and Israel? He was after all writing in a period when memories about the founder of the dynasty were still fresh. Why should he repeat things which every child knew? Even a list of his wives and children seems not absolutely necessary, especially given that he introduces them sufficiently where required, within the narrative. The succession story is self-contained and self-explanatory to such an extent that an introductory list of this kind would hardly be missed. Further, it seems barely credible that the author would have broken up the flow of the ark narrative for the sake of a few such short notices. He has no reservations about splitting up the account of the Ammonite war because in this case he can take up his story

from a particular point within the account and thus comple-
ment it. In the ark narrative, on the other hand, David
appears as the well-known king without any further introduction. And it would be surprising if the narrator of the
succession story should have added an introduction, thus
treating the famous ruler as an unknown. Further, the event
from which he takes up is recounted at the end of the ark
narrative, so that it was not necessary to destroy the flow of
the story.

Thus, looking at the problem from the perspective of the
succession story, it is most improbable that the starting point
should be sought before II Sam 6.16, the verse which dovetails
with the ark narrative. Nevertheless, at the end of our
investigations we shall deal with the question of whether the
preceding narratives themselves call for the kind of continuation provided by our succession story.

In anticipating a negative answer to this question we may
first examine the style of the succession source, taking as its
extent what we have already accepted. Coming from the
simple, terse prose of the ark narrative, we are struck all the
more by the individuality of our source. The sentences are
longer, expression is fuller, the description is richer, the
language is more sonorous and richer in imagery. The rapid
flow of the narrative is restrained. Each individual scene is
neatly detached from those adjoining. Speeches, arguments,
are no longer used merely occasionally to depict moods and
character or to underline important turning points, but they
have a purpose of their own. It will now be our task to follow
up these observations one by one.

The style of the succession narrative displays both epic
expansiveness and the detailed touch of the miniaturist which
shows itself especially when the tension increases most. A
case in point is the circumstantiality with which the
appearance on the scene of Jonathan ben Abiathar is
described in I Kgs 1.41ff. In a long speech - introduced with a
solemn: "And Jonathan answered and spoke" - he lists the
proceedings in connection with Solomon's accession which
have been related only shortly before! And this even though
an event had taken place which ruined all Adonijah's plans,
throwing him and his supporters into the greatest confusion
and driving them to rapid decisions. Or another example is
the circumlocution with which the narrator depicts David's
flight from Jerusalem, even though - as the king himself
ordered - it happened speedily! Everywhere we see this love of
description and this joy in narration which cannot have

enough embellishment.

The remarks made here about whole scenes cannot be properly appreciated until the details are scrutinized. Everywhere we find a striving towards richer expressiveness. Actions are divided into their individual phases[20] and thus verb is heaped on verb. We may compare, for example, I Kgs 1.49: "And all the guests of Adonijah trembled and rose, and each went his own way"; II Sam 14.2: "And Joab sent to Tekoa, and fetched from there a wise woman, and said to her, 'Pretend to be a mourner, and put on mourning garments and do not anoint yourself with oil, and behave like a woman who has been mourning many days for the dead'"; II Sam 13.14: "And he overpowered her and ravished her and lay with her"; II Sam 11.5: "She sent and told David and said". These examples should suffice for the many which are unmistakeable even at a cursory reading.

Alongside this accumulation of verbs is one of nouns: e.g., II Sam 11.7: "And David asked after the welfare of Joab and after the welfare of the people and after the welfare of the war"; II Sam 15.22: "And Ittai of Gath passed on, and all his men and all his family dependants who were with him." Very often the word "all" is inserted, e.g. 15.18: "And all his servants passing by at his side, and all the Cherethites and all the Pelethites and all the Gittites ..."

Clauses are also placed together in a kind of "parallelismus membrorum": e.g. II Sam 16.13b: "And he threw stones, (as he went along) opposite him, and cast dust." Infinitives absolute give a full and sonorous impression: e.g. II Sam 16.5b: "And behold, there came out a man of the family of the house of Saul, Shimei ben Gera by name - coming out and cursing as he came"; or II Sam 15.30b: "And they passed on up, weeping continually." Participles continue the idea of the main verb, e.g. II Sam 15.30a: "And David went up the ascent of the Mount of Olives, weeping as he went." There are numerous particles of every kind, הנה (behold) and גם' (also) being particularly common.

Thus the impression of richness is given everywhere. This might be, on the one hand, because of the speech rhythm of a narrator who found pleasure in full-sounding, well-rounded sentences, or who perhaps felt an inner compulsion to express his thoughts in this way rather than in any other. On the other hand, however, there does seem unmistakeably to be a certain deliberate intention here, the wish to be vividly graphic, to tell a concrete story, plus also the endeavour to increase the tension by inserting words and sentences to slow down the pace.

The obsession with graphic descriptiveness can be traced throughout. For instance, one need only think of David fleeing from Absalom, as related in 15.30; of how he takes a stroll on the roof of his place (11.2); of the characterizations of people - Hushai the Archite (15.32), Ziba (16.1) and many others. A place is described more exactly by means of a subordinate clause or an expression of time is included to give the scene a more vivid profile: e.g., 15.32: "David came to the summit, where God was worshipped" or 11.2: "It happened around about evening that David arose." In order to reflect movements, verbs are repeated over and over again; thus the word עבר (pass on, over) is heard time and again throughout the second half of chapter 15, expressing the restless withdrawal from the endangered city; or in 18.19ff. the word רוץ (run) serves a similar purpose. In addition, a succinct, metaphorical expression can be used, as when David orders Uriah to go down to his house and wash his feet. Uriah refuses, saying that it would not be proper for him to eat at home and to drink and to lie with his wife while his general was camping in the open. Similarly, the woman of Tekoa speaks of her last remaining spark being extinguished (II Sam 14.7).

The graphic quality of the narrative, however, is particularly enhanced by the use of numerous, striking images, which are scattered about like flowers on the meadows. David's behaviour when the ark is brought into Jerusalem is compared with that of a good-for-nothing (6.20). Meribaal is, in his own eyes, like a dead dog (9.8; cf. also 16.9), and is called to David's table as a royal prince (9.11). Uriah's death is compared with that of Abimelech ben Jerubbaal (11.21). Ammon acts like a fool (13.13). People are like water poured out on the earth which cannot be stopped from flowing away (14.14). David is like an angel of God (14.17, 20; 19.28). Ahithophel hopes to bring the people to Absalom like a bride to her husband (17.3). His advice is as an oracle from God (16.23). David is as strong and angry as a wild bear robbed of its cubs (17.8). He is like 10,000 of his warriors (18.3). A brave soldier has the heart of a lion (17.11). Israel is as numerous as the sand by the sea (17.11).

The use of images and similes makes us feel quite sharply the difference in the ark narrative with its lack of imagery. This difference is even more obvious when we look at the speeches.

The first thing that must be examined is the form. The

92

situation, of course, is by no means as straightforward as in the ark narrative, where nearly all the speeches consist of a simple question. Moreover the succession source exhibits a wealth of literary types: questions, summons (ranging from the plain imperative to elaborately structured admonitions), messages (both conveying some commission and as reports), descriptions and dialogue. The multiplicity of these literary types is matched by their difference of form. Sometimes the speech is restricted to a single clause - whether relatively short or long - whereas sometimes it is extended by some added motivation or qualification. Sometimes, however - and we must give particular attention to this form - it consists of a single, large inclusio ("Ploke"): a clause is motivated or extended by a subsequent one and is then repeated at the end once more so that the pattern a-b-a is formed. Examples of this form can also be found elsewhere, as for example, in Gen 50.19ff., but in that case only as an isolated occurrence. In our text, on the other hand, this pattern is so common that it can actually be regarded as a characteristic of our author. So in 11.20f., for example, he makes Joab say the following words to David: "Why did you go so near the city to fight? Did you not know that they would shoot from the wall? Who killed Abimelech ben Jerubbaal? Did not a woman cast an upper millstone upon him from the wall, so that he died at Thebez? Why did you go so near the wall?" The reader should also compare further: 11.25b; 13.32f.; 15.19f.; 16.7f. and 10f.; 18.19-31; 19.12f.; I Kgs 1.24-27; 2.42f. In addition, sometimes the speech is continued beyond the inclusio by joining on to the end some supplementary thought.[21] Thus in Hushai's speech, for instance, the verses 17.8-10 form one thought enclosed by an inclusio, namely the exposition of the situation, and vv. 11-13 follow on as the conclusion to be drawn. A similar case is provided by Bathsheba's speech in I Kgs 1.17-21.

Given the frequency with which speeches built like this occur, it can hardly be regarded as a chance occurrence; rather it must be a speech style preferred by our narrator in particular - while still being traceable elsewhere (though much less often) - and perhaps parallels to a certain extent the refrain in poetry. This observation leads us to think of it as a literary prose style not too remote from poetry, a relationship which seems not unlikely, given the pleasant, well-sounding, epic rhythm and the metre discovered by Sievers. However, it is not for us to argue the pros and cons on the question of metre, but to determine the characteristics of the narrative style of the succession story. Needless to say, the label of literary prose does give us some general idea of its character, but without providing any insights into its peculiar nature. The discussions so far have only revealed a series of individual characteristics which have been restricted to the single clause or to relatively small clusters of clauses, as just now in our examination of the forms of speeches.

The individuality of the succession story will become much more obvious if we now go on to look at some scenes from it and to compare them with similar ones in the ark narrative.

The author of the succession story has a special liking for messenger-reports, e.g. I Kgs 1.42ff.; II Sam 18.19ff.; 17.15ff.; 15.13ff. (13.30ff.); in the ark source there is also one example of this: I Sam 4.12ff. In the latter, the course of events is related simply and straightforwardly. A fugitive from the defeat comes to Shiloh with torn clothes, his news arousing shock and wild lamentation. Old Eli, his sight fading, asks what the reason is for the uproar; the messenger comes to him, tells of what he has seen and the priest, slipping backwards off his chair, falls to his death. Whereas Eli's question merely serves as a transition, the message is central to the whole narrative. There is no reply. No attempt is made to let it develop into a dialogue - neither with an introduction, nor with a concluding answer. If one takes into account that this whole scene, like the subsequent Ichabod scene, is only a shoot, a tendril on the main branch of the narrative which carries on in the Philistine camp, and that it was only intended to portray the importance of the loss, one can then clearly comprehend the subservient role of direct speech in this source.

The situation is totally different in the succession story. Particularly relevant is the scene already mentioned, I Kgs 1.41ff. Solomon is anointed as king at Gihon by Nathan and Zadok accompanied by Benaiah. The rejoicing at the coronation reaches the ears of Adonijah who is banqueting at the Serpent's Stone. Adonijah asks the reason for the uproar. While he is still speaking, Jonathan ben Abiathar rushes in. Adonijah asks him to speak. He does so and brings news of Solomon's anointing, while quoting David's words at the same time. In this case, also, the messenger's speech is followed by shocked silence. Making a hasty exit, Adonijah's guests disperse to the four winds. The king's son flees to the horns of the altar.

The greatest similarities between this scene and the one in

the ark narrative seem to be these: in both cases there is the question about the reason for the noise - in the one case the lamenting and in the other the rejoicing; in both cases there is someone who can give an answer; in both cases the effect is shocked silence. But there are also differences. It is not merely that the Jonathan scene is of decisive importance for the further development of the action. More important here is the fact that an exchange develops by means of Adonijah's request to Jonathan and that the messenger cannot refrain from quoting with particular emphasis at the end of his report two things that David had said. Direct speech is accorded much greater importance.

Looking at the messenger scene in II Sam 18 makes this even clearer. Here develops an exchange between Ahimaaz ben Zadok and Joab about the honour of bringing the news of the battle's outcome to the awaiting king; this is cut short by the general's order that the Cushite convey the message. The narrator then transfers the scene to where the messenger is running. David is sitting at the gate and we learn of the approach of both messengers through an exchange between the lookouts and the king. This is followed by Ahimaaz's report, which becomes a conversation between him and the king as does that of the Cushites later. And so the whole narrative is split up into conversations and dialogues.[22] Direct speech moves beyond a subservient role within the whole to dominate and shape the narrative, which in places is no more than a framework and setting.

Connected with this is yet one other point. In the ark narrative, direct speech was merely a transient particle within the whole context of the narrative's progress as it flowed on, sometimes faster, sometimes more slowly, like an ice floe carried along by a rushing stream in the thaw. But as soon as speech develops into dialogue, as in the succession story, this constant flow and flood is interrupted. There are calms, resting points, small eddies of seclusion. The narrative is divided into more or less clearly distinguished individual scenes whose focal points are dialogues. It is dialogue and not just direct speech in itself which has the power to create scenes. The advantage of this is that the action becomes more vivid and dramatic;[23] but there is also a simultaneous danger. It is not that of disintegration, which can be overcome by the writer's ability to mould his narrative. What he was unable to prevent, however, was the fact that even when crowds take part in the action, the plot is concentrated on the exchanges and actions of individuals.

This aspect can be seen all too clearly if we compare, for example, the description of the battles in the ark narrative, or the crowd scenes in I Sam 5 and 6, with the battle against Absalom or with the conflict between the Judaeans and the Israelites in II Sam 19.44ff. In the ark narrative we have the impression that it is the people, the masses, who are taking part; in the succession narrative it is the individual. In the former it is the Philistines, the elders of Israel, the inhabitants of Ashdod etc. - whereas here it is the "man" of Judah (איש יהודה) or the "man" of Israel (איש ישראל). In the depiction of the battle against Absalom the narrative, after a few colourless phrases, soon concentrates on the dialogue between the soldier and Joab and on the killing of the king's son. Of course, other factors could have contributed here, perhaps a certain lack of understanding or scorn for the people, which would hardly be surprising for a courtier, perhaps also the knowledge that the masses need leaders and are largely ruled by them. On the other hand, this concentration on individuals is also due to a great extent to the structuring of the scenes around dialogue.

Showing this scene-building capacity of speech means no more, of course, than that to our eyes the succession story appears to be split up into separate tableaux, though this still by no means proves that the author himself wanted to make individual scenes and form a unity by joining them on to one another like a mosaic. This is our next task.

In the messenger episode with Ahimaaz ben Zadok, already used as an example, there are two distinct scenes. The first takes place on the battlefield. Ahimaaz asks Joab for permission to bring the king the message about the outcome of the battle and manages successfully to press his request in spite of being continually turned down and the Cushite being sent by Joab. The second scene unfolds by the gate of Mahanaim, where David awaits a report from the battlefield. From the conversation between the lookout and the king we can gather that both the messengers are approaching; then stepping forward one after the other they hand over their messages, with the result in each case that there is an exchange of speech. Both scenes are introduced by the main characters being named, in the first case Ahimaaz and in the second David. But what is far more important is that the second scene, with its dialogue between the lookout and the king, starts in a quite different setting, and the approach of the two messengers, whose departure from the battle-field was described in the first scene, is first mentioned in this dialogue before they arrive and hand over their messages. In other words, they are introduced in the second scene in a similar fashion to the ark at the beginning of the ark narrative, or Samuel in I Sam 9, or Meribaal in II Sam 9, i.e., as important persons at the beginning of a new story. This is even clearer if we compare it with the messenger scene in the ark narrative. Here we accompany the Benjaminite on his flight from the battlefield, see him coming to Shiloh and going up to the old priest, Eli, to bring him, too, the news of their misfortune. The course of the narrative is not interrupted - on the contrary, the messenger is even used to provide the transition from one scene to another. The narrator of the succession story dispenses with this expedient and divides the message-taking into two scenes which are both independent of each other.

This is not the only example; cf. the Jonadab ben Shimeah scene of 13.30ff.; or I Kgs 1.41ff., although here we only learn of Jonathan ben Abiathar's arrival and are not able to follow him from his starting place which is not mentioned at all. Thus it can be shown that the author consciously refrained from connecting the two scenes directly by using the message-taking and that his dispensing with this device was no coincidence. From this it follows that the writer himself wanted his story to be divided into separate scenes.

The point can also be made by other means as well. It is no accident that the exchange in the Michal scene starts with the maids' respect for David and returns to it at the end, or that, in the Ahimaaz section, the first scene begins in v. 19 with Zadok's son wanting to bring to the king the news that Yahweh had confirmed his rights over his enemies, while the Cushite finishes the second scene (in v. 32) with a very similar phrase, even though this bracketing stretches over two scenes. Likewise, in 16.5 we are told that Shimei ben Gera came out from Bahurim cursing and throwing stones at David and his company. It can hardly have been unintentional that the scene finishes (v. 13) with almost the same words. However, that our narrator is striving to round off each single scene is demonstrated even more clearly by sentences such as: "And David came to Mahanaim. And Absalom crossed the Jordan with all the men of Israel," which are simultaneously both a conclusion and a beginning. Such usage is common, as for example in 16.14f; 15.37; 16.1.

This sectioning into single scenes does not mean, however, that the whole complex has disintegrated into disconnected pieces. In the Ahimaaz section we have already noted that both scenes were combined together to form one unit. We can find ties like this all over. Thus, for example, 14.28 and 14.24 are associated by means of the same sentence: "And he did not see the countenance of the king." Similarly the individual scenes of chapter 9 are connected by the threefold repetition of: "I wish to show him favour (for the sake of [his father] Jonathan)" (9.1, 3, 7), and further by the three, only slightly different, versions of: "You shall eat bread at my table always." (9.7, 11, 13). The separate conversations in I Kgs 1 are strung together by the constantly recurring question: "Who will be king after you and who will sit on your throne?" (1.13, 17, [20], 24, [27], 30, [46, 48]). In chapter 20 the expression "pursue Sheba ben Bichri" can be found three times (20.7, 10, 13). That רוץ (run) in 18.19ff. and עבר (pass on, over) and בוא (come, go) in 15.17ff. are significant can only be indicated here.

These ligatures, however, are even more comprehensive, going far beyond a few neighbouring scenes moulded thereby into a single act, and, too, far beyond the odd connecting word and sentence. The whole narrative complex has been forged together to make an unbreakable chain. We have already had cause to point to a) the fact that connections run backwards and forwards from I Kgs 1; b) how, on this basis, we must look for a story of the background to the succession and also the successor, and that such can be found; c) how the epilogue in chapter 2 takes up strands which can be traced right to the beginning of the succession story and back, and brings them to a gradual conclusion. There is no need to repeat once more what has already been stated to prove the homogeneity and unity of the succession story through these links and interconnections. So far we have only considered them as cementing the pieces together; we should now evaluate them in their position within the whole structure.

The succession story begins with the Michal scene. This scene has its final tense moment in the concluding words: "And Michal, daughter of Saul, had no children till the day of her death." In accordance with the rule of intensifying by antithesis there follows directly the prophecy of Nathan as preserved in the fragments 7.11b, 16. This creates tension for the reader or listener, which is all the greater when a quite different but nonetheless related thread is started in chapter 9, namely the Meribaal strand - which has its own intro- duction. This intermission in chapter 9 clarifies the situation concerning Saul's family and David's relationship to them. Its purpose is to show that there is no great threat to the continuation of the dynasty from this direction even if caution is advisable. Chapter 10 also begins with something new, with the Ammonite wars, which are just as indispensible for the beginning of the succession story as is the ark narrative. With the appearance of Bathsheba, the future queen mother becomes part of the scheme. Her importance for the further progress of the story is apparent in her being placed in the framework of the war report, which serves as an extensive introduction. The child of the adultery dies and with it the hope of regarding him as a future successor. But the second son, Solomon, is put into the charge of the prophet Nathan for his upbringing and is significantly called by him Jedidiah. Of him the writer, otherwise so reticent in giving his own judgements, testifies that "Yahweh loved him." Sapienti sat! The expert knows best! For the time being, however, this hint recedes in the face of the rejoicing at the conquest of Rabbah of the Ammonites. Solomon disappears once more into the backdrop, whence he had come for a short moment.

Two other sons, Amnon and Absalom, and the sister of the latter as well, now occupy our attention. Amnon's unbridled passion precipitates his own downfall as well as that of Tamar, his half-sister, and drives Absalom, the avenger of his sister's honour, into exile in Geshur as a fratricide. This means that two further sons of David who would have been eligible for the succession leave the scene, the one for ever and the other for several years. Eventually, on Joab's instigation, the wise woman of Tekoa is successful in persuading David to recall Absalom, pointing out that it is necessary to secure the continuation of the family line. The reconciliation between father and son does not come about, however, until years later.

And now the ambitious prince takes for himself a chariot with riders and runners, and, slowly but surely, he begins his task of subversion. The people's discontent with the growing influence of the royal jurisdiction and with shortcomings which perhaps existed give him his opportunity and at the same time a favourable soil for his evil seed. Then, after four years' preparation, he takes to armed rebellion, totally surprising the king who had guessed nothing and forcing him to take flight immediately. The tension is increased anew. Will the divine oracle delivered by Nathan be fulfilled in this way, by uprising and rebellion? And what about Solomon whom Yahweh loves?

At first the disloyal son seems to be getting the upper hand. In sharpest contrast to him is depicted the loyalty of

David's servants and especially that of the alien mercenary captain, Ittai of Gath. The ark, brought by the priests who were also fleeing the city, is sent back and the two sons of Zadok are appointed as couriers to bring the king news of the events in Jerusalem. The first ray of light! And it is soon followed by a second! At the place of prayer on top of the Mount of Olives the fugitive king meets Hushai the Archite. He sends him back into the city to offer his services to the new king in order to foil the feared advice of Ahithophel who had thrown in his lot with Absalom's party. But now Ziba comes with the bad tidings that Meribaal, his master, hopes anew for the Israelite crown. He himself brings food, drink and asses for the fugitives. Their flight continues through Benjaminite territory. Shimei ben Gera comes out from Bahurim and insults David, at the same time confirming Ziba's report of his master's expectations or at least showing it to be plausible. This narrative strand now breaks off with the king in the direst straits, fleeing his own son, insulted by his opponents, deserted.

Absalom enters Jerusalem. Hushai, suspiciously talkative, forces himself on him. Two discussions then follow. First, Ahithophel is asked about the measures to be taken next; in mean rancour, he sees the most important thing as being the violating of the ten concubines left behind by David. He then asks Absalom for 10,000 men to pursue the king. If this were granted it would mean the downfall of David. The tension now reaches it highest point. But now Absalom has the fateful idea of asking Hushai for advice, which the latter proceeds to offer with gushing eloquence. Absalom follows the traitor's advice: "And Yahweh had ordained to defeat the good counsel of Ahithophel, so that Yahweh might bring evil upon Absalom." The turning point is reached, the climax passed. It is typical of the narrator that he should use a speech to relate the decision.

Absalom's fate is soon realized. Hushai dispatches the couriers. In the light of their news David crosses the Jordan. On the eastern bank, in Mahanaim, he gets support from, among others, Meribaal's former host, Machir ben Ammiel, from the son of his former enemy, Shobi ben Nahash, and from Barzillai. He musters his troops and has them move against his disloyal son under the leadership of Joab. Absalom's downfall, begun with that conflict of words, is sealed by the battle. The king bursts into a wild lamentation as he receives the confirmation of his son's death and it is only after Joab's reprimand that he decides to review the march-past of his troops.

The long deliberations about David's return to the capital do not bode well. To be sure, Shimei does ask to be pardoned and Meribaal to be excused. Their pleas are granted. Honest Barzillai insists on accompanying the king and remains in favour after Chimham goes to court in his place. But now it comes to a conflict between the Judaeans and the Israelites, leading finally to a renewed rebellion on the instigation of Sheba ben Bichri. Amasa, Absalom's general, to whom David had given Joab's position, disappears while mustering the levy and is stabbed to death by Joab. Sheba, besieged in Abel beth Maacah, is killed by the inhabitants and his head is thrown to Joab. Thereby this further disruption of the Davidic realm is also overcome; but Nathan's prophecy still awaits fulfilment.

Meanwhile, the king has become old and his body lacks its necessary warmth. So, with his agreement, the beautiful Abishag is brought to him from Shunem. Adonijah then attempts to exploit the situation in order to gain what Absalom had failed to get. Joab and Abiathar belong to his party, whereas the latter's rival, Zadok, together with Nathan and Benaiah (who makes his first appearance here - he is probably still a young man), are supporters of Solomon. Nathan brings to Bathsheba, Solomon's mother, the news of the sacrificial meal given by Adonijah to his supporters at the Serpent's Stone and challenges her to force the old king to make a decision in favour of her son. He assures her of his assistance in doing this. The plan succeeds. David names Solomon as his successor and has him anointed as king at once. Adonijah's meal comes to an abrupt end. He himself flees to the altar and then receives a curt order to return home, hardly a good omen. David, feeling his end to be near, gives his successor various instructions concerning the rewarding and punishing of certain individuals. He then dies.

And now Adonijah desires Abishag as his wife and enlists the help of Bathsheba. Of course, David had had nothing to do with her, but as a part of the harem she is the property of his successor. Solomon regards this as an attempt on his throne and has Adonijah killed. He exiles Adonijah's follower, Abiathar, to Anathoth, and Joab, getting wind of this and fleeing to the altar, is stabbed to death in the sanctuary. Shimei's movements are put under restriction for reasons which are no longer clear and when he contravenes this he is executed without further ado. With this the kingship of Solomon is secured from within, the question of the succession solved and the narrative brought to an end.

It cannot be gainsaid that we have a quite outstanding piece of Hebrew narrative art here, perhaps, indeed, in the complexity of its plot, in the wealth of personalities taking part and in the fine organization of its structure, the most outstanding of all. It is splendid how the narrator lets the main theme be heard right at the beginning in II Sam 6.23 and never again loses touch with it. Moreover everything is subordinated to the theme, without indeed ever mentioning it expressis verbis until immediately before the end. He loves hinting at the future developments by means of occasional leitmotifs whose significance does not become clear until much later. Consider, for example, the remarkable sentence in II Sam 12.24: "And Yahweh loved him"; or I Kgs 1.4: "But the king knew her not"; or I Kgs 1.53: "Go to your house." Only once does he deviate from his habit and anticipate the development, in II Sam 14.17: "And Yahweh ordained to defeat Ahithophel's good counsel, so that Yahweh might bring evil upon Absalom." But this is also a turning point and climax in the narrative vastly more serious than any other occurring either previously or subsequently, and so it is understandable that the narrator should put aside his reserve and pass his own judgement.

The artistic skill in the structure is especially shown in the manner by which people are introduced, keep intervening in the plot, and finally leave the stage. Of the main characters, only David lacks proper introduction, is left without "kunya or nisbe" - without family name or genealogy.[24] Even the secondary characters are for the most part introduced fully. Only seldom does a minor role remain unnamed, as in the case of the maid in II Sam 17.17. All the main characters and most of the secondary characters also make a corresponding exit. Usually their fortunes are recounted until their death, as with David, Amnon, Absalom, Adonijah, Joab, Shimei, Amasa and Ahithophel, or until they leave the scene, as with Abiathar, or until they reach their zenith, as with Solomon. Between their introduction and their exit, however, they interact with great liveliness and excitement, sometimes in concert with each other, sometimes against each other. Especially in I Kgs 1[25] the characters crowd together to form a brilliant final tableau which is extended and balanced somewhat by chapter 2.[26] They are people full of life, people who can love and hate, who rejoice and mourn, who murder in cold blood and fervently fear and pray for the life of somebody else.

Here we find something which was hardly attempted in the

ark narrative, namely, the depiction of character. It is not only in the case of main actors, like David, for example, whose character, driven to and fro by barely controlled moods, is excellently portrayed. He is, incidentally, also the one who most often refers to the divine background of human action and interaction - indeed he is almost the only one who does so. True piety and strong sensuality, weakness with people he loves and strength in adverse circumstances, winning magnanimity and burning hatred, all struggle for his soul; a sense of reality, an eye for what is possible and a calculating acuteness characterize him. Against this there are his sons: the unrestrained, sensual Amnon, the ruthless, ambitious and cunning Absalom, Adonijah eager for success, the calculating, merciless Solomon. It is as if the sons were to develop without any restraint the bad characteristics which, in their father's case, had been held in check by the good ones - to be destroyed by them.

In contrast there is Bathsheba, more used than using, the energetic Nathan, the blindly devoted Benaiah, the ambiguous Meribaal, the two-faced Ziba and others as well.

We should stop here for a moment and show how splendidly Hushai the Archite is portrayed. It is a real masterstroke. With what talkativeness, which could only hide a bad conscience, does he try to insinuate himself into Absalom's confidence! How exquisite the "firstly" and "secondly" in 16.18f.! What a torrent of words meets us in the sentence: "Whom the Lord and this people and all the men of Israel have chosen, his I will be, and with him I will remain." And his advice does not come till chapter 17! What an abundance of words, what a wealth of phrases, what rich imagery and what exaggeration! A splendid garment, designed to hide his nakedness! The attempt to change a bad situation into a better one! That is the first impression. We would be tempted to make a harsh judgement if every word did not speak of his fear for David and the wish to help him. It is the words of a friend who, out of his love, takes on the unhappy role of deceiving someone else in order to save his friend.

The whole succession story reveals itself to be a lively extract from an eventful period. With the greatest skill and conscious planning, the characters are balanced against each other, their appearances determined, their actions linked one with another and connected with the major theme, the succession to David.

However, the very artistry of this construction is what brings us now to the question of whether we have here real history[27] or merely the play of fancy, whether we have fact or fiction. This question is not easy to decide. On the one hand, it must be granted that everything gives an impression of probability and realism, so much so that one would most like to maintain that long stretches of the narrative come from immediate eye-witnesses. On the other hand, the possibility cannot altogether be rejected that a writer of particular sensitivity created this work with no too great consideration for the actual events. This latter possibility is supported by the fact that the whole dramatic structure is based on dialogue, by the artistic arrangement of the individual scenes, and by the internal consistency and the fine rounding-off of the whole complex. The first possibility is made more likely by his use of the Ammonite war report which is by no means an artistic construction, by the tale of David's adultery with Bathsheba, and generally by the role which David plays here. It can hardly be assumed that somebody would later have dared to expose David in this way without sound evidence. The most probable explanation is that real historical facts are related here, but in a strongly stylized dress. Fact and fiction join hands in this succession narrative as in every work of an artistically sensitive historiographer. The task of defining which is which in particular cases and separating them out is one for a study of the history of David. For our purposes, it is sufficient to establish that this source is an historical narrative which rushes along with the excitement of a drama; it is based on actual events; it does not provide us simply with a poor imitation of reality but groups the events together around a theme, adopting them only so far and in such form as they are relevant to the basic questions of the story.

We have thus come far enough to approach the question of the writer - when he wrote and what kind of person he was. According to our earlier discussion, the terminus post quem should be regarded as the period in which the ark narrative, the account of the Ammonite war, and the oldest stratum in II Sam 7.8ff. were already in existence (even if the latter does not come from our narrator himself). These three pieces must belong to the early monarchic period, with the account of the Ammonite war, certainly, and the ark narrative, probably, attributable to the time of David. The succession story, however, could not have been written under David because it includes the first years of Solomon (at least three, according to I Kgs 2.39) as well. On the other hand it is hardly likely that the story came into being much later. Even though the tensions between the northern and southern tribes are apparent and Sheba ben Bichri is to be regarded to a certain extent as a precursor of Jeroboam, the reason for the strife - the wish to be associated with the royal household as closely as possible - is still not the same as that at the actual division of the kingdom where the issue was the aspiration to be freed from the burden of the Judaean kings. If the final rupture between the northern and southern kingdoms were already a fact of past history, the narrator would hardly have failed to stress more strongly (and perhaps even to deplore) as a prelude to future dissolution what here in his story is rated as no more than an episode and a temporary emergency, howbeit a serious one. Further, the conclusion in 2.46 gives the impression of such comfortable peace and security that there is no trace of the later upheavals which plagued David's kingdom towards the end of Solomon's reign. The most likely possibility, therefore, is the beginning of the Solomonic period.

But who was the author? Since Klostermann, people have often been concerned with him and his name. At all events what is certain is that he was a member of the royal court.[28] But whether he was Ahimaaz, as Klostermann maintains, or Abiathar, as has often been accepted since Duhm, cannot clearly be established. Good reasons can be advanced in favour of either of them. However, it does seem that an old source concerning David's rise to power finishes in II Sam 5.10 and, further, that in this narrative, in marked contrast to the succession story, Abiathar plays an important role as the constant companion of David and as the ephod-bearer. If this observation is correct, then it is likely that if any work must be ascribed to Abiathar's authorship it would be that former source. On the other hand, the succession story, in my opinion, was written despite everything else "in majorem gloriam Salomonis" - to the greater glory of Solomon.[29] The words: "Yahweh loved him" and then the speeches of David and Benaiah at his accession to the throne require this conclusion. Such goodwill, violating the limits of objectivity more than one wishes to admit, could hardly be attributed to Abiathar. Ahimaaz is far more likely. He is without doubt identical with the official in Naphthali, the son-in-law of Solomon (I Kgs 4.15). This would at least explain why the view of history as religious edification recedes markedly into the background along with the manifestations of piety in terms of the cult and oracular consultation with Yahweh; it would also explain the strong courtly influence revealed in the large number of submissive expressions of humility. Perhaps it is altogether futile to ask whether Abiathar or Ahimaaz wrote the succession story. It could just as well have been some other person who is no longer apparent, but who had a connection with court circles. In the end it is simply an argument about names which cannot change the fact that the author is one of the best narrators in the Hebrew language.[30]

Looking now at the succession story's yield for our picture of the theological outlook and the religious devotion of the early monarchy, we notice especially that only in three places (II Sam 11.27; 12.24; 17.14) does the narrator offer a judgement concerning the relationship between events on earth, on the one hand, and God's feelings and the exercises of his will, on the other. Otherwise he retires with his own opinion behind his work by placing judgements of this kind in the mouths of the characters taking part. From this and especially from the fact that there is no miraculous intervention by Yahweh, we can conclude that God's activity in history was a greater miracle for the writer than the individual miracle stories of which there was certainly no lack in that period. That and how God operates in the lives of individuals and in the fortunes of nations was for him the real miracle. And he tells us about it, without constant reference and demonstration, in such a way that the listener or reader can do nothing other than see this miracle and contemplate it with reverence. One might almost even see something of the Enlightenment's belief in providence in this work, were not the events here too potent, too sublime for this dull idea. A certain reticence with regard to the religious outlook of the people is unmistakeable. We need only think of the way in which the ark is mentioned (II Sam 11.11; 15.24ff.), or of how Ahithophel's advice is regarded as having the same value as an oracle from God. The contrast with the ark narrative or with the Abiathar source which finishes in II Sam 5.10, can clearly be discerned.[31]

If the narrator only detains us a very short time with his own opinions, so all the more does he let the characters taking part in his work say what they think on the question of the relationship between God's activity and human behaviour. Yahweh is the God of the king (II Sam 14.11, 17; 18.28; I Kgs 1.17), but also the God of Israel (I Kgs 1.30, 48). Israel is his people (II Sam 14.13) and his inheritance (II Sam 14.16; 20.19). As the God of the king, Yahweh has an especially close relationship with him. He chooses him together with the people (II Sam 16.18), makes him king (I Kgs 1.48) and the Anointed One of Yahweh - to curse him, therefore, is a crime which warrants death (II Sam 19.22). Yahweh loves him, as in the case of Solomon (II Sam 12.24f.) and stands by him, especially when he is beset with difficulties (I Kgs 1.29, 37). However this close relationship with the king does not stop Yahweh from acting against him, any more than against any other person or even the whole nation, as the preserver and protector of justice and morality. Every lapse is at the same time a sin against God, guilt before God (II Sam 12.13, 14). Yahweh punishes the sinner as the highest judge (II Sam 16.5ff.; 12.14 and 15ff.) and helps the oppressed to find justice (II Sam 19.20: Shimei notes his transgression when David returns home successful; cf. further II Sam 18.19, 28, 31; 19.2). To curse and insult someone afflicted by Yahweh brings the curser no benefit and could even result in Yahweh again showing his favour to the cursed person on that very account (II Sam 16.12).[32] Yahweh can do this because he guides human fortunes (II Sam 14.14). Humankind is in his hands (II Sam 15.25f., 31). The actions of mortals are instigated and determined by him. If it be Yahweh's will, a person can sink into a grave from which it is impossible to return (II Sam 12.15, 23). Because Yahweh, in his almighty power, is at the same time both a judging and a helping God, he can pardon and exercise mercy (II Sam 12.13f.).

It befits humankind to honour Yahweh's will (II Sam 16.10f.; 15.25f.). It is the king's particular concern as the מלאך יהוה (messenger/angel of Yahweh) to administer proper justice, like Yahweh's (II Sam 14.17, 20; 19.28). For that reason he should allow mercy to have the upper hand, out of fear of Yahweh (II Sam 14.11, 17),[33] for showing pity is divine (II Sam 9.3). Because the king in his role as judge represents God, people can swear by him (II Sam 11.11; 15.21) just as they would swear by Yahweh (II Sam 12.5; 14.11; 15.21; 19.8, 14; I Kgs 1.17, 29, 30). Blessing and cursing, wishing another person good or evil, and even wishing evil upon one's self (cf. II Sam 14.7ff.), can only be done in the name of Yahweh.[34]

Alongside moral behaviour towards one's neighbours in accordance with Yahweh's laws, there are also cultic services to be rendered - sometime used as a means of influencing Yahweh, sometimes without any selfish motives but from thankfulness. One falls down before Yahweh (12.20), prays, fasts, lies on the earth (II Sam 12.16), weeps (12.22), and refrains from putting oil on one's head (12.20); one offers sacrifice (II Sam 15.24); one undertakes vows (II Sam 15.7ff.), to make sacrifice, for instance - this is particularly so when going to foreign parts, for there no proper worship is possible (cf. here I Sam 26.19; II Kgs 5.17), but only within Yahweh's inheritance; and even here there are preferred places of prayer (II Sam 15.32). The ark is named as a cult object (II Sam 11.11; 15.24), which is sometimes taken into battle (II Sam 11.11), but which normally remains in the holy tent (I Kgs 1.39). The altar has been given a special status: it has been made with horns and provides an asylum (I Kgs 1.50ff.; 2.28f.). As a means of obtaining divine information about the future, the oracle of Yahweh was consulted (II Sam 16.23). The funeral customs also belong here because of their religious origin. People put on mourning; they no longer anoint themselves with oil (2 Sam 14.2), nor wash their feet, beards and clothes (II Sam 19.25); they rip their garments, throw ashes on their heads, put their hands on their heads and shout loudly (II Sam 13.15, cf. also 13.31, 36). The dead are buried in the family grave with their parents (II Sam 19.38; I Kgs 2.34) and in this respect even the suicide does not make an exception (II Sam 17.23).

More than anything else Yahweh is the powerful guardian of the moral law and thus religious devotion is primarily a matter of submission to God's will conditioned by the feeling of human weakness and powerlessness (II Sam 11.25; 12.23; 16.10ff.). Joy in Yahweh and hope in his saving grace are traits which recede totally into the background in this wordly piety. Religious devotion has its effect outwards in moral and cultic behaviour.

Turning finally to the question of how the narrator depicts Yahweh's intervention, it is clear that, except for sending the prophet Nathan in 12.1ff. and afflicting the baby with a fatal illness (12.15ff.), he works only in and through secondary causes. Nowhere does he intervene with a miracle, nor influence human events with oracles and prophecies. It is the secondary causes which Yahweh uses to give effect to his thoughts and to bring his plans into being. Humankind therefore has no need to consult Yahweh, as in the Abiathar source for example, but only to do whatever task Yahweh requires for the moment. Yahweh reveals himself in the course of events. His intervention is indirect.

Our narrator thus occupies a special position, contrasting with others who scrupulously place Yahweh's intervention in the foreground and stress it - as in the ark narrative, for example, especially in I Sam 5 and II Sam 6 - or who cannot have enough of accounts of dreams, revelations, the granting of oracles, the sending of prophets and men of God, of angels and spirits. He shows us how to regard human fortunes, in their simple course of passion and sorrow, as having a divine dimension, and challenges us to follow God's tracks in history. That is his mission.

The previous discussions should have demonstrated that in the succession story we have a self-contained production - that its stylistic and formal characteristics prove it to be uniform, and that the structure of the whole complex shows it to be self-contained. The same ideas run through the whole narrative. There is no need to look for something else beyond the framework provided. All characters, with the single exception of David, are appropriately introduced. They all have an appropriate exit.

Nevertheless, it could still be possible that we have here no more than a particularly unified and well-rounded part of a larger whole. This possibility should now be dealt with as follows.

If it were the case that the succession story was only a part of a larger work, there would be three feasible possibilities: 1) the whole work might have been preserved for us; 2) just separate parts and fragments might have been transmitted in addition to the section already discussed; 3) the succession story might have been the only section received into the historical books, in which case everything else, on the other hand, would have been suppressed or lost.

With regard to the first possibility, our story would need to have been preceded by accounts of David's earlier exploits and experiences, so, for instance, with his rise to power as king of Judah and Israel. In fact, there is, of course, an account of these events in the great king's life in I and II Samuel. The most important part includes the following passages: I Sam 23.1-13; 27.1-28.2; 29.1-30.26; II Sam 1.1; 2.4a; 3.20-29; 3.31-37; 4.1a; 4.5-12; 5.3; 5.17-25 (ch. 8?). An investigation of these extracts shows that they provide, without a gap, a continuous depiction of David's condition while on the run from Saul and of the events which led to his ruling over Judah and Israel and to the conquest of Jerusalem. The succession narrative, however, assumes David's residence in Jerusalem and begins with events most likely to belong early in David's Jerusalem period, as for example the Michal scene in II Sam 6.16, 20ff. This would imply that we should take both these major narrative strands together as a diptych. David becoming Saul's successor after numerous changes in fortune would constitute one side, and the other would be Solomon becoming David's successor despite all obstructions.

At first sight this view is somewhat tempting, especially as the parallels can even be extended to include details of David's succession and that of Solomon. Nevertheless, it is not feasible to take them together, for style and structure and finally also the narrator's attitude to the cult are different in both sources.

It was shown above that the speeches in the succession narrative are often constructed as inclusios with the pattern a-b-a. In the whole of the section in question there are no speeches constructed in this way. It was also established as particularly characteristic of the succession story that the individual scene concentrates and crystallizes around a conversation, a dialogue, which is its focal point. This is so pervasive that the narrative as a whole gives the impression of simply resulting from a series of juxtaposed dialogues, which were joined together by means of incidental remarks describing the situation. In the earlier David story we can see hardly anything of this dominating and creative power of direct speech. Certainly dialogue is common - a comparison with the ark narrative is proof enough of this - and even relatively long exchanges of conversation do develop; but these do not dominate the narrative. On the contrary, they have been completely accommodated to the narrative flow. They have no descriptive or dramatic effect. They are not kernels of crystallization, forming and shaping the surrounding material according to their own rules, but they remain amorphous like their context. Thus the narrative style here keeps to the middle between that of the ark narrative or of the Ammonite war report, on the one hand, and that of the succession story, on the other. One need only compare I Sam 4 (ark narrative) and II Sam 18 (succession story) with I Sam 30. Further, the speeches in the David narrative lack the brevity and power which characterize those of the succession story. In the latter, it is a question of true-to-life dialogues with quick change of speaker; in the former, people make contrived speeches, like Achish and David in chapter 29 or David in 30.23f.

There is also another factor. In the succession story everything which had to do with the cult receded somewhat into the background. Only from a chance remark do we learn that the ark was brought into the battlefield. Equally incidental is the imparting of the information that David met Hushai the Archite at the place where he used to pray

(15.32). And the remark that Ahithophel's advice was esteemed as being comparable to the consultation of Yahweh's oracle demonstrates quite clearly enough that the narrator did not think very much of such doings.

It is a different picture in the chapters which are our present concern. That the cult is in the foreground cannot be maintained, of course, but it does still provide a constant undertone which resonates everywhere. Admittedly, in the main it is only one form of cultic activity which is mentioned frequently, namely the consultation of Yahweh by means of the ephod operated by the priest, Abiathar (I Sam 30.7). We meet this method of attempting to get an indication of God's will no less than seven times (I Sam 23.2, 4, 9ff.; 30.7ff.; II Sam 2.1; 5.19, 23). In this case, to speak of coincidence does not seem possible. It has to be allowed that the consultation of Yahweh represents an important factor in the development of the story of David. David makes use of it at decisive moments: on the march to Keilah and also when in the town, concerning Saul's progress; when pursuing the Amelekites, on the return to Jerusalem, in the Philistine wars.

Now we could assume, of course, that David's own opinion about consulting Yahweh changed in the course of his life. The fact that the priests with their oracles from Yahweh retire behind the prophets who speak in the name of Yahweh without even being asked, seems to support such a change in David's attitude. Perhaps we could even venture the rather bold assertion that a writer of the Davidic period not only might have noticed this change in David's attitude but also wanted to express it in his work. If this were so, however, it would have been necessary for him at least to record in some form or another the transition from the one position to the other. And this is not the case. On the contrary, both views stand directly adjacent to each other, the more remarkably so, since we might have expected the priests of the ark and especially Abiathar, who came from Eli's family, to have gained more influence over David after the solemn entrance of the ark into Jerusalem.[35]

However, even if we had been successful in showing from this the possibility of bringing the two narratives together, it would by no means eradicate the stylistic and formal differences already established. These differences require us to separate the two narratives. Only in this way can we explain easily why the oracular consultation of Yahweh plays a large part in the story of David's rise, yet is alluded to only in a simile in the succession narrative. The difference is to be

111

accounted for by separate authorship.

If this means that the David story has nothing to do with the succession story, then every possibility is dashed of finding a connected story preliminary to the succession story. Yet even less prospect of success confronts the task of finding a connected sequel to the story. As already shown above, I Kgs 3 is followed by a description, full of examples, of Solomon's wealth and wisdom.

We should thus give up hope of linking the succession story to a larger complex handed down to us, so that it only remains for us to try to find any fragments of material which might have belonged, together with the succession story, to some other, now lost, larger whole. It will be sufficient to restrict the investigation to the Books of Samuel and the First Book of Kings. In doing this we will disregard from the start a large number of available accounts, either because at the very first glance their style and form give away their different origin, or because their fundamental outlook on life differs too much from that of the succession story.

Thus, at the most, the following chapters from the Books of Samuel come into consideration: I Sam 9; 10.1-16; 11.1-11; 15.25. [= 11.1-11, 15; 25? or 11.1-11; 15; 25? - Ed.]

A careful examination of these narratives, however, shows that their style and mode of presentation differ too much from those of the succession story for us seriously to think of them as originally belonging together. Characteristic details like the speech pattern (a-b-a) and the rounded-off scenes are totally lacking. And this is what the question really hangs on. For after all, many people can tell a story vividly and a single person can also do it in several ways. But it is out of the question that within one continuous narrative there would be such changes in the literary techniques used to present the material, that major parts of a work would receive their characteristic features through these literary techniques, whereas other parts would show not even the slightest trace of them. Thus it is impossible to find fragments in the Books of Samuel which could perhaps have belonged with the succession story in some larger work.

In I Kings we come across only one story which can be enlisted for comparison, namely the account in I Kgs 12.1-19 of the division of the kingdom at the assembly at Shechem.

Many similarities can be demonstrated here. There are alternative counsels offered and the worse one is chosen, as in II Sam 17. In v. 15, just as in II Sam 17.14, this wrong choice is revealed to be the will of God. The verse provoking the secession is the same as in II Sam 20.1. The delineation of scenes is as unmistakeable here as in the succession story. But the a-b-a speech pattern is not to be found in I Kgs 12. This warns us to be careful. And, indeed, closer examination shows the author of I Kgs 12 to follow different rules of form, which are recognized in the succession story only in I Kgs 1 whereas here they dominate and condition everything. Looking at I Kgs 1 the constantly recurring basic idea is straightway obvious: "Who should be king after you and who will sit on your throne?" Here in I Kgs 12 we have another: "Your father made our yoke too heavy; now, therefore, make the hard service and the hard yoke lighter."

There is a similarity so far between the two. But what is only a resonance in the speeches of I Kgs 1, constitutes the total content of those in I Kgs 12; and what hugs the form of the speeches in I Kgs 1 (and here especially, the speeches are excellent examples of the a-b-a pattern found in the succession story), in I Kgs 12 determines the form so much that we are almost reminded of the strophic structures and antiphon which David Heinrich Müller has identified in the prophets, cuneiform inscriptions, and the Koran.[36] Intensifying the formal structure confines the content.

This fashioning of the material into three sections of almost equal length, skilfully related to one another, shows clearly enough that we are dealing here with a rather small but nonetheless self-contained narrative which has about it something of the character of a pamphlet designed to spread the news of Rehoboam's behaviour at the assembly at Shechem to the furthest parts of northern Israel. It would be difficult to accept that this finely structured report were a part of a larger whole. It would be even more difficult to connect it to the succession narrative. There is, indeed, a certain similarity in the theme inasmuch as it is in both cases a question of succession, which can be further defined as being "of" or "to" Solomon; but otherwise there is no connection. One reason for this is that the succession story comes to a definite conclusion in I Kgs 2.46; a second is that there is nothing in I Kgs 12 which ties it to the earlier story - there is nothing even which in any way assumes the events of this story (apart, of course, from the fact of Solomon's reign).

Accordingly, we must give up as hopeless any attempt to establish a relationship between I Kgs 12 and the succession story. The similarity can be explained by the author of I Kgs 12 having the succession story to hand. Indeed, the view might even be expressed that if Ahimaaz ben Zadok is the author of the succession story, he may have been among the elders who served under Solomon, Rehoboam's father, and in this capacity may have been present at the unfortunate assembly at Shechem. If he could come into consideration as the author of our chapter then its dependence on the succession story and its comparatively elaborate form would be comprehensible.[37] Be that as it may, one thing is certain: I Kgs 12 cannot be regarded as part of a larger work including the succession story.

This also means that the final possibility of pointing to the existence of such a work also disappears. Ignoring the improbable suggestion that from the larger work the succession story alone was saved for posterity, we have no choice but to regard the succession narrative as an integrated, self-contained story. Thus we come to the same result in this present investigation of the surrounding material as we did when looking at the story itself.

It is quite obvious that this conclusion is not exactly suited to support the thesis which Hölscher and Eissfeldt adopt from Cornill and Budde, that the Yahwist and Elohist are to be regarded as the main sources in the Books of Samuel and even in the Books of Kings.[38] That view would accord them the status of mere collectors, stringing together narratives already available in fixed form, which is a role very different from that in the Hexateuch. This is quite improbable given the generally recognized creative ability of both writers. Absolute certainty as to whether there might not be a Yahwistic or Elohistic fragment here or there, could of course only be given by a stylistic examination of both strands of tradition in the Hexateuch, and we do not have the room for that here.

CONCLUSION

ow we are at an end. The finest work of Hebrew narrative art has passed before our eyes. Our task has been to isolate it and determine its limits, to study its style and structure, its historical trustworthiness, and its contribution to our knowledge of the theological outlook and religious devotion of the early monarchic period.

As a preliminary step we looked at the subsidiary sources used by the narrator: the ark narrative, Nathan's prophecy, the account of the Ammonite war, all three the products of the closing stages of the Davidic period and each having in some respect a surprising individuality. In this first blossoming of Hebrew literature we see with some amazement a series of authors fighting to carry off the laurels; and so we are afforded remarkable insight into the richly varied climate of contemporary religious thought.

Alongside the narrator of the ark source, a plain and popular storyteller with a fondness for edification and a piety strongly conditioned by the cult, there are the authors of the oldest strata of Nathan's prophecy with their deep interest in the royal house of David and their humble piety. The sober, factual account of the Ammonite war gives us a glimpse into the heart of a godfearing soldier, while the artistically structured story of the succession shows us a member of the court who views cultic life with a certain reserve and recognizes God at work in the normal course of history.

This, of course, hardly completes the picture of literary activity in the Davidic and Solomonic epochs, for the Abiathar source also belongs to the period and some individual fragments as well (such as David's last words, perhaps the Solomon story, too, and works available to the Yahwist). Only by examining these and taking them into account could we have a complete picture of the literary creativity of the early monarchic period. That, however, is a task well beyond the scope of the present undertaking.

APPENDIX · NOTES
BIBLIOGRAPHY·ETC

APPENDIX

THE VOCABULARY OF THE ARK NARRATIVE
[See pp. 13f.]

אבל   Hithp. I Sam 6.19.
Elsewhere in Sam: I Sam 15.35; 16.1; II Sam 13.37; 14.2 twice; 19.2.
Further in: Gen 37.34; Exod 33.4; Num 14.39; Isa 66.10; Ezek 7.12,
27; Dan 10.2; Neh 1.4; 8.9; Ezra 10.6; I Chr 7.22; II Chr 35.24.

אדיר   I Sam 4.8.
Further in: Exod 15.10; Jud 5.13, 25 (Song of Deborah); Isa 10.34;
33.21; Jer 14.3; 25.34ff.; 30.21; Ezek 17.23; 32.18; Nah 2.6; 3.18;
Zech 11.2; Ps 8.2, 10; 16.3; 76.5; 93.4 twice; 136.18; Neh 3.3; 10.30;
II Chr 23.20.

אחרנית   I Sam 4.18.
Further in: Gen 9.23 twice; I Kgs 18.37; II Kgs 20.10, 11; Isa 38.8.

אצל   I Sam 5.2.
Elsewhere in Sam: I Sam 17.30; 20.19, 41.
Further in: Gen 39.10, 16; 41.3; Lev 1.16; 6.3; 10.12; Deut 11.30;
16.21; Jud 19.14; I Kgs 1.9; 2.29; 3.20; 4.12; 10.19; 13.24 twice, 25,
28, 31; 21.1, 2; II Kgs 12.10; Isa 19.19; Jer 35.4; 41.17; Ezek 1.15, 19;
9.2; 10.6, 9, 16 twice; 33.30; 39.15; 40.7; 43.6, 8; Amos 2.8; Prov 7.8,
12; 8.30; Dan 8.7, 17; Neh 2.6; 3.23, 35; 4.6, 12; 8.4; II Chr 9.18;
28.15.

אתמל שלשם   I Sam 4.7.
Elsewhere in Sam: I Sam 10.11; 14.21; 19.7; II Sam 5.2. תמל שלשם in
Sam: I Sam 21.6; II Sam 3.17.
Further in: Gen 31.2, 5; Exod 4.10; 5.7, 8, 14; 21.29, 36; Deut 4.42;
19.4, 6; Jos 3.4; 4.18; 20.5; II Kgs 13.5.

בקע   Piel: I Sam 6.14.
Further in: Gen 22.3; II Kgs 2.24; 15.16; Isa 59.5; Ezek 13.11, 13; Hos
13.8; Hab 3.9; Ps 78.15.

בשׂר   Piel: I Sam 4.17.
Elsewhere in Sam: I Sam 31.9; (// I Chr 10.9); II Sam 1.20; 4.10;
18.19, 20 twice, 26.
Further in: I Kgs 1.42; Isa 40.9; 41.27; 52.7; 60.6; 61.1; Jer 20.15;
Nah 2.1; Ps 40.10; 68.12; 96.2; I Chr 16.23.

גבול   I Sam 6.12 (5.6; 6.9).
Elsewhere in Sam: I Sam 7.13, 14; 10.2; 11.3, 7; 13.18(?); 27.1; II Sam
21.5.
Further in: I Kgs 1.3; 5.1; II Kgs five times; in the Pentateuch: J six
times; E eleven times; P nine times; Book of the Covenant once; Rd.
once; D five times; sec. in Deut eight times. In Jos: E(?) once; J
once; P fifty-three times; Rd. nine times. In Jud: J twice; He. five
times. Isa 5.8; 19.19; 60.18; Jer 5.22; 15.13; 17.3; 31.16; Ezek 11.10,
11; 27.4; 29.10; chaps. 40-48 thirty-one times; Hos 5.10; Joel 4.6;
Amos 1.13; 6.2 twice; Obad 7; Mi 5.5; Zeph 2.8; Mal 1.4; Ps 78.54;
104.9; 105.31, 33; Prov 15.25; 22.28; 23.10; Job 38.20; I Chr 4.10;

6.39, 51; 21.12; II Chr 9.26; 11.13.

גלה I Sam 4.21 (22)
Elsewhere in Sam: II Sam 15.19.
Further in: Jud 18.30; II Kgs 15.29; 16.9; 17.6, 11, 23, 27, 28, 33; 18.11; 24.14, 15; 25.11, 21; Isa 5.13; 24.11; 38.12; 49.21; Jer 1.3; 13.19; 20.4; 22.12; 24.1; 27.20; 29.1, 4, 7, 14; 39.9; 40.1, 7; 43.3; 52.15, 27, 28, 30, 31; Ezek 12.3 twice; 39.23, 28; Hos 10.5; Amos 1.5, 6; 5.5 twice, 27; 6.7 twice; 7.11 twice, 17 twice; Mic 1.16; Job 20.28; Lam 1.3; 4.22; Esth 2.6 twice; Ezr 2.1; Neh 7.6; I Chr 5.26; 8.6(?), 7(?); 9.1; II Chr 36.20.

געה I Sam 6.12.
Further in: Job 6.5.

דרך Qal I Sam 5.5.
Further in: Num 24.17; Deut 1.36; 11.24, 25; Jos 1.3; 14.9; Jud 9.27; 20.43; Isa 5.28; 16.10 twice; 21.15: 59.8; 63.2, 3 twice; Jer 25.30; 46.9; 48.33; 50.14, 29; 51.3 twice; Amos 4.13; 9.13; Mic 1.3; 5.4, 5; 6.15; Hab 3.15; Zech 9.13; Ps 7.13; 37.14; 58.8; 64.4; Job 9.8; 22.15; 24.11; Lam 1.15; 2.4; 3.12; Neh 13.15; I Chr 5.18; 8.40; II Chr 14.7.

הום Niph I Sam 4.5.
Further in: I Kgs 1.45; Ruth 1.19. Qal Deut 7.23. Hiph Mich 2.12; Ps 55.3.

מהומה I Sam 5.9, 11.
Elsewhere in Sam: I Sam 14.20.
Futher in: Deut 7.23; 28.20; Isa 22.5; Ezek 7.7; 22.5; Amos 3.9; Zech 14.13; Prov 15.16; II Chr 15.5.

המון I Sam 4.14; II Sam 6.19.
Elsewhere in Sam: I Sam 14.6, 19; II Sam 18.29.
Further in: Gen 17.4, 5; Jud 4.7; I Kgs 18.41; 20.13, 28; II Kgs 7.13 twice; Isa 5.13, 14; 13.14; 16.14; 17.12; 29.5, 7, 8; 31.4; 32.14; 33.3; 60.5; 63.15; Jer 3.23; 10.13; 47.3; 49.32; 51.16, 42; Ezek 7.11, 12, 13, 14; 23.42; 26.13; 29.19; 30.4, 10, 15; 31.2, 18; 32.12, 16, 18, 20, 24, 25, 26, 31, 32; 39.11 twice, 15; Joel 4.14; Amos 5.23; Ps 37.16; 42.5; 65.8; Job 31.34; 39.7; Eccl 5.9; Dan 10.6; 11.10 twice, 11, 12, 13; I Chr 29.16; II Chr 11.23; 13.8; 14.10; 20.2, 12, 15, 24; 31.10; 32.7.

הפך Niph I Sam 4.19.
Elsewhere in Sam: I Sam 10.6.
Further in: Exod 7.15, 17, 20; 14.5; Lev 13.16, 17, 25; Jos 8.20; Isa 34.9; 60.5; 63.10; Jer 2.21; 30.6; Ezek 4.8; Hos 11.8; Joel 3.4; Jon 3.4; Ps 32.4; 78.57; Prov 17.20; Job 19.19; 20.14; 28.5; 30.21; 41.20; Lam 1.20; 5.2, 15; Esth 9.1, 22; Dan 10.8, 16.

חם I Sam 4.19 (21).
Further in: Gen 38.13, 25.

חרד I Sam 4.13.
Further in: Jud 7.3; Isa 66.2, 5; Ezr 9.4; 10.3.

יצג Hiph I Sam 5.2; II Sam 6.17 (// I Chr 16.1).
Further in: Gen 30.38; 33.15; 43.9; Exod 10.24; Deut 28.56; Jud 6.37; 7.5; 8.27; Jer 51.34; Hos 2.5; Amos 5.15.

ישר Qal I Sam 6.12(?).
Elsewhere in Sam: I Sam 18.20, 26; II Sam 17.4.
Further in: Num 23.27; Jud 14.3, 7; I Kgs 9.12; Jer 18.4; 27.5; Hab 2.4; I Chr 12.4; II Chr 30.4.

כלה I Sam 6.10.
Elsewhere in Sam: I Sam 25.33.
Further in: Gen 8.2; 23.6; Exod 36.6; Isa 43.6; Jer 32.2, 3; Hag 1.10 twice; Ps 40.10, 12; 88.9; 119.101; Eccl 8.8; Dan 9.24.

כפר I Sam 6.18.
Further in: Cant 7.12; Neh 6.2(?); I Chr 27.25.

כפות (palm of the hand, sole of the foot) I Sam 5.4.
Further in: Jos 3.13; 4.18; I Kgs 5.17; II Kgs 9.35; Isa 60.14; Ezek 43.7; Mal 3.21; Dan 10.10.

כרע I Sam 4.19.
Further in: Gen 49.9; Num 24.9; Jud 5.27; 7.5, 6; I Kgs 8.54; 19.18; II Kgs 1.13; 9.24; Isa 10.4; 46.1, 2; 65.12; Ps 20.9; 22.30; 72.9; 95.6; Job 4.4; 31.10; 39.3; Esth 3.2 twice, 5; Ezr 9.5.

כרת I Sam 5.4.
Elsewhere in Sam: I Sam 17.51; 24.5, 6, 12; 31.9; II Sam 10.4; 20.22.
Further in: Exod 4.25; 34.13; Num 13.23, 24; Deut 19.5; 20.19, 20; 23.2; Jud 6.25, 26, 30; 9.48, 49; I Kgs 5.20 twice; 15.13; II Kgs 18.4; 19.23; 23.14; Isa 14.8; 18.5; 37.24; Jer 6.6; 10.3; 11.19; 22.7; 34.18; 46.23; 50.16; Ezek 31.12.

מבצר I Sam 6.18.
Elsewhere in Sam: II Sam 24.7.
Further in: Num 13.19; 32.17, 36; Jos 10.20; 19.29, 35; II Kgs 3.19; 8.12; 10.2; 17.9; 18.8; Isa 17.3; 25.12; Jer 1.18; 4.5; 5.17; 6.27; 8.14; 34.7; 48.18; Hos 10.14; Amos 5.9; Mic 5.10; Nah 3.12, 14; Hab 1.10; Ps 89.41; 108.11; Lam 2.2, 5; Dan 11.24, 39; II Chr 17.19.

מדו I Sam 4.12.
Elsewhere in Sam: I Sam 17.39; 18.4; II Sam 20.8.
Further in: Lev 6.3; Jud 3.16; 5.10; Jer 13.25; Ps 109.18; Job 11.9.

מהומה See הום.

מחרת I Sam 5.3, 4.
Elsewhere in Sam: I Sam 11.11; 18.10; 20.27; 30.17; 31.8 (// I Chr 10.8); II Sam 11.12.
Further in: II Kgs 8.15; Jer 20.3; I Chr 29.21.

מפתן I Sam 5.4, 5.
Further in: Ezek 9.3; 10.4, 18; 46.2; 47.1; Zeph 1.9.

נגף Qal I Sam 4.3.
Elsewhere in Sam: I Sam 25.38; 26.10; II Sam 12.15.
Further in: Exod 7.27; 12.23, 27; 21.22, 35; 32.35; Jos 24.5; Jud 20.35; Isa 19.22 twice; Zech 14.12, 18; Ps 89.24; 91.12; Prov 3.23; II Chr 13.15, 20; 14.11; 21.14, 18.
Niphal I Sam 4.2, 10.
Elsewhere in Sam: I Sam 7.10; II Sam 2.17; 10.15 (// I Chr 19.16); 10.19 (// I Chr 19.19); 18.7.
Further in: Lev 26.17; Num 14.42; Deut 1.42; 28.7, 25; I Kgs 8.33 (// II Chr 6.24); II Kgs 14.12 (// II Chr 25.22); II Chr 20.22.

מגפה I Sam 4.17; 6.4.
Elsewhere in Sam: II Sam 17.9; 18.7; 24.21 (// I Chr 21.22), 25.
Further in: Exod 9.14; Num 14.37; 17.13, 14, 15; 25.8, 9, 18, 19; 31.16; Ezek 24.16; Zech 14.12, 15 twice, 18; Ps 106.29, 30; I Chr 21.17; II Chr 21.14.

סרנים I Sam 5.8, 11; 6.4, 12, 16, 18.
Elsewhere in Sam: I Sam 7.7; 29.2, 7.
Further in: Jos 13.3; Jud 3.3; 16.5, 8, 18 twice, 23, 27, 30; I Chr 12.20.

עגלה I Sam 6.10, 11, 14, (7 twice, 8); II Sam 6.3 (// I Chr 13.7).
Further in: Gen 45.19, 21, 27; 46.5; Num 7.3 twice, 6, 7, 8; Isa 5.18; 28.27, 28; Amos 2.13; Ps 46.10.

עכבר I Sam 6.4, 11, (5, 18).
Further in: Lev 11.29; Isa 66.17.

118

Appendix - The Vocabulary of the Ark Narrative

עפל I Sam 5.6, 9, 12; 6.4, 5.
Elsewhere in: Deut 28.27.

צירים I Sam 4.19.
Further in: Isa 13.8; 21.3; Dan 10.16.

צעקה I Sam 4.14.
Elsewhere in Sam: 9.16.
Further in: Gen 18.21; 19.13; 27.34; Exod 3.7, 9; 11.6; 12.30; 22.22;
Isa 5.7; Jer 25.36; 48.3, 5; 49.21; Zeph 1.10; Ps 9.13; Job 27.9; 34.28
twice; Neh 5.1.
oooo Gen 18.20; Isa 15.5, 8; 65.19; Jer 8.22; 20.16; 48.4, 34; 50.46;
51.54; Ezek 27.28; Prov 21.13; Job 16.18; Eccl 9.17; Esth 4.1; 9.31;
Neh 5.6; 9.9.

צפה Piel I Sam 4.13(?).
Further in: Isa 21.6; Jer 48.19; Mic 7.4, 7; Hab 2.1; Ps 5.4; Lam 4.17.

קסמים I Sam 6.2.
Further in: Deut 18.10, 14; Jos 13.22; Isa 3.2; 44.25; Jer 27.9; 29.8;
Ezek 13.9; 22.28; Mic 3.7; Zech 10.2.

קצר I Sam 6.13.
Elsewhere in Sam: I Sam 8.12.
Further in: Lev 19.9 twice; 23.10, 22 twice; 25.5, 11; Deut 24.19; II
Kgs 4.18; 19.29; Isa 17.5; 37.30; Jer 12.13; Hos 8.7; 10.12, 13; Amos
9.13; Mic 6.15; Ps 126.5; 129.7; Prov 22.8; Job 4.8; 24.6; Ruth 2.3, 4,
5, 6, 7, 9, 14; Eccl 11.4.

קציר I Sam 6.13.
Elsewhere in Sam: I Sam 8.12; 12.17; II Sam 21.9 twice, 10; 23.13.
Further in: Gen 8.22; 30.14; 45.6; Exod 23.16; 34.21, 22; Lev 19.9
twice; 23.10 twice, 22 twice; 25.5; Deut 24.19; Jos 3.15; Jud 15.1;
Isa 9.2; 16.9; 17.5, 11; 18.4, 5; 23.3; 27;11; Jer 5.17, 24; 8.20; 50.16;
51.33; Hos 6.11; Joel 1.11; 4.13; Amos 4.7; Ps 80.12; Prov 6.8; 10.5;
20.4; 25.13; 26.1; Job 5.5; 14.9; 18.16; 29.19; Ruth 1.22; 2.21, 23.

רוע Hiphil I Sam 4.5.
Elsewhere in Sam: I Sam 10.24; 17.20, 52.
Further in: Num 10.7, 9; Jos 6.10, 16; Jud 7.21; 15.14; Isa 15.4;
42.13; 44.23; Jer 50.15; Hois 5.8; Joel 2.1; Mic 4.9; Zeph 3.14; Zech
9.9; Ps 41.12; 47.2; 66.1; 81.2; 95.1, 2; 98.4, 6; 100.1; Job 30.5; 38.7;
Ezr 3.11, 13; II Chr 13.12, 15 twice.

תרועה I Sam 4.5, 6; II Sam 6.15.
Further in: Lev 23.24; 25.9; Num 10.5, 6 twice; 23.21; 29.1; 31.6; Jos
6.5, 20; Jer 4.19; 20.16; 49.2; Ezek 21.27; Amos 1.14; 2.2; Zeph 1.16;
Ps 27.6; 33.3; 47.6; 89.16; 150.5; Job 8.21; 33.26; 39.25; Ezr 3.11, 12,
13 twice; I Chr 15.28; II Chr 13.12; 15.14.

ריקם I Sam 6.3.
Elsewhere in Sam: II Sam 1.22.
Further in: Gen 31.42; Exod 3.21; 23.15; 34.20; Deut 15.13; 16.16; Isa
55.11; Jer 14.3; 50.9; Ps 7.5; 25.3; Job 22.9; Ruth 3.17.

שועה I Sam 5.12.
Elsewhere in Sam: II Sam 22.7.
Further in: Exod 2.23; Jer 8.19; Ps 18.7; 34.16; 39.13; 40.2; 102.2;
145.19; Job 30.24; 36.19; Lam 3.56.

שמעה I Sam 4.19.
Elsewhere in Sam: I Sam 2.24; II Sam 4.4; 13.30.
Further in: I Kgs 2.28; 10.7; II Kgs 19.7; Isa 28.9, 19; 37.7; 53.1; Jer
10.22; 49.14, 23; 51.46 twice; Ezek 7.26 twice; 16.56; 21.12; Obad 1;
Ps 112.7; Prov 15.30; 25.25; Dan 11.44; II Chr 9.6.

יצא לקראת I Sam 4.1.
      Elsewhere in Sam: I Sam 17.55; II Sam 18.6.
      Further in: Num 20.18, 20; 21.23, 33; Deut 1.44; 2.32; 29.6; Jos 8.5,
      22; Jud 20.25; II Chr 35.20.

כבדה יד I Sam 5.6, 11.
      Further in: Jud 1.35; Ps 32.4; Job 23.2.

קשתה יד I Sam 5.7.
      Further in: (Jud 4.24).

היתה יד I Sam 5.9.
      Elsewhere in Sam: I Sam 7.13; 18.17 twice, 21; 24.12, 13.
      Further in: Deut 2.15; 17.7; Jud 2.15; I Chr 21.17; II Chr 30.12.

(ותעז יד) Jud 3.10; 6.2.

(נגעה יד) I Sam 6.9.
      Further in: Job 19.21; Ruth 1.13.

(שלח יד) I Sam 24.6, 11; 26.9, 11, 23; II Sam 1.14; 24.17; Esth 8.7.

שית לב I Sam 4.20.
      Elsewhere in Sam: II Sam 13.20.
      Further in: Exod 7.23; Jer 31.20; Ps 48.14; 62.11; Prov 22.17; 24.32;
      27.23; Job 7.17.

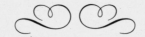

NOTES

Introduction

[Notes 1-4 in 1965 edn.]
1   Budde: Die Bücher Samuel, p.XVII.
2   According to Gunkel, it is the author and not his work which is the
concern of exegesis: Reden und Aufsätze, 12f. Against this, König: Her-
meneutik des AT, p.63.
3   On Herodotus cf. Howald: Ionische Geschichtsschreibung, pp.
127ff., and Aly: Volksmärchen, Sage und Novelle, p.113. On Thucydides cf.
Aly: ibid., p.141, and Wilamowitz-Möllendorff: "Thukydides VIII - Hermes,"
pp.598f.

NOTES TO CHAPTER ONE

The Ark Narrative

[Notes 5-74 in 1965 edn.]
1   Cf. Wellhausen: Bleek, Einleitung in das AT, pp.208ff. and 222f.
(Deleted as glosses are: I Sam 4.21b, 22; 6.5a to את־הארץ [the land] and
6.17, 18a; further 6.15. 4.18 is regarded as a redactional addition, and
perhaps also 4.15.) Löhr: Thenius, Die Bücher Samuelis, pp.LXVII and
LXVI. Nowack: Richter, Ruth und Bücher Samuelis, pp.XVII, XX, XXXIff.
Lotz ("Die Bundeslade," pp.143ff.) also divides the ark narrative similarly:
I Sam 4-6 is his Mizpah source, and II Sam 6 his David (Da) source.
2   Budde: op. cit., pp.32 and 226. (The latter deals with Cook's
attempt to distinguish two sources even within II Sam 6 ["Notes on the
Composition of 2 Samuel," pp.145-77]; Budde disagrees with this and
attributes the narrative to his unified J-source. Sellin: Einleitung in das
AT, p.74 [ET: see Bibliog.]. The quotation is from p.75.
3   Kittel: Geschichte des Volkes Israel, pp.71 and 297, note 3.
4   Steuernagel: Lehrbuch der Einleitung in das AT, pp.332ff. Gressmann: Die älteste Geschichtsschreibung und Prophetie Israels, pp.11ff. and
133ff.
5   Cf., e.g., Wellhausen: Einleitung, pp.222f.
6   Kautzsch: Die Heilige Schrift des AT, 1, p.460, notes b and c.
7   This is no more unlikely than the extension of the name for the ark,
which has generally been assumed in these narratives since Wellhausen;
but see, against this, Lotz: op. cit., pp.143ff.
8   Because of the aetiology of Perez Uzzah, the name Uzzah in II Sam
6 is certain.
9   Keil: Die Bücher Samuelis, p.260 [ET: see Bibliog.].
10   See Nowack: op. cit., pp.XV and XX; Löhr: op. cit., pp.XVIII and LIV.
11   One may compare here I Kgs 2.46, as the conclusion to the
succession story.
12   It is the intention of the author to show how the shepherd boy,
David, finally becomes king of the whole of Judah and Israel in the newly
conquered Jerusalem. Among other things, the important role given to
Abiathar and the predilection for reporting consultations of Yahweh

by David are characteristic of this author. At a guess, he could have been Abiathar, so that with appropriate reservations, we can speak of an Abiathar source.

13   II Sam 6 has no place in the story of David's rise, for this chapter is not written for the greater glory of the king but in honour of the ark which is always the focal point.

14   I Sam 6 finishes with the installation of the ark in the house of Abinadab in Kiriath-jearim. II Sam 6 begins with David's preparations for bringing it to Jerusalem. The vocabulary is closely related. Cf. עגלה I Sam 6 passim, twice in II Sam 6.3; תרועה I Sam 4.5, 6; II Sam 6.15; המון I Sam 4.14; II Sam 6.1; הציג (of setting up the ark) I Sam 5.2; II Sam 6.17. See also pp.11ff. On the style, see pp.14ff.; on the religious ideas pp.30ff.

15   See further pp.22ff.

16   See further pp.23ff.

17   With Stade and Smith as his precursors; cf. Budde: op. cit., p.32.

18   One may compare here Budde: ibid., p.33: "The fact that chapters 4-6 come from both sources is very important as this solves the problem of the gap in J. I Sam 4-6 can now follow on from the Samson story in Jud 13-16 and then all that is lacking in J up to I Sam 9 are the further details of the military successes of the Philistines, which we have already had reason to delete."

19   Ibid., p.17.

20   Ibid., p.33.

21   Cf. Baumgärtel: Elohim ausserhalb des Pentateuchs, pp.50ff.

22   Likewise Sellin: Einleitung, pp.74f. As already mentioned, he does think, however, that there is an older, underlying source.

23   See Steuernagel: op. cit., p.331.

24   See Norden: Agnostos Theos, pp.355ff.; and Aly: op. cit., Index I, under "Anapher."

25   For the linguistic connection with J and E, see p.14.

26   See Budde: op. cit., p.40.

27   Similarly Nowack: op. cit., pp.27ff.

28   Note words like מגפה (slaughter) I Sam 4.17; 6.4; מכה (smiting) I Sam 4.8, 10; 6.19; גבול (territory) I Sam 5.6; 6.9, 12; and expressions such as "What shall we do with the ark ...?" On the style, see pp.14ff., and on the religious notions see pp.30ff..

29   Op. cit., pp.27f.

30   One may compare, for example, II Sam 2.12; I Sam 29.1; I Sam 13.23 and 14.1.

31   But cf. Gressmann: op. cit., p.11.

32   But again cf. Gressmann: ibid.

33   Cf. on this, p.93.

34   See, for example: Al-Ašʿari's Kitāb al-lumaᶜ, fol. 28bf. (Kremer 101. Brit. Mus. Suppl. p.104, no. 172, Or. 3091. fol 1a, 2a-73a).

35   Cf. Dalman: "Die Nordstrasse Jerusalems," pp.75ff.

36   Gressmann: op. cit., p.12.

37   Reference to the similar events in chapter 4.6f. cannot be used to support the evidence here, because it is impossible that the Philistines could really have seen what was happening from the outset.

38   The two last words of v. 21 ("because of her father-in-law and her husband") introduce a new thought which disturbs the clear continuity effected by "because of the capture of the ark of God." Deleting these two words means also removing the whole of v. 22 which merely repeats the second half of v. 21.

39   For the change in word order compare, e.g., 4.10f. Here the two

events which are so important for the progress of the action are not connected to the preceding narrative by a waw-consecutive. Further: 4.13, 14. For the choice of words, cf. 5.6, 7, 9, 11. For the use of particles, cf. 4.13; 6.3.

40   After all, in the first battle the Israelites were defeated but not decisively beaten. After their defeat they still posed a threat which the Philistines could not ignore.

41   One could even speak of an ability to create atmosphere through silence.

42   This is the intention behind the interpretation of the name; whether or not it is right is not our concern.

43   That something was felt to be lacking here is shown by the addition (for other reasons) of the psalm in I Chr 15.8ff.

44   Cf. Schulz: Erzählungskunst in den Samuelisbüchern, pp. 8ff. [ET: see Bibliog.], citing A. Olrik: "Epische Gesetze der Volksdichtung," p.8 [ET: see Bibliog.].

45   Op. cit., pp.30ff.

46   Cf. on this Driver, Einleitung in die Literatur des AT, p.188. [English original: see Bibliog.]

47   Cf. here the interesting observations of Caspari on the "style of the opening of the Israelite Novelle," ("Der Stil des Eingangs der israelitischen Novelle," pp.218ff. [ET: see Bibliog.]), though he does not deal with our present case.

48   How and when this story became part of the larger context is not our concern here and would not affect the fact of its original independence.

49   What happened to this box is not reported. However, it probably did not remain in Beth-shemesh or in Kiriath-jearim, but was brought to Jerusalem.

50   Who the narrator was - Abiathar, David's loyal companion, Ahio ben Abinadab or Ira the Jairite or one of the sons of David or some unknown person - is a secondary matter and can hardly be determined. As we have already accepted Abiathar as the author of another source, he can hardly come into consideration here.

51   Think of the tenacity with which Church Slavonic has persisted as the liturgical language in the Russian Church and Latin in the Roman Catholic Church.

52   She is just like the unnamed neighbours who offer comfort.

53   If Kiriath-jearim in Jud 18.12 is qualified by the phrase "in Judah," this is to be explained of course as reflecting the time when this story was composed. And that Dan pitched its camp at Kiriath-jearim, does not count against the continued existence of an alliance, especially since it is expressly stated that David had no inheritance in Israel, but was seeking one.

54   II Sam 21.1ff. and II Sam 4.2f. indicate such aims on the part of Saul, motivated perhaps by the increasing endeavours of the four cities of the confederation to gain their freedom. Especially at such a time as that of the conflict with the Philistines, these individual city states and confederations would remember their former independence. Cf. Dalman: "Die Nordstrasse Jerusalems," p.84.

55   Even the return of the ark by the Philistines does not seem to be beyond the bounds of possibility. One thinks of the even more marvellous story of the Trojan horse (though the parallel is perhaps not altogether apt). Cf., however, Caspari: "Die Bundeslade unter David," p.29. Beth-shemesh seems to have been an independent city state in this period.

According to I Sam 6.12, the Philistine princes regard their task as being completed at the border of Beth-shemesh, which presumably ran between Beth-shemesh and Timnah, four km. to the west, which was Philistine according to Jud 14f. According to Jud 18.2ff., the Danites could not retain their position either in Zorah (3 km. to the north on the other side of the hollow of the Wadi es-Sarar) or in Eshtaol (5 km. to the north east) and Jud 1.35 explains that the cities Har-Heres, Aijalon (12 km. north east of Beth-shemesh) and Shaalbim could not be subdued by the house of Joseph. After the Danites withdrew, the territory of the town then bordered in the west and perhaps in the south on Philistine country, in the north on the Canaanite city-states and in the east on the territory of Kiriath-jearim, one of the members of the four-city confederation, with which it had neighbourly relations. The confederation seems to have been only loosely linked to Israel at this time so we should assume that Beth-shemesh was independent of both Judah and Israel. Cf. on this Alt: "Judas Gaue unter Josia," p.115; also "Israels Gaue unter Salomo," p.15, note 3. But against see H. Guthe: Bibelatlas, Karte 2 (depending on the possibility that Chirbet Kila north of Zora is to be identified with Keilah; but much more likely is his alternative suggestion of Chirbet Kila north of Beth Nasib) and G. Dalman: PJB 1913, pp.16f.

56   Cf. on this Gressmann: op. cit., p.135. He regards only the introduction and the end of the story as historical and thinks that what lies in between is just an imaginative creation, though he admits that some sort of connection with real events is still possible.

57   Note here especially I Sam 5. According to what the Philistines say, the ark is responsible for the disaster, but the author sees Yahweh's hand in this. Cf. further II Sam 6.7ff.

58   But cf. Volz: Das Dämonische in Jahwe, p.9.

59   It is questionable whether the consistency in the narrative can be attributed to some kind of providence.

NOTES TO CHAPTER TWO

The Prophecy of Nathan

[Notes 75-114 in 1965 edn.]

1   Wellhausen: Einleitung in das AT, p.223. Budde: Die Bücher Samuel, p.244. Sellin: Einleitung in das AT, pp.70 and 72 [ET: see Bibliog.]. Gressmann: Die älteste Geschichtsschreibung und Prophetie Israels, p.138. Kittel: Geschichte des Volkes Israel, p.123. O. Procksch: "Die letzten Worte Davids," pp.122ff.

2   Cf., however, I Chr 17.12.

3   Procksch: op. cit., pp.112ff.; Gressmann: op. cit., pp.184ff.

4   Of course this expression can also be found in the parallel passage in I Chr 17.25.

5   Budde: op. cit., p.244. Cf. also E. Kautzsch: ZAW, 1886, pp.17ff.

6   Also in I Chr 29.14 in a Deuteronomistic context.

7   But cf. Sievers: Metrische Studien III. Samuel, pp.72ff. He shows David's prayer to be metrically uniform; but, according to private correspondence, he does not maintain unity of authorship.

8   Cf. also I Kgs 3.7.

9   The structure of the Hebrew prayer does require comprehensive investigation. Such a study would have to consider especially the historical books as well as the Psalms. Greiff: "Das Gebet im AT," omitted

this in the form-critical section of his investigation where he almost exclusively uses examples from the Psalms. Doeller: Das Gebet im AT im religiongeschichtlicher Beleuchtung, does not deal with form at all.

10   Cf. on this Eissfeldt: Hexateuch-Synopse, p.84.

11   Procksch: op. cit., pp.112ff.

12   Cf. Ps 89.4ff.

13   Cf. II Sam 3.9f.; 3.18; 5.2. These passages belong to the old Abiathar source and must have some historical basis.

14   Tiktin: Kritische Untersuchungen zu den Büchern Samuelis, p.48, and Klostermann: Die Bücher Samuelis und der Könige, p.158; further Wellhausen: Der Text der Bücher Samuelis, pp.171f. But cf. Wellhausen: Einleitung, p.223; Budde: op. cit., p.232; Nowack: Richter, Ruth und Bücher Samuelis, p.178.

15   Nowack: op. cit., p.178; Löhr: Die Bücher Samuelis, p.145.

16   Tiktin: op. cit., p.48.

17   Procksch: op. cit., pp.122ff. Cf. also Kittel: op. cit., p.123.

18   Instead of לפניך (before you) read לפני יהוה (before Yahweh). לפניך surely originated in place of a לפניו (before him) under the influence of v. 26.

19   Also Sievers: op. cit., p.72, who admittedly also includes v. 17 and has v. 8f. preceding.

20   See also Keil: Die Bücher Samuelis, 260 [ET: see Bibliog.]. The switch to the future from v. 10, in LXX, Vulg. and Luther, is, of course, untenable.

21   But cf. Kautzsch: Gesenius Hebräische Grammatik, §49e [ET: see Bibliog.].

22   Ibid., §112pp-tt; Driver: Use of the Tenses in Hebrew, pp. 187ff.

23   "Gliedertanz" - Gressmann: op. cit., p.138.

24   Read with BHK & GBA למן. 11a^b should be deleted as an insertion from v. 1.

25   Cf. II Sam 24.1 (I Chr 21.1ff.).

26   Sievers: op. cit., p.72. He similarly regards vv. 9,10,13-15 as not original.

27   Cf. Steuernagel: Lehrbuch der Einleitung in das AT, pp.324f.

28   As a glance at revelations of Yahweh and prophetic oracles in the books of Samuel and Kings shows, this would appear to be a very common form (e.g. I Sam 10.1ff.; 15.17ff.; I Kgs 13.21f.; 17.14; 20.36; 22.17ff.; II Kgs 3.16ff.); but it is not the only one, as there are also oracles where Yahweh speaks in the first person (e.g. I Sam 2.27ff.; 10.17ff.; II Sam 12.7ff.; I Kgs 11.31; 14.7ff.; 20.28; 21.21f.; II Kgs 2.21; 9.6ff.; 19.6f.; 19.20ff.; 21.10ff.; 22.15). There are also those introduced by the formula "Thus says Yahweh"; these merely give an indication of what will happen without connecting the event in any way with the work of God (e.g. I Kgs 13.2; 20.42; 21.19; 21.23; 22.11; II Kgs 1.16; 4.43; 7.1; 20.16ff.). Finally there are those oracles which are direct revelations from Yahweh; these naturally have the first person (e.g. I Kgs 3.11ff.; 9.1ff.; 19.15ff.). The passage in its present shape, on the other hand, has the form of the messenger-commission, a form which in the books of Samuel and Kings appears only in I Kgs 12.22 and II Kgs 20.5ff. I Kgs 19.15 deals with Yahweh's instructions to Elijah to act, though not to speak. However, we find the messenger-commission once more in Isaiah (7.3ff.) and it is particularly frequent in Jeremiah.

29   That the author looks back over quite a long period of rule by the house of David has been recognized already by Wellhausen; on the other hand the terminus ante quem must of necessity be placed in the exile, as has already been demonstrated by Budde and Nowack.

30   Cf. vv. 10,14,15.
31   Cf. pp.39ff. Vv. 1-4a are uniform even if 1b is deleted.
32   Cf. on this Alt: PJB 21, 1925, p.18, note 3. Further Canaan: "Mohammedan Saints and Sanctuaries in Palestine," pp.55f and pp.62f.
33   Kittel: op. cit., p.210, note 3.

NOTES TO CHAPTER THREE

The Account of the Ammonite War

[Notes 115-128 in 1965 edn.]

1   H. Winckler: Geschichte Israels in Einzeldarstellungen, Part 1, p.138. Kittel, in: Kautzsch: Die Heilige Schrift, pp.464ff. Cook: "Notes on the Composition of 2 Samuel," pp.155ff. Gressmann: Die älteste Geschichtsschreibung und Prophetie Israels, pp.153ff. [ET: see Bibliog.]. Sievers: Metrische Studien III. Samuel, pp. 76ff.
2   Budde: Die Bücher Samuel, p.246. Nowack: Richter, Ruth und Bücher Samuelis, pp.XXIf. and XXXIV. Sellin: Einleitung in das AT, pp. 68ff. Steuernagel: Lehrbuch der Einleitung in das AT, pp.325f. and 334.
3   Cf. also H. Winckler: Die Keilinschriften und das AT, who admittedly adduces only a tenuous ground for such a connection in Chronicles.
4   Cf. e.g., the phrase עשה חסד (show kindness, deal loyally) in 9.1 and 10.2.
5   Sievers, it is true, finds in 10.1-6a the same metre as in 10.6bff. However, the beginning could well have been composed in the metre of the whole.
6   But cf. Cook: op. cit., p.157.
7   If an originally assumed phrase ארון אלהים (ark of God) was indeed changed for dogmatic reasons into ערי אלהים (cities of God), then at this point the presence of the ark in the camp would have been evidenced. Nor would a call to fight to protect the ark have been out of place in terms of what had been told of the earlier fortunes of the ark. On the other hand, the term "cities of God" contains ideas which can be shown to have existed at this period.

NOTES TO CHAPTER FOUR

The Succession Story

[Notes 129-172 in 1965 edn.]

1   Budde: Die Bücher Samuel, p.17.
2   Nowack: Richter, Ruth und Bücher Samuelis, pp.XXIf. and XXXIV.
3   Sellin: Einleitung in das AT, p.69 [ET: see Bibliog.].
4   Klostermann: Die Bücher Samuelis und der Könige, p.XXIf.
5   Steuernagel: Lehrbuch der Einleitung in das AT, pp.325f. and 354.
6   Caspari: "Der Stil des Eingangs der israelitischen Novelle," pp. 236ff. [ET: see Bibliog.]. Gressmann: Die älteste Geschichtsschreibung und Prophetie Israels, pp.142ff., 149ff., 157ff., 165ff., 186ff. [ET: see Bibliog.].
7   The slight deviations noted by Caspari are not enough to warrant doubting the unity here, as they could well have arisen from the narrator's wish for variation.
8   Or did Bathsheba deliberately pass on Adonijah's request in order to destroy the last serious opponent of her son?

9   It seems to be the work of the same person who wrote I Kgs 8.25.

10   The personification of the devouring sword seems quite singular.

11   Hence the content of I Sam 16.1ff; whether this applies to the form as well may be left open.

12   For בית אדניך (your master's house) in 8a read בת א״ (your master's daughter) following the Syriac b.nât with Klostermann, Nestle, Geiger and Budde.

13   Cf. on this Sievers: op. cit., pp. 79f. In his view verses 13,14,15a are secondary.

14   Cf. on this Aly: Volkmärchen, Sage und Novelle bei Herodot und seinen Zeitgenossen, p.154.

15   "Der Stil des Eingangs," pp.238ff.

16   Instead of לי (to/for me) read לו (to/for him) with Kittel (in: Kautzsch, Die Heilige Schrift, p.498) and Sievers (Metrische Studien III. Samuel, p.113). As yet Solomon has no house, but David has, as founder of the dynasty.

17   בנה (build) for עשה (make): Yahweh reveals himself directly.

18   Does this imply that the future successor has not yet been born and that the house has thus literally still to be brought into being?

19   Compare the annotators of the prophetic writings and the Pseud-epigrapha.

20   Cf. Aly: op. cit., p.142.

21   Cf. also, e.g., the Eshmunazar Inscription.

22   Cf. Aly: op. cit., p.241.

23   Cf. Windisch: "Der Johanneische Erzählungsstil," pp.174ff.

24   Cf. pp.89ff. In the case of Joab the matter is somewhat peculiar in that he is sufficiently introduced at his first appearance in the succession narrative in 14.1 as Joab ben Zeruiah; this passage, however, is preceded by the account of the Ammonite war where Joab is often mentioned but never properly introduced.

25   Following Olrik, Aly speaks of the "stern ballast" of the narratives (op. cit., p. 247).

26   Cf. Schmidt: Die Geschichtsschreibung im AT, pp.20ff.

27   Cf. here Duhm: Zur Geschichte der Alttestamentlichen Geschichts-schreibung, III, pp.132ff.; Schmidt: op. cit., II, 16, pp.23ff.; Caspari: "Literarische Art und historischer Wert von II Sam 15-20," pp.346f. [ET: see Bibliog.].

28   Cf. Caspari: ibid.

29   The seamy story of David's adultery with Bathsheba is no counter-argument, if we consider that the prostitute Rahab and the Moabite Ruth are part of David's family tree, and, moreover, that a similar story was told - and handed down in tradition - about Judah, the tribal patriarch, and his relationship with Tamar.

30   For a further characterization of the author, see the sensitive exposition of Caspari: "Literarische Art," pp.317ff.

31   In this he is somewhat similar to Thucydides: cf. W. Nestle: Thukydides und die Sophistik, p.650.

32   Perhaps the person pursued by bad luck is, as someone stricken by God, taboo?

33   Does not this imply that the king is responsible for his people, for the individual families and for the individuals themselves? In which case he cannot allow the eclipse of a family which is responsible for the cult before Yahweh. Hence he must insist on pardon - as the highest legal authority he can suspend the judgement of the law which protects the clan and thus create a new law contrary to normal legal custom (II Sam

14.4ff.). Of course this transgression of old hallowed precepts is a risky business which could under certain circumstances bring a curse (II Sam 14.9ff.).

34 A person is blessed, for instance, when taking up a new office (I Kgs 1.36ff., 39, 47) or when declining an invitation (II Sam 13.25).

35 Abiathar's fading influence makes it impossible for him to be the author of the succession story. One can much more easily attribute to him the history of David's rise.

36 Müller: Die Propheten in ihrer ursprünglichen Form; and: Strophen-bau und Responsion.

37 If he is the same as the Ahimaaz of Naphtali in I Kgs 4.15, it would be understandable why he would go over to the side of the northern kingdom after the division of the kingdom.

38 Hölscher: "Das Buch der Könige, seine Quellen und seine Re-daktion," pp. 158ff. Eissfeldt: Hexateuch-Synopse, p.85; Die Quellen des Richterbuchs, pp.38, 45, 52, 90, 98. Cornill: Einleitung in das AT, pp.108ff. [ET: see Bibliog.]. Budde: Die Bücher Samuel, pp.XVIIIff. Cf. on this Kittel: Geschichte des Volkes Israel, II, pp.294f.

ABBREVIATIONS

AT	Altes Testament
BHK	Biblia Hebraica, ed. Kittel
BWAT	Beiträge zur Wissenschaft vom Alten Testament
BZAW	Beihefte zur Zeitschrift für die Alttestamentliche Wissenschaft
ET	English translation
FRLANT	Forschungen zur Religion und Literatur des Alten und Neuen Testaments
HKAT	Handkommentar zum Alten Testament
ICC	International Critical Commentary
KHCAT	Kurzer Hand-Commentar zum Alten Testament
KKHS	Kurzgefasster Kommentar zu den heiligen Schriften Alten und Neuen Testamentes.
PJB	Palästinajahrbuch
RGV	Religionsgeschichtliche Volksbücher
ZWTh	Zeitschrift für Wissenschaftliche Theologie
ZAW	Zeitschrift für die Alttestamentliche Wissenschaft

BIBLIOGRAPHY

Alt, Albrecht
"Israels Gaue unter Salomo" in: Alttestamentliche Studien [Fest-schrift Rudolf Kittel], BWAT 13, Leipzig 1913, pp. 1-19 [= Kleine Schriften zur Geschichte des Volkes Israel, II, München 1953, pp. 76-89].
- "Judas Gaue unter Josia" in: PJB 21, 1925, pp. 100-17 [= Kleine Schriften zur Geschichte des Volkes Israel, II, München 1953, pp. 276-88].
- "Das Institut im Jahre 1924" in: PJB 21, 1925, pp. 5-58.
Aly, Wolfgang
Volksmärchen, Sage und Novelle bei Herodot und seinen Zeit-genossen. Eine Untersuchung über die volkstümlichen Elemente der altgriechischen Prosaerzählung, Göttingen 1921.
Baentsch, Bruno
David und sein Zeitalter, Wissenschaft und Bildung 16, Leipzig 1907.
Baumgärtel, Friedrich
Elohim ausserhalb des Pentateuchs, BWAT 19, Leipzig 1914.
Beer, Georg
Saul, David, Salomo, RGV II/7, Tübingen 1906.
Budde, Karl
Die Bücher Samuel, KHCAT 8, Tübingen & Leipzig 1902.
Canaan, T.
"Mohammedan Saints and Sanctuaries in Palestine" in: Journal of the Palestine Oriental Society 4, 1924, pp. 1-84.
Caspari, Wilhelm
Aufkommen und Krise des israelitischen Königtums unter David, Berlin 1909.
- "Literarische Art und historischer Wert von 2 Sam. 15-20" in: Theo-logische Studien und Kritiken 82, 1909, pp. 317-48. [ET: "2 Samuel 15-20: Literary Nature and Historical Value" in: Gunn, ed.: see under Gressmann.]
- "Der Stil des Eingangs der israelitischen Novelle" in: ZWTh 53, 1911, pp. 218-53. [ET: "The Opening Style of the Israelite Novelle" in: Gunn, ed.: see under Gressmann.]
- "Was stand im Buche der Kriege Jahwes?" in: ZWTh 54, 1912 110-58.
- "Über Verse, Kapitel and letzte Redaktion in den Samuelisbüchern" in: ZAW 33, 1913, pp. 47ff. & 116ff.
Cook, Stanley Arthur
"Notes on the Composition of 2 Samuel" in: American Journal of Semitic Languages and Literatures 16, 1899/1900, pp. 145-77.
Cornill, Carl Heinrich
Einleitung in die kanonischen Bücher des Alten Testaments, [1891] 7th edn., Tübingen 1913. [ET (from 5th German edn.): Introduction to the Canonical Books of the Old Testament, New York 1907.]
Dalman, Gustaf
"Die Nordstrasse Jerusalems" in: PJB 21, 1925, pp. 58-89.
Doeller, Johannes
Das Gebet im Alten Testament in religionsgeschichtlicher Beleucht-ung, Wien, 1914.

Driver, Samuel Rolles
A Treatise on the Use of the Tenses in Hebrew, 3rd edn., Oxford 1892.
Einleitung in die Literatur des Alten Testaments, trans. J. W. Rothstein, Berlin 1896. [English original: Introduction to the Literature of the Old Testament, 5th edn., Edinburgh 1894.]

Duhm, Hans
"Zur Geschichte der Alttestamentlichen Geschichtsschreibung" in: Festschrift für Theodor Plüss, Basel 1905, pp. 118-63.

Eissfeldt, Otto
Hexateuch-Synopse, Leipzig 1922.
- Die Quellen des Richterbuches, Leipzig, 1925.

Geiger, Abraham
Urschrift und Übersetzungen der Bibel, Breslau 1857.

Greiff, Anton
Das Gebet im Alten Testament, Alttestamentliche Abhandlungen, 5/3, Münster 1915.

Gressmann, Hugo
Die älteste Geschichtsschreibung und Prophetie Israels, Die Schriften des Alten Testaments 2/1, [1910] 2nd revised edn., Göttingen 1921. [ET pp. 153-83, 191-4: "Stories of David and his Sons" in: D. M. Gunn, ed.: Narrative and Novelle in Samuel. Studies by Hugo Gressmann and other Scholars 1906-1923, Sheffield (Almond Press) 1983.]

Gunkel, Heinrich
Meisterwerke hebräischer Erzählungskunst: I. Geschichten von Elisa, Berlin n.d.
- Reden und Aufsätze, Göttingen 1913.

Guthe, Hermann
Bibelatlas in 20 Haupt- und 28 Nebenkarten. Mit einem Verzeichnis der alten und neuen Ortsnamen, Leipzig 1911.

Hölscher, Gustav
"Das Buch der Könige, seine Quellen und seine Redaktion" in: Hans Schmidt, ed.: Eucharisterion. Studien zur Religion und Literatur des Alten und Neuen Testaments [Festschrift Hermann Gunkel], I, Göttingen 1923, pp. 158-213.

Howald, Ernst
"Ionische Geschichtsschreibung" in: Hermes 58, 1923, pp.113-46.

Kautzsch, Emil
Gesenius Hebräische Grammatik, revised by E. Kautzsch, 28th edn., Leipzig 1910. [ET: Gesenius' Hebrew Grammar, 2nd English edn. revised by A. E. Cowley, Oxford 1910.]
- Die Heilige Schrift des Alten Testaments, 4th edn. ed. A. Bertholet, Tübingen 1922.

Keil, Carl Friedrich
Die Bücher Samuelis, Biblischer Commentar über das alte Testament, II/2, 2nd edn., Leipzig 1875. [ET (from 1st German edn.): Biblical Commentary on the Books of Samuel, Edinburgh 1865.]

Kittel, Rudolf
Die Anfänge der hebräischen Geschichtsschreibung, [Rektoratsrede an der Univ. Breslau] Leipzig 1896.
- Geschichte des Volkes Israel, vol. I, 5th/6th edn., Stuttgart & Gotha 1923; vol. II, 6th edn., 1925.

Klostermann, August
Die Bücher Samuelis und der Könige, KKHS 3, Nördlingen 1887.

Köhler, Ludwig
    Deuterojesaia (Jes. 40-55) stilkritisch untersucht, BZAW 37, Giessen
    1923.
König, Eduard
    Hermeneutik des Alten Testaments, Bonn 1913.
Kosters, W. H.
    "De verhalen over de ark in Samuel" in: Theologisch Tijdschrift,
    Leiden 1893, 361-78.
Krenkel, M.
    "Einige Emendationen zu den Büchern Samuel" in: ZAW, 1882, 309ff.
Löhr, Max
    O. Thenius, Die Bücher Samuelis, 3rd edn. revised by M. Löhr,
    Leipzig 1898.
Lotz, Wilhelm
    "Die Bundeslade" in: Festschrift Sr. kgl. Hoheit Luitpold Prinzregent
    von Bayern, Erlangen & Leipzig 1901, I, pp.143ff.
Luther, Bernhard
    "Die Novelle von Juda und Tamar und andere israelitische Novellen"
    in: Eduard Meyer: Die Israeliten und ihre Nachbarstämme. Alt-
    testamentliche Untersuchungen, Halle 1906, pp. 175-206. [ET:
    "Narrative in Genesis and Samuel: Judah and Tamar and other
    Israelite Novellen" in: Gunn, ed.: see under Gressmann.]
Moore, George Foot
    "Die Eigenart der hebräischen Geschichtsschreibung im alttest.
    Zeitalter" in: 28. Bericht der Lehranstalt für die Wissenschaft des
    Judentums in Berlin, Berlin 1910, pp. 63ff.
Müller, David Heinrich
    Die Propheten in ihrer ursprünglichen Form, Wien 1896.
    Strophenbau und Responsion. Neue Beiträge, Wien 1898.
Nestle, Eberhard
    Marginalien und Materialen, Tübingen 1893.
Nestle, Wilhelm
    "Thukydides und die Sophistik" in: Neue Jahrbücher für das
    klassische Altertum, Geschichte und deutsche Literatur XVII, 1914,
    I/10, pp. 649ff.
Norden, Eduard
    Agnostos Theos. Untersuchungen zur Formgeschichte religioser
    Rede, 1913.
Nowack, Wilhelm
    Richter, Ruth und Bücher Samuelis übersetzt und erklärt, HKAT I/4,
    Göttingen 1902.
Olrik, Axel
    "Epische Gesetze der Volksdichtung" in: Zeitschrift für deutsches
    Altertum und deutsche Literatur N.F. 51, 1909, pp. 1-12. [ET in: A.
    Dundes, ed.: The Study of Folklore, Englewood Cliffs, 1965, pp.
    129-41]
Procksch, Otto
    "Die letzten Worte Davids" in: Alttestamentliche Studien [Fest-
    schrift Rudolf Kittel], BWAT 13, Leipzig 1913, pp. 113-25.
Schmidt, Hans
    Die Geschichtsschreibung im Alten Testament, RGV 2/16, Tübingen
    1911.
Schulz, Alfons
    Erzählungskunst in den Samuelisbüchern, Biblische Zeitfragen
    11/6-7, Münster in Westf. 1923. [ET: "Narrative Art in the Books of
    Samuel" in: Gunn, ed.: see under Gressmann.]

Sellin, Ernst
    Geschichte des israelitischen und jüdischen Volkes, I, Leipzig 1924.
-   Einleitung in das Alte Testament, 4th edn. newly revised, Leipzig 1925. [ET (from 3rd German edn. 1920): Introduction to the Old Testament, London 1923.]
Sievers, Eduard
    Metrische Studien III. Samuel, Leipzig 1907.
Smith, Henry Preserved
    A Critical and Exegetical Commentary on the Books of Samuel, ICC, Edinburgh 1899.
Stade, Bernhard
    Geschichte des Volkes Israel, Berlin 1881-88.
Steuernagel, Carl
    Lehrbuch der Einleitung in das Alte Testament, Tübingen 1912.
Tiktin, Harlson
    Kritische Untersuchungen zu den Büchern Samuelis, FRLANT N.S. 16, Göttingen 1922.
Volz, Paul
    Das Dämonische in Jahwe, Tübingen 1924.
Wellhausen, Julius
    Der Text der Bücher Samuelis untersucht, Göttingen 1871.
-   F. Bleek, Einleitung in das Alte Testament, 4th edn. revised by J. Wellhausen, Berlin 1878. [The section on Judges-Kings is repr. in J. Wellhausen: Die Composition des Hexateuchs und der historischen Bücher des Alten Testaments, 3rd edn., Berlin 1899.]
Wilamowitz-Möllendorff, U. von
    "Thukydides VIII - Hermes," Zeitschrift für Klassische Philologie 43, 1908, pp. 378ff.
Winckler, Hugo
    E. Schrader, Die Keilinschriften und das Alte Testament, 3rd edn. by H. Zimmern and H. Winckler, 2 vols., Berlin, 1902/3.
-   Geschichte Israels in Einzeldarstellungen, Völker und Staaten des alten Orients 2-3, Leipzig 1892-1900.
Windisch, Hans
    "Der Johanneische Erzählungsstil," in: Hans Schmidt, ed.: Eucharisterion. Studien zur Religion und Literatur des Alten und Neuen Testaments [Festschrift Hermann Gunkel], II, Göttingen 1923, pp. 174-213.

INDEX OF AUTHORS